Overcoming Modernity

WEATHERHEAD BOOKS ON ASIA
Weatherhead East Asian Institute, Columbia University

WEATHERHEAD BOOKS ON ASIA
Weatherhead East Asian Institute, Columbia University

LITERATURE
David Der-wei Wang, Editor

Ye Zhaoyan, *Nanjing 1937: A Love Story*, translated by Michael Berry (2003)
Oda Makato, *The Breaking of the Jewel*, translated and with a foreword
by Donald Keene (2003)
Han Shaogong, *A Dictionary of Maqiao*, translated by Julia Lovell (2003)
Takahashi Takako, *Lonely Woman*, translated by Maryellen Toman Mori (2004)
Chen Ran, *A Private Life*, translated by John Howard-Gibbon (2004)
Eileen Chang, *Written on Water*, translated by Andrew F. Jones (2004)
Writing Women in Modern China: The Revolutionary Years, 1936-1976, edited
by Amy D. Dooling, (2005)
Han Bangqing, *The Sing-song Girls of Shanghai*, first translated by Eileen Chang,
revised and edited by Eva Hung (2005)
Loud Sparrows: Contemporary Chinese Short-Shorts, translated and edited by Aili Mu,
Julie Chiu, Howard Goldblatt (2006)
Hiratsuka Raichō, *In the Beginning, Woman Was the Sun*, translated by Teruko Craig (2006)
Zhu Wen, I Love Dollars *and Other Stories of China*, translated by Julia Lovell (2007)
Kim Sowol, *Azaleas: A Book of Poems*, translated by David McCann (2007)
Wang Anyi, *The Song of Everlasting Sorrow: A Novel of Shanghai*,
translated by Michael Berry (2008)

HISTORY, SOCIETY, AND CULTURE
Carol Gluck, Editor

Takeuchi Yoshimi, *What Is Modernity? Writings of Takeuchi Yoshimi*, edited and translated
with an introduction by Richard F. Calichman (2005)
Contemporary Japanese Thought, edited and translated with an introduction
by Richard F. Calichman (2005)

RICHARD F. CALICHMAN
EDITOR AND TRANSLATOR

Overcoming Modernity

CULTURAL IDENTITY
IN WARTIME JAPAN

Columbia University Press

New York

COLUMBIA UNIVERSITY PRESS

Publishers Since 1893

New York   Chichester, West Sussex

Copyright © 2008 Columbia University Press

All rights reserved

Library of Congress Cataloging-in-Publication Data

Kindai no chokoku. English.

Overcoming modernity : cultural identity in wartime Japan / Richard F. Calichman,
editor and translator.

p.   c.m

Translation of articles under the title of Kindai no chokoku, originally appeared
in Bungakukai, Sept. and Oct. 1942 issues.

Includes bibliographicsl references and index.

ISBN 978-0-231-14396-7 (alk. paper) — ISBN 978-0-231-14397-4 (pbk. : alk. paper)

1. Japan—Civilization—1926–1945—Philosophy.   2. Japan—Civilization—Western
influences.   3. World War, 1939–1945—Moral and ethical aspects—Japan.

I. Calichman, Richard F.   II. Title.

DS822.4.K51613 2008

952.03′3—dc22

2007041381

Columbia University Press books are printed
on permanent and durable acid-free paper.

Printed in the United States of America

c 10 9 8 7 6 5 4 3 2 1

Contents

Preface

IN DECEMBER 2006, Japan's upper house of parliament approved the passage of two highly controversial laws, one revising the 1947 Fundamental Law of Education and the other elevating the status of the nation's Defense Agency. Enacted two years after Japan's defeat in the Fifteen-Year War (1931–1945), the 1947 law sought to prevent the reemergence of nationalist sentiment as promoted by the wartime state education system, with greater emphasis placed on individual autonomy than on individual self-sacrifice in the name of emperor and country. The current revision of this law requires that classroom teaching once again involve instruction in patriotism, with particular focus on fostering among students "an attitude that respects [Japanese] tradition and culture, that loves the nation and home country." Meanwhile, the upgrading of the Defense Agency into an independent ministry has taken place alongside a greater prioritization on overseas missions, despite the fact that Article Nine of the constitution prohibits the country from maintaining armed forces. Critics have rightly condemned the passage of these two laws as signaling the beginning of a return to the militarism and ultranationalism of the 1930s, when Japan actively sought to expand its colonial holdings in Korea and Taiwan by invading the Chinese mainland. For such critics, the threat of a repetition of Japan's militarist past appears symbolized by the fact that the recently resigned prime minister, Abe Shinzō, is the grandson of the former prime minister Kishi Nobusuke, who, during the war, served in Japan's puppet government in Manchuria before being imprisoned by the Occupation authorities as a Class A war criminal. Led by Abe's Liberal Democratic Party, the conservative government insisted on the need for Japan to overcome its lingering war guilt, arguing that such guilt has effectively stunted a sense of national pride among Japanese citizens, which in turn has prevented the country from seeking a more prominent place in world affairs.

This resurgence of nationalism in Japan, with its predictable nostalgia for tradition and culture, invariably brings to mind the 1942 symposium Overcoming Modernity (Kindai no chōkoku). The gradual erosion of the postwar pacifist ideals brought about by the end of the Cold War and the changing needs of U.S. foreign policy—despite the fact that, ironically, it was the United States that originally laid the framework for these ideals—makes it incumbent upon us today to critically reexamine the ultranationalist discourse of the wartime years. Few texts offer a better chance to understand the complexities of this discourse than the proceedings of Overcoming Modernity.

The symposium must above all be understood against the backdrop of the Meiji period (1868–1912), when Japan sought to defend itself against the threat of Western imperialism by embarking upon a rapid process of modernization. This plan centered on the policy of "civilization and enlightenment" (*bunmei kaika*), which involved the wholesale incorporation of Western rationalism, science, and technology with which to construct the vast institutional framework of the modern nation-state. For the symposium participants, "civilization and enlightenment" was regarded in primarily negative terms due to its denigration of Japanese traditional culture. Yet these intellectuals seem to have been less aware that Japan's path of modernization also required that the country adopt the same colonialist policies in Asia as those maintained by the Western powers it sought to imitate. For it was this link between modernity and colonial violence that most fully accounted for the historical circumstances in which the symposium participants then found themselves. The fact that the symposium took place only seven months after the start of the Pacific War was emblematic of a major pattern of Japanese modernity, one that could easily be neglected, however, in the mourning over the loss of the premodern past.

This pattern began, following the formation of the Meiji state, with the Sino-Japanese War of 1894–1895, from which Japan acquired Taiwan and gained greater influence in Korea. The Russo-Japanese War (1904–1905) later yielded to Japan the southern half of Sakhalin Island as well as virtually total control over Korea, which was finally annexed in 1910. Thereafter Japan turned its attentions to a weakened China, gaining numerous concessions there through its infamous Twenty-one Demands of 1915. It gradually increased its influence in China (particularly Manchuria) throughout the next decade, but it was the global depression of the late 1920s that brought about a dramatic escalation of Japanese expansionism in the region, as government officials believed that control over northern China would bring an end to the economic troubles Japan was then facing. The puppet state of Manchukuo was established in 1932. Five years later war with China—referred to euphemistically as the China Incident (*Shina jihen*)—broke out as Japan aimed to create a puppet government throughout the entire country. By the summer of 1942, it seemed all too clear that, in its drive for modernization, Japan had consistently sought to ward off the threat of Western imperialism by competing directly with the West for colonies in Asia.

In the Overcoming Modernity symposium, the modernity to be overcome was associated with the West itself, such that overcoming modernity and overcoming the West were seen as essentially the same thing. In this way, the symposium participants refused to acknowledge that Japan's course of modernization, with its nearly fifty-year history of colonial acquisition, already represented a certain fulfillment of modernity. The modern West was to be vanquished by pursuing the same policy of Asian expansionism it itself had introduced, but this of course revealed the immense difficulties and contradictions contained in the project to overcome modernity. While the symposium largely focused on the need to restore Japan's traditional culture and spirit, it is important to grasp that this appeal to cultural nationalism and the country's military expansionism were in fact two sides of the same coin. From today's perspective, we can see that one of the great values of Overcoming Modernity is the relationship it exposes between a nation's heightened stance of militarism and the nostalgia of its culturalist discourse. Military means are utilized to confront what is perceived to be a foreign threat while culturally the nation responds by consolidating what belonged to its own traditional past. Bringing together a group of experts from such diverse fields as literature, science, film, philosophy, theology, history, and music, Overcoming Modernity offers a rare glimpse into not only the considerable breadth of Japan's intellectual discourse of the wartime years but also, more urgently, the manner in which the desire for cultural identity is given shape by military expansionism.

The symposium Overcoming Modernity took place in Tokyo over the course of two days, July 23–24, 1942. The original idea for the symposium had been conceived approximately six months earlier by the literary critic and former left-wing activist Kamei Katsuichirō, who subsequently drew up plans for its organization together with two other members of the group that had formed around the journal Bungakkai (Literary World), the literary and social critics Kawakami Tetsutarō and Kobayashi Hideo. Participants were selected from among some of the leading figures in Japan at the time in the fields of thought, the arts, and science, and invitations were sent out in May. All those invited accepted with the notable exception of Yasuda Yojūrō, the leader of the Nihon roman-ha (Japanese Romantic school). In addition to these three organizers of the symposium, participants included the following: the composer and music scholar Moroi Saburō, the Catholic theologian Yoshimitsu Yoshihiko, the Kyoto school religious philosopher Nishitani Keiji, the philosopher of science Shimomura Toratarō, the film critic Tsumura Hideo, the atomic physicist Kikuchi Seishi, the Kyoto school historian Suzuki Shigetaka, the literary critic and scholar Nakamura Mitsuo, the former proletarian literature writer Hayashi

Fusao, and finally the poet Miyoshi Tatsuji. Collectively these individuals represented three more or less distinct groups or affiliations: the *Bungakkai* group (Kamei, Kawakami, Kobayashi, Nakamura, Miyoshi, and Hayashi), the Kyoto school of philosophy (Nishitani, Suzuki and, more loosely, Shimomura), and the Japanese Romantic school (Kamei and Hayashi).

The symposium proceedings first appeared in print in the September and October 1942 issues of *Bungakkai*, with essays by Nishitani, Moroi, Tsumura, and Yoshimitsu appearing in September and those by Kamei, Hayashi, Miyoshi, Nakamura, and Suzuki, as well as a transcript of the two roundtable discussions, appearing in October. (The essays by Miyoshi and Nakamura were written as "impression pieces" after the symposium, whereas the remaining seven essays were written beforehand, as requested by the organizers, who then printed and distributed them to all of the participants for their perusal). The Tokyo publishing company Sōgensha published the conference proceedings in book form the following year, but Suzuki's essay was omitted—apparently by personal request—and essays by Shimomura, Kikuchi, and Kawakami added. The Sōgensha edition, from which the currently used Fuzanbō edition, the basis of this translation, was produced in 1979, numbered three hundred pages and ultimately went through forty-six printings, with an initial run of six thousand copies.[1]

The primary aim of the symposium was to go beyond what was considered to be the facile and unreflective discourse on Japan's new spiritual order so as to examine in more substantive terms the phenomenon of Japanese modernization and westernization since the Meiji period. As Kawakami, who acted as chair of both roundtable discussions, memorably put it in his brief essay "'Kindai no chōkoku' ketsugo" (Concluding Remarks to "Overcoming Modernity"), "We wanted to discuss 'how' we were present-day Japanese."[2] What Kawakami seems to mean by this statement is that the task of the symposium lay in part in analyzing the tensions implicit in the relation between the Japanese people and the present day given the considerable threat that the latter posed to Japanese cultural identity and the traditions that historically supported it. Much of this threat consisted in the extreme degree of specialization forced upon the various branches of culture and knowledge by the demands of modern life, resulting in the widespread sense of alienation among intellectuals and others. Such specialization was perceived by many as particularly damaging to the social fabric of Japan's national community, as could be seen in the changes then taking place at the levels of language and aesthetic sensibility, for example. The fissures that had thus been exposed could not continue to be ignored by ideological appeals to the superiority of the Japanese spirit but rather had to be realistically confronted in such a way that a particular kind of Japanese modernity that was true to both the nation and the exigencies of technological advances and social transformation could be forged out of this experience. Kawakami specifically mentions December 8, 1941, the day that Japan declared war against England and the United States, as crucial in this regard.³ For this event, which marked the official beginning of the Pacific War, was seen as essentially the first step in Japan's collective accounting of itself on the part of the intellectuals, who had now recognized the need to more effectively consolidate their efforts for the good of the nation. It seems clear that the organizers envisioned the symposium as continuing in this direction of increased solidarity so as to provide a more rational and practical solution to the problem of Japanese modernization.

Two very different symposia must be mentioned as direct forerunners of Overcoming Modernity: the Entretiens (Conversations) sessions held primarily throughout the major cities of western Europe under the auspices of the League of Nations' Committee on Intellectual Cooperation during the years 1932–1938 and the *Chūō kōron* (*Central Forum*) symposia of 1941–1942 that took place in Kyoto. The Entretiens sessions were intermittently chaired by Paul Valéry and numbered among its participants such luminaries as Aldous Huxley, Thomas Mann, Johan Huizinga, and Julien Benda. Part of their recorded proceedings was published in two monographs, *The Future of the European Mind* (1933) and *The Education of Modern Man* (1935), which appeared in Japanese translation in 1936 and 1937, respectively.⁴ In his essay, Kawakami makes direct reference to these sessions, criticizing them quite harshly for attempting to conceal, under the guise of culture, the decline of Europe despite the fact that Europe's political reality at the time so clearly exposed that decline. Yet it is evident that Kawakami to a large degree modeled Overcoming Modernity on these sessions and, moreover, that he believed the Japanese conference had succeeded where its European precursors had failed. As for the symposia published in the journal *Chūō kōron*, they were limited in participation to the Kyoto school, specifically four scholars of the younger generation who were then teaching at Kyoto Imperial University: Nishitani Keiji, Suzuki Shigetaka (both of whom also participated in the Overcoming Modernity symposium), Kōsaka Masaaki, and Kōyama Iwao.⁵ The first symposium was entitled "The World-Historical Standpoint and Japan" (November 26, 1941), the second "The Ethical and Historical Nature of the East Asia Co-Prosperity Sphere" (March 4, 1942), and the third "The Philosophy of Total War" (November 24, 1942). Unlike the text of Overcoming Modernity, which consists of both the transcripts of the roundtable discussions and individual essays, the published version of the *Chūō kōron* symposia (which first appeared in the journal between January 1942 and January 1943 and was published in book form in April 1943 under the title *Sekaishi-teki tachiba to Nihon* [*The World-Historical Standpoint and Japan*]) includes only the transcripts of the three roundtable discussions. These symposia also differed from Overcoming Modernity in that topics focused almost exclusively on the relation between philosophy and history without branching off into the various realms of culture. The influence of Nishida Kitarō, the founder of the

Kyoto school, was naturally quite profound. As could be expected, the content of discussion was on the whole considerably more abstract or conceptual than that of Overcoming Modernity and, given the shared background of the participants, the flow much smoother.

Regarding the topics discussed in the Overcoming Modernity symposium, it is clear that Kawakami organized the roundtable discussions in such a way as to encourage active debate and equal time among all the participants, without any overt bias in favor of his own *Bungakkai* faction. The first day's topics included "The Modern Meaning of the Renaissance," "Modernity in Science," "The Link Between Science and God," "Our Modernity," and "Modern Japanese Music"; on the second day the participants discussed "History: The Mutable and the Immutable," "The Problem of Civilization and Specialization," "The Essence of Civilization and Enlightenment in the Meiji Period," "The West Within Us," "Americanism and Modernism," and "Possibilities for Present-Day Japanese." In his closing comments at the end of the second day, Kawakami confessed to having prepared too many topics but that, given the total duration of eight hours devoted to the roundtable discussions, he wanted to ensure that conversation remained lively and covered sufficient ground.[6]

There seems to have been a general consensus that the symposium failed to achieve the goals it had originally set for itself. The notion that, amid the intellectual confusion that reigned at the time, "it was with unspeakable joy . . . that the Overcoming Modernity symposium appeared like a beacon that faintly pierced these walls [of the metaphorical prison that effectively isolated Japanese intellectuals from one another] and shone into our eyes," as Kawakami wrote, is belied by the tensions and real differences that can be discerned in both the roundtable discussions and some of the postsymposium essays.[7] There are at least three reasons the conference did not appear to live up to expectations. First, the guiding concept of modernity yielded widely disparate interpretations, as the organizers quickly realized before the roundtable sessions had even begun when reading through the individual essays. Rather than actively explore these disparities in the discussion and thus possibly arrive at a more essential grasp of this problem of the overcoming of modernity, the participants more or less skirted the issue. Second, in contrast to the *Chūō kōron* symposia, the interdisciplinary ambitions of Overcoming Modernity resulted in a mode of discourse that all too often sacrificed depth for breadth. Although there were moments when participants went beyond their own fields in search of a more general form of questioning (one thinks, for example, of the several fascinating exchanges between Nishitani and Kobayashi on the second day), it is difficult to escape the sense that disciplinary boundaries were somewhat excessively respected, thus hindering more synthetic or comprehensive analyses. And third, a serious division emerged in the roundtable sessions between the *Bungakkai* writers and the Kyoto school scholars or thinkers. This division can be perceived in the quite different approaches to the topics under discussion: whereas the former camp tended to speak about their own personal experiences, the latter generally sought a more conceptually rigorous means of expression. The inability to bridge this gap between the concrete and the abstract was implicitly seen as constitutive of the difference between literature and philosophy, without any middle space existing between them.[8]

In conclusion, I offer some remarks on the manner in which Overcoming Modernity has been received in postwar Japanese intellectual history. Rather than providing a comprehensive survey of the relevant secondary literature, I would like simply to call attention to two important texts that merit discussion in any extended treatment of the symposium: the critic and Chinese studies scholar Takeuchi Yoshimi's 1959 essay "Overcoming Modernity" and the social and literary critic Karatani Kōjin's 1994 essay of the same name. As is generally acknowledged, Takeuchi's essay was a landmark piece that was crucial in reviving questions about Japan's modernization and westernization at a time when such questioning was seen as outdated if not indeed politically suspicious and any mention of the symposium was accompanied by angry denouncements of its fascist character.[9] Takeuchi tried to demonstrate that Overcoming Modernity could hardly be understood in such simplistic terms, which rather suggested an underlying repression regarding Japan's relations with the West on the part of postwar Japanese as opposed to a more rational or balanced assessment of the symposium. Significantly, Takeuchi insisted that this symposium be examined alongside the *Chūō kōron* discussions in order to grasp as fully as possible the concrete circumstances of wartime intellectuals, and this subsequently became the standard practice among scholars.[10] In thinking about the notion of overcoming modernity in this context, Takeuchi believed, it was imperative to recognize that Japan's Fifteen-Year War was irreducibly double: although it represented a legitimate struggle against Western imperialism, the attempt to overcome such imperialism ended up repeating it in the form of Japan's own colonial aggressions throughout Asia. This logic in which the non-West (Asia) must essentially become Western in order to resist the West, or—what was seen as the same thing—become modern in order to resist modernity, was, in Takeuchi's view, never sufficiently problematized either during the war or thereafter, despite its central importance in thinking through the question of East-West relations as well as, indeed, modernity in general. This logic was inextricable from what Takeuchi called the aporias (*aporia, nankan*) of modern Japanese history, which appeared in such oppositions as reactionism vs. restoration, isolationism vs. the opening of the country, East vs. West, and so on.[11] The Overcoming Modernity symposium should justly be credited with raising these crucial issues, Takeuchi declared, which must continue to be discussed and reflected upon so as to better understand this vital notion of resistance (*teikō*) in all its political and philosophical implications.

Karatani Kōjin's "Overcoming Modernity" article is quite unlike Takeuchi's essay composed several decades earlier.[12] Beyond the widely different historical circumstances that immediately shaped these texts, to which both writers were sensitive, Karatani chose to treat the Overcoming Modernity conference in and of itself, apart from the *Chūō kōron* symposia. In so saying, however, it must be recognized that this "in and of itself" was interpreted by Karatani in the most expansive manner possible, no doubt as a result of his insight into the fundamental alterity of all historical objects, which always exceed their objectification. In order to grasp what is at stake in this symposium, then, it becomes necessary as a kind of calculated reading strategy to detour from it and touch upon not only Takeuchi's and Hiromatsu's previous studies but also such apparently unrelated topics as Kantian aesthetics, the Meiji writer Natsume Sōseki's 1906 work *Bungaku ron* (*Theory of Literature*) and the Marxist philosopher Tosaka Jun's critique of liberalism. Karatani made several valuable points in his reading. He emphasized, for example, that the notion of overcoming modernity was actually problematized well before the 1942 symposium, that already in the 1930s such thinkers as Nishida Kitarō were turning their thoughts explicitly in this direction—to say nothing of the related attempts then being made in Europe, such as those by Heidegger. Karatani also drew attention to the rift that emerged in the symposium between the literature and philosophy camps, as represented by the *Bungakkai* group and the Kyoto school. Other commentators have pointed to this tension as well, but Karatani interpreted it as an opposition between French thought and German thought, given that most of the writers were educated in modern French literature and criticism while the scholars or thinkers had all received extensive training in German philosophy. Here Karatani put forth three provocative ideas: (1) this opposition between literature (French thought) and philosophy (German thought) should properly be understood as a difference in aesthetics, which he believed opens up the political dimension of the symposium; (2) the focus on France and Germany in this context must also be regarded as a neglect of England and the United States, with which Japan was then at war. For Karatani, the general neglect or dismissal of these two countries throughout the symposium pointed to an unspoken conviction on the part of the participants that Japan would, in fact, eventually lose the war; and (3) given that, in comparison with the Kyoto school thinkers, it is the *Bungakkai* writers who demonstrate greater clarity of thought (which is seen as grounded upon their own life experiences and so distinguishes itself sharply from abstract theorizing), literature here must be regarded as more philosophical than philosophy. Now this third idea involves, in typical dialectical fashion, an ultimate reversal or inversion (*tentō*) that in a sense repeats the very aim of the Overcoming Modernity symposium itself in the participants' desire to advance beyond the West. In other words, this idea remains informed by precisely the same logic that Takeuchi warned against; to wit, that in the context of the oppositional relation, *one inevitably becomes that which one opposes.* Karatani's argument thus appears to be on rather tenuous ground here. Yet it seems that Karatani realized this trap in his determination of aesthetics as "that which surmounts and unifies actual contradictions at an imaginary level."[13] In this obvious critique of dialectics, both the *Bungakkai* group and the Kyoto school are condemned for viewing the war as just such a resolution, or sublation, of contradictions. It is on this basis that one must agree with Karatani's judgment that the symposium participants fell prey to constructing an aesthetics that was used for disastrous political ends.

NOTES

1. These figures are cited in a footnote by Takeuchi Yoshimi in his 1959 essay "Kindai no chōkoku" (Overcoming Modernity), in *What Is Modernity? Writings of Takeuchi Yoshimi*, ed. and trans. Richard F. Calichman (New York: Columbia University Press, 2005), p. 104, n. 1.
2. Kawakami Tetsutarō "'Kindai no chōkoku' ketsugo," in *Kindai no chōkoku* (Tokyo: Fuzanbō, 1979), p. 167.
3. Kawakami Tetsutarō, "Roundtable Discussion: Day One," in *Kindai no chōkoku*, pp. 171–172.
4. Watanabe Kazutami, "Re-reading 'Overcoming Modernity,'" trans. Kevin M. Doak, *Poetica* 56 (2001): 58.
5. For a study of the *Chūō kōron* symposia in English, see Horio Tsutomu, "The *Chūō kōron* Discussions, Their Background and Meaning," in *Rude Awakenings: Zen, the Kyoto School, and the Question of Nationalism*, ed. James W. Heisig and John C. Maraldo (Honolulu: University of Hawai'i Press, 1994), pp. 289–315. For a more critically incisive reading of part of these symposia, see Naoki Sakai, *Translation and Subjectivity: On "Japan" and Cultural Nationalism* (Minneapolis: University of Minnesota Press, 1997), pp. 163–170.
6. Kawakami Tetsutarō, "Roundtable Discussion: Day Two," in *Kindai no chōkoku*, p. 270.
7. Kawakami, "'Kindai no chōkoku' ketsugo," p. 167.
8. As Nishitani Keiji remarked in the second roundtable discussion, "What I find so unfortunate in contemporary Japanese literature and philosophy is the absence of any major figure who occupies a middle space between philosophy and literature, such as Pascal or Nietzsche. It is the fault of both literature and philosophy that we have not prepared the ground for the emergence of such figures" (*Kindai no chōkoku*, p. 249).
9. The significance of this work in intellectual history appears to be cemented by its inclusion in the Fuzanbō edition of *Kindai no chōkoku* (pp. 274–341). In fact, this

volume is prefaced with an introduction by Matsumoto Ken'ichi, one of the foremost scholars of Takeuchi.

10. For example, despite his severe criticisms of Takeuchi's essay, this approach was also adopted by the Marxist philosopher Hiromatsu Wataru in his book "*Kindai no chōkoku*" *ron* (*On "Overcoming Modernity"*) (Tokyo: Kōdansha, 1989).

11. Takeuchi, *Kindai no chōkoku*, pp. 145–147.

12. A translation of this essay appears in Richard F. Calichman, ed., *Contemporary Japanese Thought* (New York: Columbia University Press, 2005), pp. 101–118.

13. Ibid., p. 114.

Acknowledgments

THIS WORK WAS supported in part by a grant from the City University of New York PSC-CUNY Research Award Program. Funding was also provided by the Weatherhead East Asian Institute of Columbia University.

I am happy to express my gratitude to Takeshi Kimoto, who checked my translations with great skill and with whom I shared many valuable discussions on the Overcoming Modernity symposium. Carol Gluck supported this project from beginning to end, and through her example I have learned better what it means to contribute to a field of study. Chris Hill kindly showed me a draft of a translation he had made several years earlier of Nakamura Mitsuo's symposium essay. Likewise, Kevin Doak showed me drafts of translations he had previously undertaken of the essays by Hayashi Fusao and Kamei Katsuichirō. Kevin also generously read my translation of the Yoshimitsu Yoshihiko essay and offered several expert suggestions for revision. Akiko Ishii provided assistance with some passages in classical Japanese and helped secure materials at the Diet Library. Ben Middleton read my introduction and offered helpful criticisms; I am grateful for both his candor and his hospitality. This project also benefited from the reviews of two readers, one of whom remains anonymous; the other, John Kim, read the work scrupulously and offered several important suggestions for improving the manuscript. Finally, I give my sincere thanks to Madge Huntington of the Weatherhead East Asian Institute and Jennifer Crewe of Columbia University Press.

The book is dedicated, once again, to M.

Overcoming Modernity

Introduction: "Overcoming Modernity"

The Dissolution of Cultural Identity

CULTURE AND THE GENERAL NOTION OF IMPURITY

In the closing lines of his contributing essay for the Overcoming Modernity symposium, entitled "Kinnō no kokoro" (The Heart of Imperial Loyalty), the writer Hayashi Fusao directly addresses the figure of Japanese literature:

> Japanese literature, return to your true nature! You are the progeny of the country. You are the valiant son who, born from your country, can now exalt it. You must succeed to the proper lineage and genealogy of Japanese literature. Reject all the filth of contemporary literature! The true purity sought by literature can be found in the heart of imperial loyalty. You must cultivate only this sense of imperial loyalty as lies within your own heart! Do not look anywhere else; just walk straight on the path as revealed by this loyalty.[1]

These remarks, which Hayashi described as a prayer or supplication (*inori*) also directed to the Japanese gods, were prompted by a situation in wartime Japan that was seen by Hayashi, as well as all of the other symposium participants, as nothing less than a national crisis. This crisis went beyond the Fifteen-Year War, which ended only three years later with the nation's defeat in 1945, to include Japanese modernization itself. This modernization brought with it such a profound level of Western influence that Japanese cultural identity was perceived as at risk of disappearing. Externally, this threat of modernization or westernization manifested itself in, for example, the pervasive spread of capitalism, the introduction of machine civilization, and the importation of such political systems or ideas as liberalism and democracy. Internally, it was the influence of individualism, rationalism, and utilitarianism that was seen as most directly responsible for the decline of spirit. Such decline was to be found in all of the arts in Japan, but nowhere was this more apparent, according to Hayashi, than in the field of literature. The need for an overcoming of modernity in this field could be understood by witnessing the dominance of such schools as naturalism and proletarian literature, for these originated in the West and thus functioned strictly to conceal or repress the Japanese spirit that otherwise found its proper mode of expression in a Japanese literature that remained faithful to its roots.[2] The question arose, then, of how to most effectively accomplish this overcoming. For Hayashi, the problem demanded first of all that one make a distinction between Japan in its actual existence and Japan in its essential being, for his entire project consisted in reducing the former to the latter, or rather in allowing the potential contained within the latter to express itself in such a way as to reshape or transform the former. Japan as it existed had become foreign to itself as a result of the widespread implementation of the Meiji-period policy of *bunmei kaika* (civilization and enlightenment) which it was forced to adopt in order to ward off the threat of Western imperialism and remodel itself into a modern nation-state as based on the Western powers. Since in Hayashi's view the ills of the country were necessarily reflected in its arts, Japan's existence was thus one in which it had lost sight of its true nature (*honzen no sugata*). This nature had since the time of Meiji gradually become buried beneath what he called the filth of contemporary culture and must be unearthed in order for "true purity" to be restored.

There can be no question here of the filth contained in Japan's modernized society possibly contaminating the essential purity that lay at its core, since for Hayashi essence and actual existence were to be rigorously distinguished from one another according to what is, in fact, a classical hierarchy that endows the former with the power to shape the latter, rather than the reverse. Nevertheless, it must be pointed out that Hayashi encountered certain difficulties when he attempted to locate the historical source of Japan's impurities as a necessary step leading to their eradication. On the one hand, the reduction of such impurities and the concurrent revealing of the country's true nature took place as part of the project of overcoming modernity, which is to say that these impurities were seen as first emerging in Japanese society with the onset of westernization and modernization. On the other hand, however, Hayashi was forced to acknowledge, in seeking the antecedents of such impurity, that Japan's spiritual decline extended all the way back to the Heian period, that is, centuries prior to the introduction of Western modernization. Referring to the families that dominated Japan's imperial court politics during this period (and, later, the shogunate politics of the Kamakura period), Hayashi wrote, "The Fujiwara, Taira, and Hōjō clans were all ruined by the effeteness [*bunjaku*] of their sons, who were raised in luxury. It is also said that the long decline of imperial authority from the medieval period was due to the effeteness of the court nobility."[3] He went on, in regard to literature: "From the late Meiji to the Taishō and Shōwa periods, Japanese literature has certainly not revived the country; rather, it has made the individual forget his country. Such tendency may be traced back to the merchant literature of the Edo period and even the court literature of the Heian period."[4]

Had Hayashi simply located the origin of Japan's impurities—that is, those elements that hinder the full expression of the country's true nature—at the beginning of Western modernization, then his argument could be understood as essentially one with the widespread "Japanism" of the time in its naive identification of the foreign with that which contaminates the otherwise pure cultural space of Japan. No doubt such a view did occupy a certain place in Hayashi's thought, but what complicated matters was the fact that the filth of contemporary literature and culture in Japan could be traced back to the early stages of the country's history. That is to say, Hayashi was forced to recognize that impurities, those elements that prevent a culture from fully actualizing itself, were to be found at its source not simply *outside* but rather *within* that very culture. This insight is a crucial one for any understanding of the symposium, and yet it is important to fully grasp what is at stake here, for the determination of cultural impurities strictly as *historical phenomena* (for example, the westernization of Japan in the Meiji period, the emergence in the Heian period of a literature that putatively diminished the bonds between individual and country, and so on) leaves intact Hayashi's distinction between existence and essence and all that this distinction implies. What it implies, first and foremost, is that impurities either may or may not befall a culture, for they are no more than empirical accidents that take place depending upon the external circumstances at the time. In this way, cultural entities in their essential grounding remain ultimately exempt from all threats, which as merely historical and empirical are to be understood as external dangers only and are thus easily defended against. However, it seems that Hayashi's difficulty in locating the exact origin of Japan's cultural impurities goes beyond the relatively narrow question of historical periodization. What caused him to attribute the filth of contemporary literature and culture to Japan's incorporation of Western modernity while *also* tracing back the historical antecedents of this filth to the Heian period cannot be reduced to the inconsistencies or insufficiencies of his own historical research. Far from pointing to any subjective shortcomings of Hayashi's work as a historian, this problem of determining the source of Japan's cultural impurities ultimately derives from the real or "objective" relation between culture and the notion of impurity itself.

Although this relation is never explicitly treated in Hayashi's essay (nor, it should be added, throughout the symposium as a whole, despite its direct relevance to this topic of overcoming modernity), Hayashi did gesture toward something like the beginning of a logic through which we are better able to account for the problems that arise at this point in his argument. Here the issue concerns what is regarded as the taint or corruption of naturalist literature, which entered Japan during the Meiji period but continued to exert a strong influence thereafter:

> The strong attraction to literature on the part of Meiji and Taishō youths is above all due to the fact that literature served as their mouthpiece. During this horrible time, it was perhaps only literature that deplored and struggled against Japan's vulgarization and loss of purity. Although this struggle was weak, it is a fact that literature fought this fight desperately. Without knowing why, young people were thus attracted to it. It was through literature that they tried to guard their own spiritual purity. Unfortunately, however, the corruption of literature that accompanied society's corruption took place rapidly. *Or rather, this deadly poison was already inherent in naturalist literature from the beginning [saisho kara sono tainai ni mōdoku wo fukundeita]*.[5]

Once again, a certain hesitation or inconsistency can be discerned in the way Hayashi lays out the problem. Initially it appears to him that the corruption or poison of literature is something that affects literature from the outside; in this instance, the source of contamination is determined as Japanese society itself, against whose "vulgarization and loss of purity" Japanese literature originally struggled. At a certain point, however, literature comes in the course of this struggle to be infected by the corruption that had previously restricted itself to society. Yet Hayashi considers this possibility of literature's external corruption only to quickly reject it: "or rather" (*iya*: literally, "no" or "nay"), as he writes, such literature in fact contained that corruption within itself. Hence, even in its struggle against society's corruption, literature was *already*, however latently or unwittingly, acting as an agent for that which it sought to eradicate. What must be emphasized here is Hayashi's discovery that, despite appearances, the impurities that contaminate an entity have their source *within* that entity as opposed to befalling it from outside. In other words, following the traditional distinction to which Hayashi makes appeal, such impurities originate not at the level of actual or empirical existence but rather in the essential being of that entity itself. It is this logic that is able to resolve the problem Hayashi earlier encountered in trying to determine the origin of the filth contaminating Japan's literature and culture. Despite the slightly different contexts of these discussions, it becomes clear that the relation between cultural entities and the notion of impurity (filth, corruption, poison) is an intrinsic, or essential, one. In Hayashi's language, this impurity is what may be said to constitute the *honzen no sugata* (true nature) of any given culture. As soon as a culture comes into being, in other words, it is necessarily already corrupt: this corruption informs both its essence and existence.

This is not, however, to enact a simple reversal in the relation between essence and existence, such that the alterity of the latter now comes to overwhelm in its diversity or manifoldness the purity of the former. As is well known, reversals of this type solve nothing if they do not involve a radical transformation of the terms themselves. Rather, it is a question of seeking something like the common root or ground from which this opposition between essence and existence originally emerges. For Hayashi, as we have seen, Japan in its essential being (that is, its true nature) was opposed to its existing state, which was determined as corrupt. Any simple privileging of this latter, contra Hayashi, risks repeating the same classical gesture in setting forth an oppositional relation in which one term carries dominance over the other. Yet in reading Hayashi's text, it is apparent that the impurity he denigrates poses a much greater risk to Japanese culture—and, indeed, to any cultural entity in general—than its assigned status as merely historical or empirical would otherwise suggest. For in speaking of this impurity, he explicitly refers to its capacity to shape entities "from the beginning" and "from within" (*saisho kara sono tainai ni*). That is to say, despite his intentions, Hayashi recognizes that the notion of impurity possesses an innate or essential status as well, and this is precisely why it is so dangerous. Impurity, then, is to be found at the levels of both existence and essence. Because of the coincidence of these different levels or registers, however, the notion of impurity must be said to precede this very distinction, since the terms of this distinction—as with the terms of any distinction, of course—have meaning only by opposing themselves to one another. The most obvious consequence of this is that Japan's true nature, that to which not only Hayashi but indeed all of the symposium participants make appeal (in one form or another) in order to resolve the national crisis at the time, revealed itself to be *already* contaminated by the impurity they wished to eradicate. Hence, it is not that the notion of Japanese spirit or identity simply disappears or becomes nonsensical in this process; more precisely, what might be conceived here as a general notion of impurity ensures that such cultural essence remains haunted by that which ultimately makes it impossible.[6]

REPRESENTING JAPAN: FIVE CONTRADICTIONS

If Hayashi's text helps us better understand the dynamics of impurity in relation to particular cultural entities, then it is also instructive in explicating the role of a certain kind of prescriptive force in the subject's self-formation. One notes, for example, that Hayashi's direct address to Japanese literature as quoted earlier consists of a series of imperative statements: return to your true nature, succeed to your proper lineage and genealogy, and so forth. Yet it is no less important to recognize the appeal to subjective formation in these same lines. As Hayashi insists, "You must cultivate only this sense of imperial loyalty as lies within your own heart!" Here it is the term "cultivate" (*sodateru*) that expresses the notion of such formation, or *Bildung*. In this regard, it is no exaggeration to claim that this term, or rather the logic contained in it, functions as the motivation behind all of these imperatives, if not indeed of the entire symposium itself. By cultivating a sense of imperial loyalty, the subject of course cultivates himself—that is to say, he forms himself into a properly Japanese subject. Let us confirm this point by turning to some of the prescriptive statements issued by several other participants of the symposium. The following, for example, is a passage from Kamei Katsuichirō's essay "Gendai seishin ni kansuru oboegaki" (A Note on Contemporary Spirit), in which Kamei also makes reference to the emperor in the course of harshly criticizing the current state of language in Japan:

> I find it unbearably distressing that the abuse of slogans has created a situation in which language is made increasingly utilitarian, such that even the most meaningful words can be understood only as slogans. This tendency to standardize everything through such vulgarization must be described as a terrible crisis for spirit. Without knowing the situation in other countries, I can say that in our nation the only great words that *should spread* throughout the people's hearts are those of the imperial edicts.[7]

The composer Moroi Saburō, discussing the correct standpoint to adopt in reading the Japanese classics in his essay "Wareware no tachiba kara: kindai no chōkoku ni kansuru ichi kōsatsu" (From Our Standpoint: Reflections on Overcoming Modernity), says the following:

> However, the pursuit of the [Japanese] classics *must not be* simply retrospective. The notion that "things are good because they are old" is tantamount to antiquarianism; it is impossible to see any creativity here. In our pursuit of the classics, we *should adopt* the attitude of "restoration is renewal," for any simply reactionary or retrospective attitude *must be* thoroughly *avoided*. The notion that Japan's true spirit existed only in the past and is not present today is most dangerous and *must not be* the standpoint from which we pursue the classics.[8]

It should be pointed out that, whereas Hayashi's prescriptives are regularly expressed in the *meireikei*, or imperative form of the verb (*torikaese* [return!], *tsuge* [succeed to!], *kyozetsu seyo* [reject!], *sodateyo* [cultivate!], *ayume* [walk!]), Kamei uses the auxiliary *beki*, meaning "should," "ought," or "must" (*shintō sasubeki* [should spread]), while Moroi employs a combination of this auxiliary (*torubeki* [should adopt], *nasubeki de nai* [must not be or do]) and the prohibitive verbal expression *naranai* (*de atte ha naranai* [must not be], *sakenakereba naranai* [must be avoided]). Beyond these linguistic differences, however, it is clear that a common rule of conduct is being laid down that states, in effect, "you must become Japanese." It was necessary to issue such prescriptive statements because, as we have seen, contemporary Japanese society was perceived as having lost its properly Japanese character due to the excessive incorporation of Western methods and ideas. In this heightened sense of anxiety over the loss of cultural identity, one can detect an awareness that identity cannot be understood in such putatively empirical terms as, for example, race, ethnicity, or language. Were identity something natural or immediate, there would be no need for these prescriptives and the process of subjective formation that they are intended to effect. Or rather, from a slightly different perspective: if identity can be understood only as immediate, then this awareness on the part of the symposium participants is of the strange impotency of this notion. This strangeness, in fact, conceals a series of contradictions that lie at the very heart of the symposium. On the one hand, for example, Japanese cultural identity is regarded as the source or origin of Japanese society. As the essence (or true nature) of this society, such identity possesses an ontologically privileged status in relation to all that actually exists in Japan, and this is particularly true given the nation's contamination by the modern West, which has made Japan, so to speak, *less Japanese* and so triggered the national crisis. In this way, the participants reveal their conviction in the ultimate force of this identity, for it is capable of anchoring the entire nation and its long history to itself. On the other hand, however, this origin that is Japanese identity is acknowledged to be more or less powerless, incapable of preventing the spread of westernization and the contemporary crisis. In the face of the historical waning of this origin, the conference participants were forced to come to its aid by prescribing the correct course of action for people to return to it. For Hayashi, this meant that the Japanese people must recover their "heart of imperial loyalty" that lies buried within them, beneath the sedimented layers of westernization. For Kamei, it required halting the circulation of slogans and all that promoted the vulgarization of language so as to focus attention more exclusively on the imperial edicts. And for Moroi, the task at hand involved transforming the manner of interpreting the Japanese classics so as to reflect the fact that Japan's true spirit did not simply lie in the past but also lived on in the present day.

These figures of the emperor, the Japanese language (which reached its highest form in the imperial edicts), and the Japanese classics, respectively, must be understood as representatives of that original Japanese identity that was otherwise absent. In other words, they functioned to ideologically direct the people back to that original site that could not, however, be said to exist anywhere else but in its represented forms. Clearly, this return to original identity on the part of the Japanese people could not be achieved directly given its absence or obscuration in modern society. The return could only be effected, therefore, by introducing a process of subject formation whose telos of producing Japanese citizens who fully embody their essential identity was to be reached sometime in the future. Finally, the transition from original identity to those historical figures whose role it is to represent this origin was perceived as necessary but dangerous. It was necessary because of the origin's decline, as I have stated, but the danger lay in the fact that these representations could always represent poorly or badly, they could always go astray. Indeed, Kamei made precisely this point regarding the current state of the Japanese language, which had unfortunately yielded to the pressures of modernization in such a way as to become vulgar and ridden with slogans. Ideally, the language should convey a sense of pure Japanese identity, for this is the task that it was intended to fulfill.[9] Linguistic reform must, it was reasoned, take place in view of this ideal or essential origin, but the far greater problem was that the Japanese language should never have lost sight of its origin to begin with. It fell to Kamei and the other symposium participants to restore this essential quality to the language, and this was accomplished through the use of prescriptives: the Japanese language should—or must, ought to—be what it (originally) was, not what it (presently) is. Although the very need for these prescriptives signified that original Japanese identity was somehow defective, they were nevertheless seen as capable of bridging the gap between the ideal origin and the fallen present.

For the sake of clarity, I enumerate in the following some of the contradictions or inconsistencies revealed in this relation between original Japanese identity and those historical figures (the emperor, the Japanese language, the Japanese classics) that functioned as its representatives.

1. Whether referred to as Japan's "true nature" (Hayashi) or "true spirit" (*Nihon no hontō no seishin* [Moroi]), original Japanese identity was seen as the primal force uniting the country throughout the various permutations of its history. It is this original identity, for example, that distinguished Japan and the Japanese people from all other nations and peoples. Beginning with the importation of Western modernity into the country in the Meiji period, however, this identity had somehow become eclipsed to the point of disappearing, as could be seen in contemporary society in the loss of imperial loyalty, the vulgarization of the Japanese language, and the merely antiquarian readings of the Japanese classics. These historical signs indicated a certain powerlessness or defectiveness at the essential core of Japan which required in response an intervention on the part of the country's cultural authorities—the symposium participants. Indeed, the conference itself was organized in part precisely as such an intervention. Yet this begs the question of the status of Japanese identity in its essence or origin: given the force of this origin, which was capable of negating

all relevant historical differences as moments contained strictly within the internal development of the nation, why was it seen as under threat by foreign influence? How is one to explain this sudden fragility of what was otherwise so powerful? Above all, what can possibly account for this reversal of power relations, for in effect the ground (original identity) needed to appeal to the grounded (the historical manifestations of this identity) for support?

2. The appeal made by the symposium participants on behalf of Japanese identity to the people, urging that they return to their original identity so as to become, in effect, *more Japanese*, carried certain risks of which the participants were not unaware. Here it is important to recall the fact that, as a result of Japan's extensive colonial expansion during the course of its modernization, the notion of Japanese identity had radically opened up and become accessible to not only so-called native Japanese, but also Taiwanese and Koreans, for example (given the annexation of Taiwan in 1895 and that of Korea in 1910, among other territories).[10] Hence, this ideology of identification qua Japanese, as can be seen to have informed, for instance, the prescriptive statements quoted in the preceding, was considerably broadened. No doubt this broadening of Japanese identity beyond the confines of native Japanese was perceived as carrying its own risks, but what I would like to emphasize here is that the very attempt on the part of the Japanese people to aid or restore the origin that essentially determined who they are inevitably put that origin in jeopardy. The reason for this is to be found in the suspect quality of the people themselves. Specifically, the Japanese people were seen as insufficiently Japanese; they were too foreign. For example, beginning in the Taishō period, with the continued erosion of traditional Japanese culture through the ongoing dissemination of civilization and enlightenment, the Japanese had gradually fallen victim to what Tsumura called the "infection" (*kansen*) of Americanism. Indeed, this infection had, in the early part of the twentieth century, spread throughout the world to affect Europeans as well as the Japanese. As a film critic, Tsumura naturally focused on his own field: "American film spreads American customs, embracing countries in a longing for the American way of life. With its jazz, eroticism, and optimism, American film spreads both its powerful toxins and *considerable charm*."[11] This foreign infection that had become part of Japanese society and people could in turn infect the essential origin of Japanese identity in the very attempt to restore it. In other words, the national crisis of the time was a situation in which the inside (original Japanese identity) needed to appeal to a kind of immediate outside (the Japanese people) in order to overcome its own self-alienation, but this outside was feared to be, given the infection of foreign elements, *too outside*, or at least more outside than inside. The exteriority of the Japanese people vis-à-vis their original identity needed to be accepted according to the logic of representation, but only on the condition that this

exteriority be an *outside of an inside*, in which the bond that tied these people back to their point of origin was privileged, as opposed to an *outside of an outside*, in which they were linked more tightly to the foreign as that which was doubly outside the ground of Japan. In any event, what is clear is that the possibility of infection was not simply limited to the spread of Americanism in Japan but rather emerged more generally in the very restoration of original Japanese identity.

3. A division inherent in the structure of representation allowed for these figures of the emperor, the Japanese language, and the Japanese classics to function as the signs of an original or essential Japanese identity that had no natural existence and was not to be found anywhere else except in these signs. This division set in motion a kind of circular referral between these figures and the Japanese essence that they represented, the force of which was all the greater because of its tautological nature. The tautology can be summed up as follows: "These figures represent the essential ground of Japan because that is where they originate," and, conversely, "This essential ground of Japan can be understood through the mediation of those figures because they are its representational expressions." Such statements, in their obviousness, require no empirical testing or proof, which indeed would almost certainly have been criticized at the symposium under the name of positivism (*jisshōshugi*), as, for example, Kobayashi criticized positivism in the field of literature.[12] My intent here is not to defend positivism; rather, I would like to draw attention to the fact that Kobayashi, in his opposition to this method, makes a direct appeal to Plato and his theory of ideas. Specifically, what attracts Kobayashi to Plato is the transcendence of concrete history, for it is only beyond history that one can understand the immutable and true nature of things. Kobayashi illustrates his view of Platonism as follows:

> No matter how much we interpret or criticize history in our modern fashion, we can never approach its beauty. The beauty of history lies in the fact that such dead men as Kusunoki Masashige existed in such a form as to surpass all our interpretations of him. To see this form is to understand history. For example, it is absolutely impossible to understand the Kamakura period by determining its nature, how it emerged as a result of the Heian period, and then how it influenced the next period. Regardless of how we explain the Kamakura period, either through such causal interpretations or dialectical interpretations, its form remains unmoved. I have come to understand the importance of sensing this form. No matter how one interprets Mount Fuji, it is necessary when sketching it that one's interpretation not change the mountain's form. It is an important secret that historical facts be seen in just this manner.[13]

Despite Kobayashi's rather unorthodox interpretation here, it seems clear that his notion of "form" (*katachi*) refers to the Platonic eidos/idea, meaning essence, idea, or form. (After this passage Kobayashi translates eidos/idea more traditionally in its phoneticized form as *idea*). It will perhaps be recalled that eidos/idea in Platonic philosophy signifies the universal forms of things that transcend the phenomenal world and belong properly to the noumenal world, the world of the real and eternal. However, this division between noumena and phenomena, eidos/idea and appearances, universal and particular, abstract and concrete, and so on is not a simple one since these latter terms exist in a mimetic relation to the former; that is, their change or movement is motivated by a desire for self-perfection that, although ultimately unattainable, nevertheless always binds such singular instances to their ideal forms, of which they are then the imperfect copy. Kobayashi's otherwise innocuous referral to the Platonic idea reveals, I believe, that the logic of the various figures of Japanese identity (the emperor, the Japanese language, the Japanese classics, and others) in their relation to what is essentially Japanese is, precisely, a mimetology.[14] A closed system is presented here in which origin (the real, the eternal) and copy (the simulated, the fluctuating) refer interminably back to each other, one reinforcing the next in circular form. In this regard, the constant appeal on the part of the symposium participants to the historical figures of Japanese identity must be understood as *ideological* in the profound sense of this term, for both these appeals and figures derive from the *idea* of Japanese identity itself. Many scholars have denounced the symposium's ideological character, and these indications are valuable, particularly in the light of the various political defenses of Overcoming Modernity put forth by conservative thinkers. Nevertheless, it is important to grasp that ideology in this context is, first and foremost, a question of a mimetic relation to the otherwise transcendent idea of Japan. The circularity of the referral between this idea and those figures that represent it is such as to also contain within itself the very propagators of this ideology, that is, the symposium participants, for in their view they are as fully informed or imprinted by this idea as these figures themselves.[15]

4. A strange temporality emerges here in what is, literally, the *project* (*project*) to restore Japanese identity through the mediation of various historical figures. According to this temporality, the return to the origin of one's cultural identity can be effected only by moving further into the future, since the present is, in this case, determined as the time of formation as or into Japanese subjects. To refer once again to Hayashi's language, the return takes place through a process of "cultivation," such that one becomes in the future that which one most originally is or was. In other words, telos and origin are seen as one, they are the twin points that enable the construction of a narrative of Japanese identity as, precisely, a tale of presence, loss, and recovery. For the sympo-

sium participants, Japanese identity historically existed at one time in all its fullness and immediacy. With the intervention of Western modernity in the Meiji period, however, Japan suffered a fall from this idyllic time in which the country's actual existence remained yet close to its essence. Modernity is thus determined as the period of Japan's alienation from itself, which is to say, then, that the overcoming of modernity is seen as the path of self-restoration, in which all exteriority to Japanese identity is either eliminated or absorbed in the return to one's proper nature.[16] Two comments must be made in this connection: First, the logic according to which *the origin can be approached only by further distancing oneself from it* demands that the link remain open between past and future. Since the past is retroactively imagined to be the site where the Japanese spirit manifested itself most fully, it will be held out as an ideal for the future. For this reason, it becomes necessary to harshly condemn those who close off this link and dwell excessively on the past. We can see such condemnation in Moroi's remarks, as quoted earlier:

> However, the pursuit of the [Japanese] classics must not be simply retrospective. The notion that 'things are good because they are old' is tantamount to antiquarianism; it is impossible to see any creativity here. In our pursuit of the classics, we should adopt the attitude of 'restoration is renewal,' for any simply reactionary or retrospective attitude must be thoroughly avoided. The notion that Japan's true spirit existed only in the past and is not present today is most dangerous and must not be the standpoint from which we pursue the classics.

The poet Miyoshi Tatsuji perceived exactly this same threat to the Japanese spirit, but, unlike Moroi, he specifically attributed such reactionism to the Japanists: "This morbidly zealous tendency of the so-called Japanists fully runs the risk of hindering the future of the Japanese spirit. The fervor and effort with which the nation as a whole is trying to advance toward the future are matched only by the Japanists in their advance toward the past. For them, the past has in fact become their future."[17] In their narrow focus on tradition, the Japanists and other reactionaries failed to understand the projective nature of subject formation. They did not grasp the paradox whereby absolute fidelity to the Japanese spirit risks suffocating it. This spirit requires *difference* in order to expand and develop, which is why one must allow for the Japanese past to now give way so that the Japanese future may emerge from it. Second, between the origin and telos of Japanese identity there stretches the span of Japanese history, which both is and is not equivalent to that identity. Japanese history partakes in that identity, which is after all what provides it with its specifically Japanese character, but in its historical aspect it has become radically opened up to difference and all that is foreign. This distinction between original Japanese identity and history presupposes what is, in fact, a classical metaphysical-theological notion: *history as fall*. Here historical difference is recognized strictly on the condition that it be derivative of a prior unity. Such a difference is thus merely temporary or even aberrant, for it remains always in view of that unity from which it emerges and to which it is destined in advance to return. This notion, or logic, can be seen to inform certain historiographic interpretations on the part of several symposium participants, who abstract this distinction between histori-cal difference and transcendent unity or identity so as to bring it to bear on intrahistorical differences—that is to say, history itself becomes the arena in which is played out the difference between difference and unity. In the follow-ing two passages, for example, Nishitani Keiji and Yoshimitsu Yoshihiko con-ceive of the collapse of unity that brought about the end of the Middle Ages and the beginning of modernity. Nishitani:

> In the West of the Middle Ages, these three concepts [of God, world, and soul] formed an undivided harmony as united in Christianity. Despite the many disturbances throughout medieval intellectual history, it can be said that this foundation itself was solid. However, the loss in relationality between these three concepts resulted in the collapse of the medieval spirit along with the imposing structure of its worldview.[18]

Yoshimitsu:

> In this sense as well, what had existed in the living *total unity* of the Middle Ages (such unity was rooted in the ethos and living nature of the simple society of the people, and corresponded to its social reality) lost its ground of original life in modernity, insofar as this was an atomistic or atomistic-collective consciousness of the *isolated and abstract individual*. Thus, with the inhuman application of the technological intellect, modern Western society followed its fateful path toward the "slave society" of capitalist self-interest, or rather plutocratic rule.[19]

What is of concern here is not the particular object of inquiry, the Middle Ages and its transition to modernity, but rather the methodology itself. For change and difference are conceived in these instances entirely on the basis of unity, their force domesticated by the various forms or structures that both precede and control it. This relative unimportance of the object of inquiry vis-à-vis the guiding methodological principle of unity can be confirmed by examining Nishitani and Yoshimitsu's treatment of other objects in precisely the same fashion. Yoshimitsu, for example, views human history in toto according to the theological narrative trajectory of God's presence, the loss or forgetting of Him, and finally His return. Nishitani, for his part, conceives of the influence of westernization in the Meiji period as a destruction of a prior Japanese unity (which will, however, be recovered upon the overcoming of Western modernity): "It is simply that Western culture, with all its discordant divisions, infiltrated throughout such places as post-Restoration Japan, thereby bringing about the danger of *splitting apart the very foundation of the nation's unified world-view formation* such that people would fall into confusion in their self-understanding."[20] In both cases, a tripartite structure is elaborated in which the loss of original presence signifies a crisis of negativity that is ultimately resolved by the origin's repetition or re-presencing. What must be underscored here is the repression (or an unthought) in both Yoshimitsu and Nishitani of a conception of violence—or force, difference, change—as itself originary, such that the loss of primordial unity and identity is properly recognized as nothing more than a retrospective fantasy.[21]

5. In order to appear in its effectivity, the origin is forced to give itself not as it truly is but rather strictly in the form of representation, which must be understood as a necessarily diluted or attenuated repetition of itself. The embodied figures of Japanese identity are thus not to be confused with Japanese identity itself, for they are no more than its historical proxies or agents. The element in which such figurative representations appear is the world, in which their movement is governed by contingency. Yet this opening to contingency is what constitutes the freedom of things, for although they are constrained to represent the origin from which they derive, their removal from that origin means that representation can always be seduced and led astray, as it were. Other forces are at work on these figures, and their interactions with them produce traces of these encounters that are never completely eradicable. The Japanese language, for example, exists in a world where it invariably encounters other languages, and the contact that it experiences with these others *affects* it, that is to say, it leaves behind marks that ensure that Japanese is never quite the same language it was before that contact. This simple phenomenon is perhaps best illustrated by the presence of *gairaigo* (loanwords) that derive from outside Japan but subsequently become part of the Japanese language: such terms are the product of an "interlingual" encounter that in some way alters Japanese and makes it less purely itself.[22] A similar example can be found in the Japanese classics. Although these texts are generally thought to represent the Japanese spirit, they can nevertheless always be read in such a manner that their link back to this spirit becomes severed or otherwise jeopardized. This freedom on the part of things in their representational function is indivisible from their exposure to the world's alterity, but this is also to say that such a function is essentially threatened by the world. Representations are distinguished from their represented origin by virtue of their lack of force. A Japanese classical text, for example, can be lost to history, but the Japanese spirit or identity that it represents is in no way harmed by this merely contingent and empirical loss. Paradoxically

enough, however, it is precisely this lack of force that constitutes the representational object's force. By being in the world, these objects acquire the potential to become other than what they originally or essentially are. What is crucial here is the recognition that the origin, in its desire to double itself and thus appear effectively in the world, has no choice but to *relinquish its propriety over what is otherwise its own representations*. This means that representation can always fail, that indeed this failure of representation exists as a kind of structural (or essential, formal) component of representation itself.[23] It is noteworthy how resistant the symposium participants were to this logic of representation, but it is at the same time entirely understandable given the earnestness of their desire in this period of national crisis to restore Japanese identity to its proper unity. This desire can be realized only through the means of representation, that is, through the various figures of Japaneseness to which the participants ideologically appealed, and yet this very vehicle upon which they depended constantly threatened to sabotage their project from within. Once again, it is a question of seeing past the diverse topics the participants happened to be treating at the time in their individual essays or during the roundtable sessions so as to discern the common underlying principles that shaped their thought. Tsumura Hideo, for example, criticized the popularity of Western cinema among Japanese youths during the Shōwa period because this medium illegitimately usurped or supplanted the literary classics on which it is occasionally based: "A frivolous situation has come about in which a great many youths watch the American films *Crime and Punishment* and *Resurrection* with the intention of understanding Tolstoy and Dostoyevsky."[24] Tsumura's point is that a proper understanding of these writers is possible only by returning to the source, the literary works themselves, for any cinematic or other adaptation invariably distorts the author's original meaning. A similar sentiment can be found in Kamei Katsuichirō, who denounced the contemporary practice of making photographic reproductions of ancient Japanese art objects, since something valuable is unavoidably lost in this transition from thing to image: "In their confidence that objects are accurately reproduced, spectators have lost sight of the astonishing inaccuracy resulting from the loss of those shaded emotions lying within the object's depths."[25] However, this threat of representation is of course not limited to such modern technological innovations as the camera. Any time an origin is repeated, resulting in the division between a referent and its representation, the possibility emerges of the latter somehow betraying the former, taking on its own life and signifying otherwise. This possibility is addressed, in very different contexts but with essentially the same attitude, by Hayashi Fusao and the literary critic Nakamura Mitsuo. In the following passage, Hayashi chastises those biographers of the iconic samurai figure and leader of the Satsuma Rebellion Saigō Takamori for their belief that the question of Saigō's lineage is an unimportant one: "I have frequently encountered the argument that, since the genealogy of the Saigō clan . . . is not so much a fabrication as a mere subsequent discovery on the part of biographers, it is sufficient to recognize Saigō Takamori's greatness without regard to his lineage. For me, however, such an argument represents the common sense of modernism in its destruction of tradition, and is utterly unrealistic. With the advent of 'civilization and enlightenment,' the Japanese people forgot the value of tradition and lineage."[26] For Nakamura, the origin in question is not so much temporal as it is spatial. Unlike Hayashi, he is not concerned in the following lines with a figure of the Japanese past whose links back further into this past are neglected by scholars of the Japanese present; rather, Nakamura wishes to remind contemporary Japanese people that the everyday objects they use originally came not from Japan but from the West. Here, interestingly, Hayashi's dialogue with Saigō's biographers is mirrored by Nakamura's dialogue with those Japanese for whom the question of an object's origin has become irrelevant: "I imagine people might respond as follows: 'Indeed, it is true that these things were originally imported from the West, but they have now become Japanized to such an extent that no one considers them to be Western. Since the people have now grown sufficiently familiar with these things, there is no longer any need to look into their background.' On the contrary, however, I believe that our current failure to realize that these things are Western reveals how deeply this influence has permeated our lives."[27] In all these four cases, one can perceive a sense of moral indignation with the deceit and usurpation of representation vis-à-vis that which is represented: film adaptations not only distort the meaning of the literary works on which they are based, but they have also supplanted these works as the means by which people acquire an understanding of the original authors; photographs of art objects give people a false sense that they have understood these objects, when in fact such representations are unable to capture the essential elements of this art; biographers of historical figures neglect the genealogical origins from which they come, because of which their interpretations of these figures are deficient and misleading; and finally the gradual Japanization of everyday objects that first came from the West misleads people into believing that these object are Japanese rather than foreign. Caught in these contradictions of representation, the symposium participants had no choice but to speak of its enormous promise in restoring Japanese identity to itself while, at the same time, they warned in the direst of tones of the threat it posed to origins in general. The message was this: Return to the long-neglected Japanese spirit by earnestly devoting yourself to its representations, such as the emperor, the Japanese language, and the Japanese classics! However, do not trust representations, for they are inherently deceitful and can lead you astray! This situation would be comical if one did not keep in mind the explicitly national-culturalist ideology promoted throughout the symposium. It is precisely because of the destructive historical effects of this ideology that one must, I believe, become attentive to its underlying contradictions.[28]

THE MOVEMENT ACROSS:
TRANSMISSIONS AND TRANSPLANTATIONS

As can be seen in the enormous complexity of these contradictions, the question of overcoming modernity presented no easy solutions for the symposium participants. Nevertheless, it is remarkable how acutely these individuals understood that this question demanded of them a kind of self-critique, since it was no longer possible in twentieth-century Japan to speak of Western modernity as simply foreign or alien. Shimomura's remark that "the overcoming of modernity is the overcoming of ourselves" was echoed by many others, who stressed that the gravity of the problem was directly related to the fact that it now concerned Japan's own interiority. As Nakamura Mitsuo concluded, "A sound first step toward overcoming modernity consists in clearly recognizing such spiritual crisis as an internal enemy [*miuchi no teki*: literally, "an enemy within the body"] to be fought."[29] Kamei Katsuichirō confirmed this point during the discussions when he commented on the manner in which "the poisons we received from the West have circulated within our body [*wareware no tainai ni*] since the time of civilization and enlightenment."[30] For Kawakami Tetsutarō, following the traditional mind-body distinction, the modern Japanese intellectual had himself become the site of a dualism between his "Japanese blood" and "Europeanized intellect": "We intellectuals were certainly at a loss then [during the first year of the Pacific War], for our Japanese blood that had previously been the true driving force behind our intellectual activity was now in conflict with our Europeanized intellects, with which it had been so awkwardly systematized."[31] Finally, the historian Suzuki Shigetaka asserts in his essay "'Kindai no chōkoku' oboegaki" (A Note on "Overcoming Modernity") that "this issue of overcoming modernity must in one sense be seen as related to us, since European civilization has today already become deeply internalized [*naizaika seshimerare*] within our country and is no longer merely an alien civilization but actually now a part of us. That is to say, the modernity that is to be overcome exists not only in Europe but indeed within us as well."[32]

At its most fundamental level, Japan's national crisis thus revealed itself to be a crisis of the self. This self experiences the loss of its integrity and knows itself to be divided, for now another force exists within it. The difficulty, however, is that this foreign invader cannot be easily identified, since it lacks any substantial form and, like a poison, enters the bloodstream only to circulate throughout the entire body. Typically, the symposium participants recognized this breach of interiority strictly in its historicist sense: by determining the breach to have occurred at a certain moment in history, it was reduced to nothing more than an empirical aberration, an evil that supervenes upon a preexisting good. In other words, Japan's normal state of affairs was regarded as one in which the border between the self and its outside remains inviolate, such that domestic elements are never confused with the foreign. At no point in the conference was the possibility ever considered that the source of the crisis might not simply be historical in this sense, that rather the self (however defined, as either an individual or collectivity) exists *in principle*—that is to say, at all times—in crisis given its exposure to an alterity over which it has no control. The self's crisis is thus the "normal" state of the self since it never exists in the world otherwise. In its threat to the sovereignty of the self, however, this basic exposure to alterity must be disavowed—just as, according to the Freudian notion of *Verleugnung*, the male child is forced to disavow his own perception of the absence of the penis in the female out of fear of being castrated himself, just as she evidently was earlier.[33] Such disavowal bespeaks a desire: in the case of Overcoming Modernity, this desire involved the elimination of those traces of the other that prevented the self from being itself in all its imagined purity and absoluteness. The symposium participants readily perceived this absence of pure Japaneseness in Japan, and yet they had to deny the fundamental nature of this impurity in order to maintain their fantasy of cultural identity. This operation of disavowal can very clearly be read in the several passages just quoted from Nakamura, Kamei, Kawakami, and Suzuki. The compromising of Japan's borders by foreign elements created a situation in which cultural interiority and exteriority could no longer be neatly delineated. The participants knew this—such knowledge appears unambiguously in these passages—and yet they simultaneously shielded themselves from this knowledge by organizing the hybridized space of Japan in the oppositional terms of native and foreign. This gesture of organizing the noncoincidence of the self with itself according to the distinction between *authentically internal* and *inauthentically internal* is a classical one and can be found in all nationalist ideologies. The lesson to be derived from this gesture concerns the relation between difference and oppositionality: namely, the notion of oppositionality emerges retroactively as an attempt to disavow the originary "fact" of difference. In this way, oppositionality retains its status as difference, but strictly on the condition that it be recognized as difference disavowed.

It is this disavowal of difference in the form of oppositionality that allows the self to maintain its fantasy of absolute sovereignty. In the context of the symposium, this can be seen even in the essay of Nishitani Keiji, who was without question the most powerful thinker of subjectivity in attendance. Nishitani lays out the problem of subjectivity quite succinctly, in a manner that reveals the impressive clarity of both his ideas and means of expression. The task was to determine the precise nature of true subjectivity, what Nishitani called, following his teacher Nishida Kitarō, the "standpoint of subjective nothingness" (*shutaiteki mu no tachiba*).³⁴ In order to arrive at this elemental level of the self, Nishitani declared, it is necessary to go beyond the scientific standpoints of biologism and psychologism. True subjectivity is not to be found either in the physical body or in consciousness, to say nothing of such classical notions as the mind or soul, both of which have been definitively superseded by modern psychology. The body and consciousness can be objectified by science, which thus presupposes the existence of a deeper level of subjectivity that acts as the ground of such objectification, and which is not itself apprehensible as an object. This deeper subjectivity can be found in the operation of a "self-interiority" (*jiko naimen*) that expresses itself in free and spontaneous acts. Since these acts do not follow the principle of causality in the manner of actually existing entities, one must recognize that subjectivity is ultimately not an ontic phenomenon; rather, a fundamental shift is required here from the register of being to that of nothingness.

Nishitani was forced by reason of economy to move quickly in his explanation of this notion of subjective nothingness and to show how the everyday conception of the self is, in its merely ontic (or substantialist) nature, derivative and misleading. All of this is explained much more elaborately in his first book, *Kongenteki shutaisei no tetsugaku* (*The Philosophy of Elemental Subjectivity* [1940]). What must be emphasized here, however, is that Nishitani's account of subjectivity remained ultimately framed in the oppositional terms of East and West. As he argues at the conclusion of section 2 in his essay, "As goes without saying, this standpoint of subjective nothingness is a feature of Oriental religiosity. Only Oriental religiosity resolves the difficulties of the relation between culture and science as contained in the religiosity of the post-Renaissance West. True liberalism can be realized only in this kind of freedom. This is Oriental liberalism."³⁵ Yet the question demands to be asked: why did Nishitani, after offering such a forceful critique of any ontic or regional understanding of the subject, appeal to an oppositional logic that is in fact fully enabling of modern conceptions of subjectivity? As Nishitani doubtless understood, the relation between man and world comes in the modern era to be conceived in explicitly theoretical terms as an opposition between the epistemological subject (*shukan*) and object (*taishō*). Modern man seeks to establish his own subjectivity by positing an opposition between himself and other entities. It is through this act of positing that others are negated in their inherent difference or alterity and transformed into objects. This process can be understood in part etymologically, since the object is that which the subject projects opposite (ob- [*tai*-]) itself so as to constitute itself reflectively in relation to it.³⁶ On the basis of this logic, however, it is clear that, in the context of the East-West relation to which Nishitani refers, each of these terms, East and West, determines itself in its identity strictly by negating its oppositional other. The East, that is to say, is what it is only by posing itself against the West, and vice versa. In this sense, it appears puzzling why Nishitani clung to a logic that his notion of subjectivity otherwise ungrounds and exposes as derivative. As we saw earlier in the case of various contradictions existing within the relation between Japanese identity and its representational figures, however, such inconsistencies conceal a *desire*. For Nishitani, this desire is that Japan and, more broadly, Asia (the Orient) as a whole be seen in its unique identity as a simple outside of the West.

However, it is not difficult to see that this desire is a profoundly reactive one. That is, the wish for an exclusively Japanese or Eastern identity emerges as a reactionary response to the desire for an exclusively Western identity. In its reactivity, the former desire simply *repeats* the exclusionary violence of the latter, no matter how much it wishes to distance itself from it. This scene of positing a proper space for Japan is, I believe, ultimately a product of ressentiment, in which the slave (Japan) triumphs over the master (the West) by outmastering him, by, in other words, beating him at his own game. The problem, however, is that the rules of this game of cultural identity—which is, of course, a form of *subjective* identity, regardless of its grounding in nothingness—remain entirely in place, internalized all the more deeply in this overcoming of one's historical subjection. Here we can understand how the disavowal of difference in the form of oppositionality ensures that the dialectic between the master and slave remains always one in which the notion of subjective identity emerges as the real victor.[37]

What logic, then, can be mobilized "against" the more derivative and theoretically based oppositional logic whose destructive effects can be seen throughout the symposium? This other logic must be capable, in its generality, of accounting for the oppositionality that undergirds East and West cultural identity, but it must also, by virtue of this same generality, be able to *unground* that oppositionality, open it up to the alterity that is its true or proper element. It will perhaps come as no surprise to learn that such logic did not simply exist *outside* the symposium but rather operated within it in a kind of repressed or disavowed form. This logic is that of transmission. One of its clearest articulations can be found in the writings of Paul Valéry, the French poet and essayist who, in the 1930s, chaired several of the Entretiens sessions, which were so influential in the formation of Overcoming Modernity. In his foreword to the first edition of *Regards sur le monde actuel* (*Reflections on the World Today* [1931]), for example, Valéry begins by recalling that he first became conscious of Europe as a distinct entity in the final years of the nineteenth century when he heard news of two wars, the Sino-Japanese War (1894–1895) and the Spanish-American War (1898): "One was the first act of power by an Asiatic nation remodeled and equipped on European lines; the other was the first act of power against a European nation by a nation derived and, as it were, developed from Europe."[38] In considering this paradox in which Europe was, so to speak, taken out of itself and applied in contexts that were completely different from those it originally intended—and indeed, in the case of the Spanish-American War, appropriated for use *against itself*—Valéry was forced to rethink the relation between Europe and science, for it was science in its applied forms that so crucially determined the development and outcome of these two wars: "Europe founded science, which has transformed life and vastly increased the power of those who possess it. But by its very nature science is essentially transmissible; it is necessarily reducible to universal methods and formulas. The means it affords to some, all can acquire. . . . So the artificial imbalance of power on which European predominance has been based for three hundred years is tending rapidly to vanish."[39]

Europe thus creates something that is inherently capable of transcending Europe. Given that it is "essentially transmissible," science possesses the strange ability to betray the site from which it originates without losing anything at all in that transmission. Its promiscuity, as it were, means that anyone can use it regardless of differences in time and place and it will remain the *same* science. This is why, of course, it is absurd to speak of science as in any way regionally determined: there is no such thing as Canadian physics, Thai biology, and so on. Science in its universality (its "universal methods and formulas," as Valéry writes) radically ungrounds such regional determinations, in apparent contrast to the cultural or human sciences (*jinbun kagaku*), where such things as *Japanese* literature or *Japanese* history, for example, function as legitimate objects of inquiry. As is well known, this distinction between the natural sciences and historical sciences was central to neo-Kantianism.[40] Yet even here, major differences emerged regarding the place of universality in these latter culturally or historically based sciences, and this question is still vigorously debated today. What is in any case clear is that Valéry's notion of European science illustrates that a certain kind of universality is able to be produced from an empirically contingent point of origin. Valéry commonly associated the European with universality—a point that was surely not lost on those symposium participants who were familiar with his work—but what reveals itself in these passages is that the link between universality (understood here as that which is able to transcend its own empirical context and still retain the same functionality) and regional determination is an exceedingly fragile one. By transcending the original site and circumstances of its production, European science quickly sheds its parochial beginnings and becomes, depending upon its employer, *Japanese* science or *American* science, to cite only the two particular sites of appropriation or usurpation mentioned by Valéry. In such cases, the empirical origins of science, along with its various empirical destinations, become utterly irrelevant, which means that universality in the course of its movement threatens these regional determinations, which are no more than its temporary points of transit. This is not to claim, of course, that this movement of universality in its transcendence of particular sites results in the effacement of these latter. Such would be the trap of formalism in its indifference to the markings of empiricity. Nevertheless, it seems undeniable that this power of transcendence does create certain effects in these particular regional sites. For this force does not simply respect these sites in their integrity; on the contrary, its very operation takes place by violating that integrity, penetrating within those sites in such a way as to leave its borders fundamentally unsettled.

For all of Valéry's importance in the formation of the symposium, he is in fact mentioned by name only three times, twice by Kawakami and once by Yoshimitsu. The first instance occurs in Kawakami's essay, where Valéry and the Entretiens sessions in which he participated are mentioned as more or less a model for Overcoming Modernity. Kawakami notes with contempt that Valéry and others "skillfully contrived that the topic for discussion be 'How Are Europeans Possible?' First-rate intellectuals thus exhausted their minds in trying to strip the body from the intellect."[41] The second instance is to be found in the day two roundtable discussion, where Kawakami remarks that "all of Valéry's conclusions in his theory of civilization reveal that he is nothing but a mystic of machinery, and for this reason I find him ultimately trivial."[42] The third reference to Valéry appears in the course of Yoshimitsu's denunciation of the various critiques of modernity to be found in the West; Yoshimitsu calls attention to "the new *myth of the intellect* on the part of such 'Godless mystics' as Alain and Valéry, who in their desperate faith of self-reliance try like Ulysses to save themselves from drowning by resolutely throwing themselves into an ocean of despair."[43] Such comments have their own interest and value, no doubt, but what I would like to pursue here is the logic—or perhaps quasi-logic—that Valéry unearths in his reference to Japan and the notion of European identity in its relation to the transmission of scientific universality. In this context, it is important to understand that science represents but one form of this universalism. While it is significant that Valéry singles out this particular form in its historical consequences, we must not fail to grasp that the crucial feature of this universalism lies in the fact that it is "essentially transmissible," as he writes— that is, it is capable of transcending its originating context and functioning in the same manner elsewhere. What is so threatening about such universalism is its indifference to particular cultures: once unleashed, as Valéry perceives, not even Europe wields control over European science. Clearly, this threat affects the status of the whole-part relation that is so fundamental to the maintenance of cultural identity. For culture is generally regarded in spatial terms as a kind of whole that is composed of its various parts. Accordingly, these parts *belong* to the whole and do not make sense outside of it. In his example of science, however, Valéry (wittingly or otherwise) reveals the inherent defectiveness of this conception. Rather than restricting itself in its functionality to the whole

(Europe) that is its proper context, the part (science) shows that it is capable of transcending that whole and operating elsewhere. That is to say, the part shows that it is in fact greater than the whole: the part becomes a whole in which the original whole is now just a part.

However, this reversal or inversion between the whole and its parts is by no means a simple one. Here we are not dealing with the paradigmatic relation between the master and slave, in which the dialectical reversal enacts nothing more than a calculated readjustment of the terms, thereby leaving intact the general principle of their relation. On the contrary, the transcendence of the part beyond the whole, along with its subsequent penetrations and utilizations both of and by other wholes (for example, Japan, the United States, and so on), exposes the structural weaknesses of these wholes and thus the problematic status of the notion of belonging itself. Determinate cultures reveal themselves in this instance to be oddly porous, and it is this porosity—that is, the essential openness to alterity that at all time works to loosen the hold of its borders—that ultimately calls into question the stability of its determinateness. At bottom, I believe, this is what accounts for the fear of this force or movement of universality: namely, this force *undermines the determinate nature of cultures*. Significantly, and perhaps counterintuitively, such fear exists within both those cultures that act as the source of the dissemination of universality and those that are its recipients. The former fear is expressed by Valéry: Europe risks losing its global hegemony by exporting the products of Europe, for in certain cases the universality of these products is what ensures their anonymity, that is, their potential to be appropriated by anyone, even the non-West, regardless of their identity. Such products have the capacity to ultimately turn back and threaten their producer. With regard to the notion of European identity, this phenomenon poses the difficult question, How can Europe be Europe when that which it creates is, in the mode of potentiality, essentially non-European? The latter fear is expressed by the symposium participants: Japan risks losing its particular cultural identity by importing the products of the West, for these products come to take root in the native soil, thereby creating a critical situation in which foreign elements become inextricably mixed with the native. The very condition for this transcendence of Europe and subsequent naturalization in Japan is the universality possessed by certain cultural products. As Tsumura Hideo writes, "When we consider how Europe has been able to maintain its status as world culture for so long, it seems to me that, in addition to its cultural traditions, its very universal power of expression is what has enabled this culture to spread throughout the world. Europe's defense and dissemination of this universal power of cultural expression. . . ."[44] With regard to the notion of Japanese identity, then, the following question must be asked: How can Japan be Japan when its culture is essentially incapable of preventing the internalization and use of things that are non-Japanese in origin?

Despite these differences in positionality—which can, and indeed often do, reverse themselves, such that the West becomes the recipient of essentially transmissible cultural products that originate in Japan—it is important to remark on the underlying similarity between the standpoints of Valéry and the symposium participants. What above all brings them together is their *desire for cultural propriety* and the fear that this propriety might someday be lost. In this regard, I would like to show that the logic of transmission is not limited to Valéry's example of European science in its universality. In the course of the symposium, the participants were in fact constantly confronted with this same logic, but it manifested itself far more broadly in the attention to language and cultural flow in general. The notion of universality was opened up beyond the scope of Valéry's intentions, and in such a way that its force was seen in the transcendence of various kinds of elements beyond their originating context while yet preserving their same functionality. This logic was naturally perceived as threatening and so repressed, but, as with all repressions, its effects are nevertheless still legible throughout the symposium. While Valéry specifically referred to this logic with the word "transmissible," it can be understood as renamed in the context of Overcoming Modernity by the word "transplantation" (*ishoku*).

Let us look at two examples from the symposium. For Nakamura Mitsuo, it was no longer possible in the twentieth century to equate modernity with the West. This meant, among other things, that the notion of "overcoming modernity" could not simply involve a return to Japan, which was already irrevocably westernized. Nevertheless, it is important to remember that modernity was originally for Japan a transplantation from abroad: "Given that this so-called modernity is a hasty foreign transplant, however, it already differs in character from European modernity. Whereas modernity is at the very least a kind of European domestic product, in our country it is above all an import. Isn't it true that this imported character is the most significant feature of our country's 'modernity'?"[45] Moroi Saburō expressed essentially this same view in terms of Japan's importation of Western classical music. For the absence of such a musical tradition in Japan had unfortunately encouraged a superficial practice of random transplantation: "Japan's tardiness in music composition has perpetuated our borrowing of Western music and created all kinds of confusion in our music culture. It has also produced an extremely dangerous absence in our understanding of the essence of Western music. People thus leap at classical music, romantic music, modern music, and medieval music without any proper links between them. Even in terms of performance, the various schools of Western music are randomly transplanted as based on individual circumstances, as it were."[46]

It should be apparent in these passages that, despite their different historical contexts, the notions of transmission and transplantation designate fundamentally the same logic. As can be seen in their shared prefixes, this logic is properly *transcendental*. In this instance, however, "transcendental" does not refer to Kant and his analysis of the conditions of possible experience. Rather, transcendental signifies the possibility of any element repeating itself beyond the empirical circumstances of its original production and functioning elsewhere. Such transcendentality is not an incidental or additional feature of elements but in fact constitutes an essential part of their very appearing. When an element comes into being, in other words, its meaning can be known strictly by virtue of its capacity to strip from itself the immediate circumstances of its production and resituate itself in other contexts. The element's identity is not to be determined on the basis of the site of its initial emergence, since what is even more originary to it is, paradoxically, its innate ability to divide or cut itself from that site and give itself repetitively to different times and places. This is precisely why it is a transplant, for it exists only in the process of its cutting and replantation elsewhere. In this sense, all elements in their transplantation belong most properly to the future, understood here as the time of alterity. Prior to its belonging to any empirically determinable context, an element in its exposure to the world (to space and time) exists as a kind of X that can only be identified later and elsewhere in the course of its ongoing trajectory.

Nakamura and Moroi (together with all of the symposium participants) feared this logic of transplantation in much the same way that Valéry feared the logic of transmission. For the transplant represents something like the inner outside, that which, while inhabiting an entity (Japan or Europe), is nevertheless essentially improper to it since it is from its inception always pointing elsewhere, toward other spatiotemporal points or regions from which it has come and to which it will go.[47] In the case of Valéry, the emergence of European science always already refers away from Europe to other destinations that are the equally improper sites of its future development and use. In the case of Nakamura and Moroi, the cultural products of modernity refer away from Japan and to the West as their putative source, for they fail to realize that this transcendental movement of transplantation can have no fixed point of origin, just as it can have no fixed destination. In their eyes, the arrival in Japan of these transplanted products inevitably came with a cost: the loss of traditional Japanese culture and spirit, which were effectively supplanted by the transplant. The cost of Western modernity in Japan could also be seen in the latter's superficial modes of reception, for everything from Western science to Western music was introduced in Japan without the benefit of native traditions that gradually and, as it were, *naturally* fostered the development of these products in the West. The sudden appearance in Japan of Beethoven's symphonies, for example, could only lead to misunderstanding in an environment that lacked the tradition of classicism, for it is only as a reaction against classicism that the birth of romanticism could properly be grasped. Hence it is not simply that cultural objects possess authenticity or inauthenticity depending upon their point of origin; the misunderstandings that developed around these objects in their transplantation from the West to Japan revealed ultimately that Japanese modern culture was itself inauthentic.[48] In this way, authenticity is reserved only for the proximity an object (music, science, and so forth) bears to its original site of production (Europe). The relation between transplanter and transplantee exactly parallels that between authenticity and inauthenticity. In the context of the symposium, this logic of transplantation was thus seen as threatening to the sovereignty of the self, which can maintain authenticity only by ruling over all that exists within the borders of its realm.

A similar phenomenon is detected in the field of language in modern Japan. This is hardly surprising given the radical transformations that took place with regard to language in all nations upon the advent of modernity. Indeed, as has been widely documented, the formation of the nation-state typically occurs in history alongside the production of a unified national language as part of the state's attempt to create a homogeneous national space for its citizenry, one that exists as distinct from other, like spaces. In such cases, the linguistic heterogeneity that previously existed in the nation (or, rather, pre-nation) has had to be violently eradicated through the use of such state-sponsored institutions as, for example, the school system. In Overcoming Modernity, the modern transformations of the Japanese language were seen as uniformly negative. Specifically, modernity was denounced as responsible for the superficialization of language, the traces of which could be found everywhere in contemporary Japanese society. As Kamei Katsuichirō remarked, "What I find most troubling in our present crisis is the decline in man's sensitivity and efforts regarding language. The tendency to play around only with 'words' as results is now much more deeply rooted than an accurate understanding of the facts or the attention given to the efforts required in forming a single word. This is the age of daydreaming about 'language.' There has never been a time in which large words have been so abused as now. Contemporary man has lost the presence of mind to reflect accurately on the infinite meanings contained within a single word."[49] For Tsumura Hideo, the decline in the Japanese language needed to be understood in terms of the harmful influence of Americanism: "Japanese culture has lived without losing its own traditional spirit while absorbing abundant amounts of both American material civilization and an old European culture imbued with the modern spirit. Even now the word 'culture' [*bunka*] is used very cheaply and in strange ways: in the Taishō period a 'new-style house' [*bunka jūtaku*] still meant something positive, while such phrases as 'new-style rice dish' [*bunka donburi*], 'new-style shorts' [*bunka sarumata*], and 'new-style kitchen range' [*bunka konro*] were quite popular. Even here it is clear how Japan was negatively influenced by American material civilization."[50]

Both Kamei and Tsumura reveal in these passages how thoroughly their notions of language are informed by a sense of nostalgia for a purer form of Japanese that putatively existed prior to modernity and the introduction of American materialism. As we have seen, such nostalgia for a lost Japaneseness haunts the symposium from beginning to end. Kamei and Tsumura represent this fantasy of a vanished cultural plenitude according to its typical spatiotemporal coordinates: spatially, impurity comes from without in the form of the West; and temporally, impurity takes place at a certain moment in history (that is, modernity), which presupposes the existence of an age of cultural purity or interiority that lasted up until this time. In this way, they remained blind to a more essential notion of language as transplantation, conceived not—as with Nakamura and Moroi—on the merely derivative basis of an empirically determinate origin and destination but rather as the initial exposure to alterity "itself." For language is in its structure nothing other than relationality to the other. That is, language refers necessarily away from itself to other times and places that allow it, as a general system of marks, to come into being and signify. As ideal units of meaning, linguistic signs emerge from their originating empirical context strictly on the condition that they be repeatable. Without this repeatability, the markings of language are unable to transcend their uniqueness or singularity and function as signs. In the botanical terms of transplantation, these marks must contain the innate capacity to uproot themselves from their native or home soil so as to be replanted elsewhere, in entirely different environments, and take root anew. In this regard, the ideal objectivity of signs, that is, their ability to retain the same meaning in widely disparate contexts, implicitly points to the by right limitless number of contexts that constitute their differential trajectory.

In his naïveté, Kamei wishes to determine the meaning of the Japanese language as a whole on the basis of the empirical site of its birth, which he believes to be Japan itself. Since Japan has lost its cultural autonomy with the introduction of Western modernity from the Meiji period, however, the return of Japanese to its original birthplace is no longer possible. For Kamei, it is this distance or gap that has opened up between language and its original site of production that above all accounts for language's decline and decadence. Similarly, Tsumura in his examination of some of the diverse uses to which the word "culture" has been put in contemporary Japan (as a descriptive modifier of houses, shorts, rice dishes, and so on) condemns this linguistic practice as a negative influence of American consumerism. While such a critique of what is now called cultural imperialism is not without its merits, we must nevertheless not fail to see in this denunciation a classical and reactive desire for words to maintain their stable identity throughout their different contexts. The problem, however, is that words acquire meaning only through their repeated use over the span of different contexts, which means that linguistic identity is, in its exposure to empiricity, inherently instable. That is to say, the word "culture" is, because of its internal divisibility, in principle exposed to the alterity of its future transplantations (or remarkings, recontextualizations). The exteriority that it contains within itself opens this word to its always possible transformations and translations as, for example, "new-style shorts," *bunka konro* (new-style kitchen range), and so on. Such transformations are not, contra Tsumura and Kamei, the fall of a word from its original and proper meaning; rather, they are simply the differential repetitions of a prior exposure to difference that the word necessarily experienced in order to signify at all.[51]

Yet perhaps there do exist certain moments in Kamei's text when he himself seems able to teach us something about the unpredictable effects of transplantation in language. Despite his mourning over the loss of linguistic sensitivity in contemporary Japanese society, Kamei alerts us to another possible interpretation of language. In the following, for example, he criticizes the simplistic tendency of adulating the Japanese classics: "The classics are of course splendid, and I do not doubt the sincerity of those who tell us so. Once expressed, however, this praise turns against one's will in being instantly defaced—as if struck by a machine rotating at extremely high speed—with the resulting scattered fragments becoming standard catchphrases. People curtail their own thinking and attempt to make judgments based solely on slogans and catchphrases."[52] I repeat this middle sentence in order to underscore its importance: "Once expressed, however, this praise turns against one's will in being instantly defaced—as if struck by a machine rotating at extremely high speed—with the resulting scattered fragments becoming standard catchphrases." Four distinct if interrelated aspects regarding the operation of language can be abstracted from this line: (1) language can always possibly turn against the will (*ishi ni han shite*) of the speaker, (2) meaning is defaceable (*mametsu sare*), (3) there is something essential to language that gives itself to be thought through the metaphor of machinery (*kikai ni fureta yō ni*), and (4) any word or phrase can always become scattered and fragmented (*hisan shita hahen*) so as to mean something different than it did originally. All of these aspects combine to reveal that signification is necessarily an open-ended process that begins from a point that is already divided from itself in its exposure to different times and places. The machine that Kamei envisions here that is equipped with rotating blades powerful enough to take originally meaningful and well-intended phrases and violently cleave them so that they scatter forth away from the speaker in the form of defaced shards and fragments is, in fact, nothing other than an instrument of transplantation. Kamei typically conceives of this process in empirical terms, for the utterance suffers its decline in meaning only at the moment of its worldly expression ("once expressed": *hitotabi hyōgen sareowaru yainaya*), but in fact any linguistic element in its belonging to a general system already experiences its loss of unity—that is, its status as a discrete unit—prior to such expression, in its originary referral to other markings through which alone it is able to constitute itself as (never) itself. Above all, it is strange that Kamei does not recognize that it is precisely this machine that would help him achieve his goal of having contemporary man comprehend, or at the very least marvel at, the "infinite meanings contained within a single word," as I quoted him earlier. For the production of future transformations and translations of any single word, the possibility of which is already inscribed within the word itself, reveals that it contains "infinite meanings." Such meanings can be released or set free only upon the defacement of the speaker's original intentions, but this defacement already takes place by virtue of the essential divisibility of any linguistic mark. The "resulting scattered fragments," as Kamei puts it (or rather, in all rigor, as I have *translated* him as putting it, since Kamei of course never used these exact words), represent the dispersive effects of this process, or what might be understood as the anonymous products of this transplanting machine.

CONCLUSION

I would like to conclude this introduction to the Overcoming Modernity symposium with a glance at some of the discursive effects it has produced, as these effects constitute the history of its reception. In the English language scholarship, the two most influential works to date are Minamoto Ryōen's "The Symposium on 'Overcoming Modernity'" and Harry Harootunian's "Overcoming Modernity." Both works offer fine summaries of the various standpoints represented in the symposium and the occasional debates that took place among the participants, and they also provide useful information regarding the immediate historical circumstances surrounding the event. Nevertheless, it must be said that both essays fail to rigorously address the notions of cultural transmission and subjective identity that were so crucial to the symposium. Without sufficiently questioning these notions, Minamoto and Harootunian ultimately come to repeat certain logics that govern the thinking of the symposium participants—logics that I have reconstructed and analyzed in the foregoing. It should be noted that this is a far greater problem for Harootunian, whose critical standpoint toward the symposium contrasts sharply with the attitude of Minamoto, whose views seem to largely conform to those of the participants. Yet both writers equally approach their work on the basis of a theoretical framework in which East and West exist strictly as oppositional entities, and neither writer seems especially aware of the various contradictions that result in positing empirical collectivities in such an avowedly theoretical fashion. In the case of Harootunian, it is this act of *theoretical positing*, which allows him to recognize East qua East and West qua West, that effectively subverts his otherwise admirable attempt to elaborate something like a notion of eventfulness as historical singularity.[53] Despite appearances, such positing of cultural entities in their collectivity does not reflect an already present and preconstituted reality; on the contrary, it functions in its practical effects to *create* that reality. The overriding problem with this discourse is that it claims to present an empirical reality of "everydayness" that exists prior to all theoretical inquiry, and yet it finds that it can do so only by disavowing its own profoundly theoretical presuppositions. In this sense, Minamoto's conclusion to his essay about bringing "the marvelous intellectual and religious traditions formed in the East and the West into relation" represents a view that the *logic* (not simply the *intent*, which would be quite different) of both his text and Harootunian's shares with the text of Overcoming Modernity itself.[54]

It thus remains a matter of the utmost importance to continue to read this text of the symposium so as to understand how our own ideas about such things as cultural transmission, subjective identity, East-West relations, and so forth are still informed, in all too many cases, by the same presuppositions that haunted Overcoming Modernity. But here I am merely repeating the words that Takeuchi Yoshimi already uttered nearly a half century ago. As he wrote then, "To discard the idea of 'overcoming modernity' by identifying it with its legend [that is, its status as "a symbol of war and fascist ideology"] would be to abandon those problems that we might still succeed to today, and this would act against the formation of tradition. I think we should reclaim the legacy of those ideas with the greatest breadth possible."[55] With this suggestion, Takeuchi reminds us that history can never be reduced to a thing of the past, since the present takes its shape entirely on the basis of this past, to which it must refer back in a kind of deferred or disjunctive self-dialogue. However, this repetition of Overcoming Modernity that Takeuchi is enacting in his essay of the same name very intentionally *intervenes* in the symposium, that is, it comes between the symposium and itself by creating a critical space from which to read and judge it. In this way, Takeuchi ensures that the "legacy" (*isan*) that he "reclaims" (*toraenaosu*) marks a difference from the symposium, for he fervently disapproves of its reactionism and complicity with wartime ideology. Here, I believe, it is imperative that in our reading of the symposium and its various afterlives (for example, the commentaries by Takeuchi, Karatani, Minamoto, Harootunian, and so on), we continue this process of differential remarking. In relation to Takeuchi, for example, it would be necessary to take seriously his words about reclaiming the symposium's legacy "with the greatest breadth possible" (*atau kagiri no kanōsei no haba de*), as he writes. For despite the considerable merits of his essay, Takeuchi in certain respects fails to grasp what is at stake in this legacy with sufficient *generality*, which is what I understand his "greatest breadth possible" to mean. His restriction of this generality relates, in fact, to his notion of transplantation in the context of language, which he articulates in his 1948 essay "Kindai toha nanika" (What Is Modernity?). Let me quote here at length:

> Proof of this can be seen by viewing the history of words in Japan, for words here either disappear or *fall into decay*. The word "civilization" becomes the name of a sponge cake while that of "culture" becomes the name of an apartment or cooking pot. Such apartments *decay* from ferroconcrete to wood, they never advance from wood to ferroconcrete. It is true that new words are born one after another (while new words become necessary inasmuch as words *fall into decay*, they at the same time cause the *decay* of old words), but this is due to the fact that they are originally rootless. Thus while it appears that new words are born, in fact they are not. Do words exist that have sprouted new shoots through growth and ripening, splitting apart naturally from the weight of their content? Of course there are some words that have neither disappeared nor *fallen into decay*. Yet a close look reveals that these words have been nourished externally and live only as long as such nourishment is not cut off. Such words are not productive in themselves.
>
> Given that words are the representation of consciousness, doesn't the fact of their rootlessness mean that spirit itself is not developmental? . . . There have been people who argue that new words have roots, while others argue that they do not. The former locate these roots in the various substance-like things that they bring. While I might find this argument persuasive, it seems to me that roots themselves do not move. The latter attempt to transplant the various roots that they introduce externally, but I have yet to see a case where transplanted roots actually grow. In addition, there have been those who argue in favor of growing words from their native soil since transplanting is unsuccessful. But this soil can be introduced only externally; no sprouts have yet to emerge from it.[56]

Here we can see, among other things, that Takeuchi's inheritance of certain aspects of the symposium in fact overflows the borders of his essay about it. Specifically, Takeuchi's example of several items (apartments and cooking pots) designated by the word "culture" refers back, whether intentionally or otherwise, to Tsumura's example of similarly named items (houses, rice dishes, shorts, and kitchen ranges). Further, Takeuchi's use of the notion of transplantation to describe the history of words in modern Japan recalls the use of this term by Nakamura and Moroi in the context of cultural flow. I draw attention to these similarities not because I would like to show how Takeuchi was in any way influenced by the symposium, as such a line of questioning is ultimately of little interest. Rather, what is at stake here is the logic of transplantation, and the danger that I perceive is that Takeuchi's understanding of this logic follows all too closely that of the symposium in its disavowal of its generality. As I have stressed, such a disavowal reveals a desire, and in the case of Takeuchi and the symposium participants, this desire is to preserve a sense of cultural identity that is strictly proper to Japan. Like Tsumura and Kamei, Takeuchi seems to mourn the loss of authentic language in modern Japanese society. Authenticity is described here as equivalent to natural phenomena. As he rhetorically asks, "Do words exist that have sprouted new shoots through growth and ripening, splitting apart naturally from the weight of their content?" If the emergence of new words in Japan follows such a natural course, then they are authentic and true. For Takeuchi, the natural creation of words derives from their rootedness, which refers in this context to something like a native linguistic or literary tradition. Indeed, it is this tradition to which he points in his essay when he speaks of what he calls, significantly, "the formation of tradition." Clearly, this tradition is a Japanese tradition, one from which words and cultural products alike are created naturally. In contrast to this rootedness (and its conceptual chain of nature, native, tradition, authenticity, and so forth), the absence of roots in words is what is responsible for such modern linguistic aberrations as "civilization sponge cake" (*bunmei kasutera*) and "culture (or new-style) apartments" (*bunka apāto*). In his remark that "I have yet to see a case where transplanted roots actually grow," Takeuchi is in effect rejecting the possibility that foreign words can ever truly take on a new life and thrive when replanted on Japanese soil.

As in the case of the symposium participants, one must read Takeuchi's words here while keeping in mind the real threat of Western imperialism (both political and cultural) to which he was responding. Such circumstances, I believe, form the proper context of Takeuchi's remarks. Nevertheless, the logic of transplantation is precisely that which reveals the impossibility of any utterance possessing its own proper context. As goes without saying, Takeuchi's discussion of transplantation is not exempt from the general logic of transplantation in its radical deprivileging of particular empirical contexts with regard to meaning. As we have observed, linguistic signs acquire meaning strictly by virtue of their ability to transcend their own originating contexts, for otherwise they could not be understood in their mute singularity. Meaning is for this reason never determinable by context, for a deeper, more subterranean movement is already at work that effectively makes the linguistic mark point elsewhere, to other transplantable contexts in time and space. Without such transplantation, of course, there can be no reading of the symposium. This means that Takeuchi (together with the symposium participants) unwittingly rejects that logic that makes his (and their) own discourse possible. The mark's internal divisibility is what opens for it its future, but this future in its alterity means that the mark can always come to be remarked otherwise, beyond the scope of original intentionality and, indeed, beyond all propriety or ownership whatsoever. Hence the word "culture" can one day become attached in its worldly trajectory to such otherwise unrelated objects as cooking pots, apartments, and shorts, despite the apparent incongruity of this linking. For precisely this same reason, the symposium opens itself in its internal exteriority, or divisibility, to be read and translated in utterly different contexts. This, then, is what is at stake in the logic of transplantation: it is not a game or some theoretical abstraction involving plants or words, and so on. Transplantation names the possibility of repetition in different times and spaces. Ultimately, this is why there can be no notion of Japanese culture or identity (or tradition, language, spirit, and so forth) in its purity. External elements have from the beginning taken up residence within these entities, thereby rendering all borders porous and exposed.

NOTES

1. Hayashi Fusao, "Kinnō no kokoro," in *Kindai no chōkoku*, pp. 110–111.
2. This more authentic form of Japanese literature includes, according to Hayashi, such ancient texts as the *Kojiki* (*Records of Ancient Matters* [compiled by imperial order in the year 712]) and *Jinnō shōtōki* (*Chronicle of Gods and Sovereigns* [written by Kitabatake Chikafusa in 1339]), as well as, more recently, the *Meiji tennō gyoseishū* (*Collected Poetry of the Emperor Meiji* [1922]).
3. Hayashi, "Kinnō no kokoro," p. 101
4. Ibid., p. 105
5. Ibid., pp. 107–108. Emphasis mine.
6. Let us be clear here: this general notion of impurity as revealed in Hayashi's text necessarily informs the symposium as a whole. Any attempt to see this essay as exceptionalist, as "totally different from the others" (p. 214), as Minamoto Ryōen has written, would thus have failed to grasp this logic. Such a reading can be attributed to two factors: (1) Minamoto is concerned here simply with presenting a thematic summary of the symposium, and so his understanding follows closely the intentions or most overt meanings of the participants; (2) Minamoto himself views cultural entities in substantialist terms (one quotation must suffice here: "Even with my little knowledge of music, I find it easy to understand what [Moroi] is trying to say. As a Japanese, he finds something unsatisfying about Western music" (p. 208) and so would naturally determine cultural impurities to be mere empirical accidents ("The Symposium on 'Overcoming Modernity,'" in *Rude Awakenings: Zen, the Kyoto School, and the Question of Nationalism*, ed. James W. Heisig and John C. Maraldo [Honolulu: University of Hawai'i Press, 1994], pp. 197–229).
7. Kamei Katsuichirō, "Gendai seishin ni kansuru oboegaki," in *Kindai no chōkoku*, p. 9. Emphasis mine.
8. Moroi Saburō, "Wareware no tachiba kara: Kindai no chōkoku ni kansuru ichi kōsatsu, in *Kindai no chōkoku*, p. 55. Emphasis mine.
9. Kamei, of course, is not alone in this belief, which rather permeated the entire symposium. One of the best examples of this can be found in the exchange

between Nishitani and Kobayashi regarding the proper style of Japanese philosophical prose. What is in question here is the current foreign or non-Japanese quality of this prose. As Kobayashi remarked in the second roundtable session: "To slightly change the topic, both your essay and that of Mr. Yoshimitsu are extremely difficult. I would go so far as to say that these essays lack the sensuality of the Japanese people's language. We feel that philosophers are truly indifferent to our fate of writing in the national language. Since this language is the traditional language of Japan, no matter how sincerely or logically expressed, its flavor must appear in one's style as that which can be achieved only by Japanese people. This is what writers always aim for in their trade. It is linked to literary reality, and so either moves people or leaves them unmoved. Thought is contained within this literary reality. Philosophers are extremely nonchalant in this regard. If this attitude is not conquered, however, it strikes me that Japanese philosophy will never truly be reborn as Japanese philosophy" ("Roundtable Discussion: Day Two," in *Kindai no chōkoku*, pp. 247–248).

    I undertake a reading of these lines in *Contemporary Japanese Thought* (New York: Columbia University Press, 2005), pp. 13–18. For a rather different reading of this passage, see Sun Ge, *Takeuchi Yoshimi toiu toi* (*The Question of Takeuchi Yoshimi*) (Tokyo: Iwanami shoten, 2005), pp. 240–241.

10. Significantly, the question of Japanese imperialism and colonial acquisition was almost entirely repressed in the symposium. In his essay "Nani wo yaburu beki ka" (What Is to Be Destroyed?), the film critic Tsumura Hideo refers without elaboration to "the birth of an East Asian cultural sphere" (*Kindai no chōkoku*, p. 121) and "the founding of a Greater East Asian life sphere under Japanese leadership" (ibid., p. 128), while the theologian Yoshimitsu Yoshihiko, in his "Kindai chōkoku no shingakuteki konkyo: Ikani shite kindaijin ha kami wo miidasu ka" (The Theological Grounds of Overcoming Modernity: How Can Modern Man Find God?), alludes to the building of "a new East Asian spiritual civilization" (ibid., p. 79). The clearest statement on this issue, however, doubtless comes from Nishitani. In his "'Kindai no chōkoku' shiron" (My Views on "Overcoming Modernity"), he writes: "However, the construction of Greater East Asia must of course not mean for our nation the acquisition of colonies, just as the founding of a new world order must be a just one" (ibid., p. 32).

    Some context is necessary to understand Nishitani's apparent warning against colonialism, for these lines are followed slightly later in the essay by a defense of the notion of *hakkō ichiu* (the whole world under one roof), which was widely used at the time to legitimate Japanese imperial expansion: "This also seems to explain why the idea of 'the whole world under one roof' has today again come to be recognized as our national doctrine, for this is fundamentally different from world empire through conquest in that it allows each nation to take its own place" (ibid., p. 34). A close reading of Nishitani's essay reveals, I would argue, that his support of both Japanese nationalism and imperialism is in fact fully informed by his universalism. There is no contradiction whatsoever between these positions, as some scholars appear to believe.

Finally, I would like to mention in passing that it is one of the great merits of Takeuchi Yoshimi's essay on the symposium to have explicitly touched on this issue of Japanese imperialism, for he shows that it was essentially no different from the Western imperialism on which it was modeled: "The Greater East Asia War was at once a war of colonial invasion and a war against [Western] imperialism. Although these two aspects were united in fact, they must be separated logically. . . . While imperialism cannot be overthrown by imperialism, it is nevertheless also true that imperialism cannot be judged by imperialism" ("Kindai no chōkoku" [Overcoming Modernity], in *What Is Modernity? Writings of Takeuchi Yoshimi*, p. 124).

11. Tsumura, "Nani wo yaburu beki ka," p. 126. Emphasis Tsumura's.

12. "I have learned many things about Dostoyevsky in examining his path from social revolution to his discovery of the Russian people and Russian God, but for our present purposes I would like to speak about only one of these: this is that Dostoyevsky was *not* someone who expressed modern Russian society or nineteenth-century Russia. . . . Rather, Dostoyevsky successfully fought against these things; his works stand as a record of triumph over them. When one realizes this fact, one begins to see with particular clarity the shortcomings of positivist and scientist forms of literary scholarship, which were quite fashionable when we began studying literature" (Kobayashi, "Roundtable Discussion: Day Two," p. 218).

In the *Chūō kōron* symposia, Nishitani referred to positivism as a particular feature of modern European civilization that contrasts with the Chinese "scientific" influence in Japan prior to the Meiji period (*Sekaishiteki tachiba to Nihon* [The World-Historical Standpoint and Japan] [Tokyo: Chūō kōronsha, 1943], pp. 24–25).

13. Kobayashi, "Roundtable Discussion: Day Two," pp. 222–223.

14. On this point, see Philippe Lacoue-Labarthe, *Typography: Mimesis, Philosophy, Politics*, ed. Christopher Fynsk (Cambridge, Mass.: Harvard University Press, 1989), especially pp. 43–138.

15. Much more remains to be said on this topic, but at the very least let me add that the Platonic idea is accessible through a kind of seeing—eidos means, literally, "that which is seen"—that goes beyond that which is merely perceptible by the senses to target the true, unchanging forms that lie behind worldly things. The idea involves, therefore, a *theoretical* rather than practical relation. It is important to keep this in mind in order to understand Nishitani's response to Kobayashi, for this reply is motivated by a clear privileging of the *practical* over the theoretical. Nishitani's reply comes immediately after Kobayashi's claim that he has "finally understood Plato's greatness" and runs as follows: "One can of course regard such eternity in terms of, say, beautiful form or aspect (sō). As you remark, those who have truly come in touch with eternity from within history did so directly by surpassing in a single leap their own period and its various conditions, whatever these may be. However, these men encountered eternity not through such completed things as form and aspect in their eternal beauty, as you state, but rather by virtue of their own efforts or spirit, which created that form and aspect. . . . It is *we* who must possess the effort or spirit through which eternally beautiful form and aspect are created" ("Roundtable Discussion: Day Two," p. 223).

However, it seems to me that this opposition between the theoretical and practical is an invalid one. What neither Kobayashi nor Nishitani states here is that the mimetology of the Platonic idea is what inextricably binds the theoretical and practical together. In the case of the idea of Japaneseness, for example, it is the theoretical seeing of this idea that sets in motion the practical acts involved in imitating and participating in it. What is at stake here, in other words, is the link between the Platonic idea and the notion of subject formation.

16. The sense of nostalgia for a purely Japanese past as yet untainted by the West can be seen throughout the symposium. This nostalgia has in fact been well documented in the secondary literature. See, for example, Bernard Stevens, *Le néant évidé: Ontologie et politique chez Keiji Nishitani: Une tentative d'interprétation* (Louvain, Belgium: Éditions Peeters, 2003), pp. 87–88; and Harry Harootunian, *Overcome by Modernity: History, Culture, and Community in Interwar Japan* (Princeton, N.J.: Princeton University Press, 2000), pp. 34–94.

17. Miyoshi Tatsuji, "Ryakki" (A Brief Account), in *Kindai no chōkoku*, p. 142.

18. Nishitani, "'Kindai no chōkoku' shiron," p. 21.

19. Yoshimitsu, "Kindai chōkoku no shingakuteki konkyo," pp. 73–74; emphasis Yoshimitsu's. It should be noted that Yoshimitsu was quite conscious of this similarity between Nishitani's thought and his own, as can be seen in his summary of their views during the roundtable discussion: "As Mr. Nishitani discusses in his essay, a unity existed in the Middle Ages between religion, culture, and national ethics, whereas in modernity this unity disintegrated when these individual moments each came to seek their own autonomous principles. In other words, what in the Middle Ages existed publicly in a single, unified fashion was now destroyed with the emergence of modernity, or perhaps the universal logic that had earlier united these individual elements now disappeared. As such, despite the division between the Middle Ages and modernity in terms of unity and the loss of unity, the questions here are ultimately the same. *I believe that today, when the problem of 'conquering modernity' is often discussed, we have come to the question of how to newly revive this universal principle of unity [fuhenteki tōitsu genri].*" ("Roundtable Discussion: Day One," in *Kindai no chōkoku*, p. 181; emphasis mine).

Yoshimitsu spells things out very clearly here: the narrative of history begins in unity (presence, identity) but is then negated by the fall or loss of unity. However, this negativity comes itself to be negated in the ultimate restoration of unity.

20. Nishitani, "'Kindai no chōkoku' shiron," p. 21. Emphasis mine.

21. This notion of originary violence that I am articulating here is not, of course, simply foreign to the symposium. Perhaps its closest expression can be found in the fascinating essay presented by the thinker Shimomura Toratarō, "Kindai no chōkoku no hōkō" [The Course of Overcoming Modernity]. In it, Shimomura returns to this question of the Middle Ages as if in reply to Nishitani and Yoshimitsu: "Was the time preceding the post-Renaissance period [that is, the Middle Ages] strictly spiritual and the people focused strictly on their interiority? Can one really say this without some kind of idealization (*risōka*)? . . . Wasn't the post-Renaissance period really a fall *of* rather than *from* the Middle Ages? Or rather, wasn't this period the *development* of something that was implied within the Middle Ages and yet

neglected and negated then? Wasn't the post-Renaissance period the development of the Middle Ages themselves?" ("Kindai no chōkoku no hōkō" [The Course of Overcoming Modernity], in *Kindai no chōkoku*, pp. 113–114; emphasis Shimomura's).

Shimomura introduces here an extremely powerful logic whose traces can be found throughout his essay and in connection with themes that go beyond the theme of the Middle Ages. This logic can be understood in terms of the notion of self-alterity, in which difference does not at one time or another *befall* historical entities since these entities are already, from the very moment of their appearing, "internally" exposed to that difference. What Shimomura is questioning here, in other words, is the very ground of the entity's integrity or unity.

Nevertheless, it remains clear that Shimomura does not draw all the necessary consequences of this insight. Despite his understanding that "Europe is no longer a mere other [*tasha*]" (p. 112) and "modernity is us, and the overcoming of modernity is the overcoming of ourselves. It would be easy if the overcoming of modernity were simply a question of criticizing others" (p. 113), Shimomura still ultimately regards this difference between self and other in the oppositional terms of Japan and the West. A critical reading of the symposium as based on Shimomura's thought would thus require, I believe, a radicalization of certain of his ideas.

22. This notion of interlinguality must be used with quotation marks, since the very distinction between one linguistic entity and another (for example, Japanese and Korean) presupposes that each possesses its own unity and totality. That is to say, this notion involves a purely theoretical rather than practical understanding of what constitutes the interiority and exteriority of particular languages. In fact, however, such a distinction between one language and another can only be made *retroactively* through the subjective act of positing. This positing of difference attempts to erase the more originary difference that is ceaselessly at work in language and that effectively overflows the borders erected by this positing, hence disturbing the otherwise regulated flow between its inside and outside. In this sense, one must conclude that the outside of a particular language necessarily precedes the formation of that language as a particular entity. In other words, strangely enough, *gairaigo* in its most general aspect by right exists prior to Japanese.

For a critique of this notion of interlinguality, see Naoki Sakai, *Translation and Subjectivity: On "Japan" and Cultural Nationalism* (Minneapolis: University of Minnesota Press, 1997), especially pp. 1–17.

23. See Jacques Derrida, *Of Grammatology*, trans. Gayatri Chakravorty Spivak (Baltimore: Johns Hopkins University Press, 1974).

24. Tsumura, "Nani wo yaburu beki ka," p. 124. For Tsumura, more generally, the danger posed by American popular culture to both classical Japanese and European culture lay in part in this inauthenticity of representation, which he linked to modern massification and the spread of democracy.

25. Kamei, "Gendai seishin ni kansuru oboegaki," p. 12.

26. Hayashi, "Kinnō no kokoro," pp. 91–92.

27. Nakamura Mitsuo, "'Kindai' he no giwaku" (Doubts Regarding "Modernity"), in *Kindai no chōkoku*, p. 154. Let us note here that everything at stake in this passage

of Nakamura's as well as in the just quoted passages of Tsumura, Kamei, and Hayashi is encapsulated, in a certain sense, in Nakamura's phrase "look into their background" (*mimoto wo arau*). This phrase is used in connection with performing a background or identity check. However, the verb *arau* has the more common meaning, when used independently, of "to wash" or "to wash away." In other words, this washing away or effacement of something's background seems to haunt as an impossibility the very project of determining that background. In this way, the condition of something's appearance can be said to be the disappearance, or concealing, of its origin.

28. In the context of the symposium, the one significant exception to this general distrust of representation is Shimomura, or rather, more accurately, certain moments in Shimomura's text. I quote here one especially important passage: "The experimental method of modern science originally sought to reveal that which does not exist naturally, or in nature, and it shared this spirit with magic. The aim of this knowledge is not the intuition of essential forms [*honshitsu keisō no chokkan*] but rather the development of nature's potential. Modern machinery is a product of this method. This represents the reconstruction or remaking of nature, as opposed to its mere application or utilization. What comes into being in this building of modern machines is not merely a subjective independence or freedom from nature but rather a truly *objective* freedom and independence" ("Kindai no chōkoku no hōkō," p. 115; emphasis Shimomura's).

A fundamental shift in emphasis takes place here in the movement away from the "intuition of essential forms" to a pursuit of the effects produced in the "development of nature's potential." What is particularly striking here is the link Shimomura makes between the notion of freedom and the break from the immediacy of nature. When something remains too close to its immediate origin, its potential becomes stunted. This potential is released only by departing from that origin, such that a thing's own internal development requires sacrificing that interiority and exposing itself to difference. Nevertheless, it must be asked of Shimomura whether he regards this process of self-differentiation to be ultimately appropriable by the self. An important issue in this connection involves, I believe, Shimomura's relation to Hegel, but this same tension can be found in the Kyoto school as a whole.

29. Nakamura, "'Kindai' he no giwaku," p. 164.

30. Kamei, "Roundtable Discussion: Day One," p. 201.

31. Kawakami Tetsutarō, "'Kindai no chōkoku' ketsugo," in *Kindai no chōkoku*, p. 166.

32. Suzuki Shigetaka, "'Kindai no chōkoku' oboegaki," *Bungakkai* (October 1942), p. 42.

33. Sigmund Freud, *An Outline of Psycho-Analysis*, trans. James Strachey (New York: Norton, 1949), pp. 59–60.

34. Nishitani, "'Kindai no chōkoku' shiron," p. 24.

35. Ibid., p. 26.

36. Cf. Nishitani: "Neither, of course, does the reality of an 'object,' in the sense that traditional brands of realism or materialism think of it . . . express the original selfness of a thing. Such reality is represented as the point within things appearing on the

field of sensation as objects of sense perception which goes beyond immediate perception and beyond perceiving subjectivity. But this manner of representation stems from a field on which the subjective and the objective are set in opposition to one another, from the field of objects and their representations. *What pretends to go beyond the opposition of subject and object is, in fact, still being viewed from within the perspective of one of the two opposing orientations*—namely, that of the object. To that extent, we have yet to rid ourselves of thinking in terms of the opposition of subject and object" (*Religion and Nothingness*, trans. Jan Van Bragt [Berkeley: University of California Press, 1982], p. 120; emphasis mine. This text was originally published in 1961 under the title *Shūkyō toha nanika* [*What Is Religion?*]).

My questioning of Nishitani on this point of a concealed oppositionality existing within the very critique of the oppositionality of the subject-object relation thus reveals itself to have a certain affinity with Nishitani's own thinking. In other words, the basis for his critique of classical materialism as remaining yet tied to oppositional logic despite its wish to overcome it can be mobilized, in the context of the symposium, against Nishitani himself. The difference, however, is that here "the perspective of one of the two opposing orientations" is that of the subject rather than the object.

37. This reactivity of identifying with Japan as a response to one's encounter with the exclusionary self-identification of the West is given its sharpest expression by Moroi Saburō: "When I went to study in Europe, I, too, very much felt that Europeans think about how different they are from others in order to express their selves. I found it intolerable that Europeans devoted all their efforts to this. Art certainly does not consist in distinguishing oneself from others by poking so finely at individual differences. First of all, it is crucial to understand that people are about 90 percent the same. I actually couldn't stand being in Europe. In a musical sense, Japan is very limited, and in many ways one is blessed to be in Germany. But I felt strongly about returning to Japan" ("Roundtable Discussion: Day Two," p. 236).

38. Paul Valéry, *History and Politics*, trans. Denise Folliot and Jackson Mathews (New York: Bollingen Foundation, 1962), p. 4.

39. Ibid., p. 17. In his 1919 essay "La crise de l'esprit" (The Crisis of the Mind), Valéry expresses this same fear that the transmission of European science outside the borders of Europe would invariably result in the end of European global hegemony (ibid., pp. 34–35).

Ukai Satoshi draws attention to this former essay in his article "Colonialism and Modernity" (in *Contemporary Japanese Thought*, p. 268), whereas Karatani Kōjin discusses the latter essay in the specific context of the symposium, concluding, significantly: "Thus technology represented an applicability [*ōyō kanō*] outside Europe, it was something that could corner Europe. . . . This is because technology is applicability. If technology is a European product, then, Europe has conquered the world, even if Europe were to be destroyed by it" ("Overcoming Modernity," in Calichman, *Contemporary Japanese Thought*, p. 115).

40. The physicist Kikuchi Seishi essentially endorsed this neo-Kantian standpoint when he insisted that science must leave room for spirituality. Somewhat predict-

ably, this caution about the limits of scientific universality gave way to a notion of cultural particularism as based on the nation: "The absence of a world outside of such a [materialist] scientific worldview would mean the disappearance of both the Japanese spirit and the concept of national polity [kokutai]. This would be horrible." ("Kagaku no chōkoku ni tsuite" [On the Overcoming of Science], in *Kindai no chōkoku*, p. 146).

41. Kawakami, "'Kindai no chōkoku' ketsugo," p. 166.

42. Kawakami, "Roundtable Discussion: Day Two," p. 263. In the secondary literature, Valéry's influence on the symposium is widely documented. Specifically, writers have focused on the manner in which his Eurocentrism was found deeply offensive by the symposium participants, which contributed (among many other things) to the formation among them of a reactive sense of Japanocentrism. See Watanabe Kazutami, "Re-reading 'Overcoming Modernity,'" trans. Kevin M. Doak, *Poetica* 56 (2001): 55–68; Kevin M. Doak, "Paul Valéry, Japan, and 'Overcoming Modernity,'" *Poetica* 56 (2001): 69–90; and Karatani Kōjin, "'Kindai no chōkoku' wo megutte" (On "Overcoming Modernity" [this is a roundtable discussion conducted with Hiromatsu Wataru, Asada Akira, and Ichikawa Hiroshi]), in *Symposium* (Tokyo: Shichōsha, 1989), pp. 181–235.

43. Yoshimitsu, "Kindai chōkoku no shingakuteki konkyo," p. 67. Emphasis Yoshimitsu's.

44. Tsumura, "Nani wo yaburu beki ka," p. 118. It should be noted that, for Tsumura, such a universal power of transmission was not limited to Europe, as the United States possessed a similar power: "Yet the American cinema's lack of any sense of traditional culture has created, on the one hand, the appeal of universality and, on the other, a different appeal, that is, the novelty of the social customs of this 'new world' so bereft of traditional culture" ("Roundtable Discussion: Day Two," p. 256).

45. Nakamura, "'Kindai' he no giwaku," p. 152.

46. Moroi, "Wareware no tachiba kara," pp. 49–50.

47. This logic is what Derrida calls, among other names, "quotation," but its traces must be sought prior to deconstruction in the central phenomenological relation between retention and protention, understood here as that which divides the punctuality of the present from itself in the movement back to the past and into the future (*Limited Inc*, ed. Gerald Graff [Evanston, Ill.: Northwestern University Press, 1988]).

48. It should be noted that the inauthenticity of cultural objects can also derive from their functionality, or rather misfunctionality, as media. Western film techniques and even film itself, for example, are unsuitable in their role as transplants because they are unable to represent native Japanese content. As Tsumura explained, "In fact, these difficulties are very familiar to the top filmmakers in Japan. While Japanese film techniques were basically learned from American and Soviet films, most of what was expressed through these techniques has been fake, showing neither real Japanese customs nor the Japanese heart. There are now people working hard to devise Japanese-style film techniques to express the Japanese spirit, and we are seeing the chaos of this transitional period today. Yet even if we try to express the

Japanese heart through film, we ultimately run into problems, since this mechanism of film originally came from abroad" ("Roundtable Discussion: Day One," pp. 211–212).

49. Kamei, "Gendai seishin ni kansuru oboegaki," p. 7.

50. Tsumura, "Nani wo yaburu beki ka," p. 123; emphasis Tsumura's. This term *bunka jūtaku* (culture/new-style house) refers to those dwellings built from the late Taishō to early Shōwa periods that were modern in design and considered convenient to live in, in contrast to more traditional structures. The other objects Tsumura lists here were produced and perceived along similar lines, that is, new, simple, and convenient.

51. This trajectory of a word, or even a part of a word, in its resituation within different contexts is best illustrated by Hayashi Fusao in his essay "Kinnō no kokoro" (pp. 87–88). Here Hayashi recalls his early school years, when students were required as part of their English language education to recite from Shakespeare's play *Julius Caesar*, and in particular Marc Antony's speech delivered at Caesar's funeral. Hayashi misquotes Antony's famous line, "Brutus is an honorable man" as "Julius Caesar was an honorable man." However, this doesn't affect the humor of the incident, as Hayashi recounts the bawdy laughter he and his classmates shared upon hearing the Japanese pronunciation of these last three words: *an onara-buru man* (*onara* means "fart" in Japanese).

Aside from the not inconsiderable interest of the fact that a right-wing intellectual (Hayashi was, by all accounts, ideologically the farthest right at the symposium) discussed such scatological matters in the context of a wartime essay about loyalty to the emperor, what must be noted here is the radical recontextualization of language that took place in the context of this joke. Hayashi used English to (mis)quote in an essay otherwise written in Japanese a line from an English play about a Roman military and political leader. The source for Shakespeare's play was a 1579 English translation of a French translation of Plutarch's *Lives*, which was originally written in Greek. By virtue of an interlingual pun, Shakespeare's word "honorable," which is repeated several times by Antony as a rhetorical device to turn the Roman people against Brutus for his slaying of Caesar, comes now to be repeated in a different country several centuries later to mean, in a different language, "fart." It is, I believe, precisely this crosscutting between linguistic, national, and cultural traditions that functions to jeopardize the unity and determinate nature of these traditions, ensuring that they are never fully closed off to their outside.

52. Kamei, "Gendai seishin ni kansuru oboegaki," pp. 5–6.

53. Harootunian, *Overcome by Modernity*, pp. 34–47.

54. Minamoto, "Symposium on 'Overcoming Modernity,'" p. 229.

55. Takeuchi, "Kindai no chōkoku," p. 118.

56. Ibid., p. 61. Emphasis Takeuchi's.

A Note on Contemporary Spirit

KAMEI KATSUICHIRŌ

I. ON THE ENEMY OF SPIRIT

It seems that all manner of remedies for the crisis in spirit have already been discussed. To take one example near our own country, there are a great many ideologies that, in the emergence of new spiritual paths following the imminent demise of Communism, claim to be wonder drugs leading to a recovery of the present age. Innumerable prophets have come forth, and the words of both Eastern and Western sages recalled all at once. Everything from ancient Greece to the dying stages of European thought, including of course our own classics and Buddhist texts, has been offered up as reference points. Contemporary man seems to have become increasingly garrulous as he abuses the "wonder drugs" concocted by these prophet-chemists. Clearly there exists a sense of crisis, but this is a crisis of *what*?

There are those in the world for whom the awakening to faith is at once a blindness to reality. And there are not a few who cherish the illusion that they alone can escape the present confusion of thought by clinging to the words of the sages. My own training of late consists in rejecting the particular egoism of those who seek salvation.

Since the China Incident, the spirit of our classics has been extolled and submission to foreign culture strictly forbidden. The classics have engaged in a mass attack, and Anglo-American trends and materialism seem to have gradually retreated. There can be no doubt that the outbreak of the Greater East Asia War has, at the very least, brought about a resolution to the previous confusion. However, has there been any decline in our spiritual crisis? The following scene frequently unfolds before me under the pretext of ideological warfare: a brilliantly constructed picture-card show spreads throughout the minds of the public in which the hero "Japanese spirit" and villain "foreign thought" battle it out with stock phrases until finally the hero is cheered when the villain falls over like a puppet. Shall we call this scene a rosy delusion brought about by our military victories? Such delusion, which is bound up with the particular egoism of those who seek salvation, hinders any accurate understanding of contemporary spirit. We are thus overrun by an infirm spirit masquerading as bravery.

I am not all that interested in what is now called "thought" and "spirit," as what is discussed there can be understood by reading. Rather, I am primarily concerned with the various forms in which thought and spirit live and die in the present era. I am troubled by the notion that heroes and villains are to be distinguished from one another as apparently complete opposites when they are, at bottom, merely twins of the same form who share the same fate. The classics are of course splendid, and I do not doubt the sincerity of those who tell us so. Once expressed, however, this praise turns against one's will in being instantly defaced—as if struck by a machine rotating at extremely high speed— with the resulting scattered fragments becoming standard catchphrases. People curtail their own thinking and attempt to make judgments based solely on slogans and catchphrases. In other words, they live by swift understanding and swift forgetting. The words of the sages have suffered the same fate. What, then, is the origin of this form of spiritual life—or rather, its speed of death?

I believe that our greatest enemy is that swiftly changing mode of civilization that, ever since the influx of the West's dying culture of "modernity," has steadily violated the deepest recesses of spirit while producing all manner of daydreams and garrulity. My fear is that all thought might be permeated by this poison and thereby homogenized and mechanized. As this poison exists within ourselves, people will happily fall victim to it without necessarily becoming aware of its symptoms. Compared to this bewitching power, today's Anglo-American "enemy thought" is really insignificant. For those who are convinced of their engagement in ideological warfare through sermons, propaganda, and slogans, it is crucial to discover whose puppet they have become. I shall speak of a few symptoms that I have perceived around me regarding those distortions and debilities that "modernity" has wrought upon our spirit.

II. ON THE CRISIS OF LANGUAGE

Are we uttering normal human words? Are the political jargon and intellectual terminology that we use so casually really human language, or are they rather the marks that simulate human language? Some have already pointed to the confusion surrounding contemporary language, but it is words that reveal most directly the sign of spirit's decline. This problem cannot be corrected by restricting the use of Chinese characters or by adopting the attitude that language be made more "easily understandable."

Language originally comes into being in the pain of trying to give voice to the flood of emotions that can never be fully expressed. These are piercing events to which one devotes one's whole soul, such as love and grief. There may be something infinitely unsatisfying in expressing an inexpressible thought. One is haunted by something like the regret of being unable to realize one's desires. This can be described as attachment to life or obsession with art. Yet language comes into being when man has done all he can, in other words, when Providence decrees it. Vengeful ghosts also exist in language. It is only in this way, however, that language is first given beautiful expressions and deep shadows.

One's life is at stake in language. I feel a strong nostalgia for language's original value, that is, when it existed vividly in all its many poses and shadows, like the dance of a dancing girl. Among all the words man has ever uttered, love poems and death poems are the most beautiful. These are not necessarily limited to poetry, however. In all the workings of spirit, is there anything other than love poems and death poems?

What I find most troubling in our present crisis is the decline in man's sensitivity and efforts regarding language. The tendency to play around only with "words" as results is now much more deeply rooted than an accurate understanding of the facts or the attention given to the efforts required in forming a single word. This is the age of daydreaming about "language." There has never been a time in which large words have been so abused as now. Contemporary man has lost the presence of mind to reflect accurately on the infinite meanings contained within a single word.

Relatedly, our handwriting has declined to an astonishing degree. How uncharacteristically poor are the brushstroke characters written even by our so-called writers! This is shameful. As for characters written by pen, these are no longer characters at all but instead mere office markings to be typed out. I am not here vainly calling for a return to the past. Rather, I am troubled by the loss of that ardor with which one seeks out the mystery and abyss of language. For example, men of old copied out the sutras and classic texts as important acts of faith because they wished to fully experience the superb spirit residing within each word, *not* because printing technology was as yet undeveloped. The decadence of language is at once the decadence of thought. Even in regard to the spirit of our classics, it is insufficient to merely speak about it. Everything depends upon how one experiences as well as how beautifully one conveys to posterity the infinite thoughts that reside within even a single word of these texts. It is meaningless to simply discuss the classics. And yet contemporary man evaluates these texts strictly through such discussion. This is how he evaluates everything. In regard to such thinking, whereby signs or marks are mistaken for language, leftist and rightist ideologies are identical. Here as well, as I have stated, apparently opposite positions reveal themselves to be at bottom merely twins of the same form.

What accelerates this trend is so-called enlightened consciousness and the abuse of slogans. There are certain heedless groups that defile the original beauty and severity of language by speaking in an "easily understood" manner, as based on the dogmatic belief that the masses are illiterate. Previously this was the Left, but who is it now? No matter how illiterate, the people know the depths of love and sorrow. They want for nothing in respect of love poems and death poems, which attests to their sound instinct that elevated language is to be received with tears rather than through interpretation. This is proven quite beautifully in our own time, when many soldiers are being sent off to battle only to return home as war dead. Are there spirits that are so weak as to doubt the traditions that flow within the people's hearts?

Slogans are an even worse form of this "enlightened consciousness." As the product of modern democratic politics, which seek to employ language in the most utilitarian way possible, slogans are a propaganda device that never previously existed in our tradition but which gradually became popular from the Taishō to Shōwa periods of liberalism and Communism. They are the worst of all the imports from the West. I find it unbearably distressing that the abuse of slogans has created a situation in which language is made increasingly utilitarian, such that even the most meaningful words can be understood only as slogans. This tendency to standardize everything through such vulgarization must be described as a terrible crisis for spirit. Without knowing the situation in other countries, I can say that in our nation the only great words that should spread throughout the people's hearts are those of the imperial edicts. Poetic feeling is the one thing that does not simply issue from the emperor and circulate among the people but also naturally leads up to the emperor. How grievous, then, that slogans should exist in a nation so blessed by language!

III. ON THE DECLINE OF SENSITIVITY

Especially noteworthy among the evil wrought by modern civilization is the decline in sensitivity. I have already discussed the crisis in language, but this crisis also signifies the loss of silence. Those who understand the true nature of language also understand the sorrow of silence. Healthy language dwells within a healthy silence.

Yet contemporary man has forgotten this silence and become terribly garrulous. He is dissatisfied if he does not say something about everything, and here we can see something like a natural force of coercion operating within the form of contemporary civilization. I shall tentatively call such signs of decline in sensitivity the trend toward exposure. Modern civilization has brought about a violence that has ruthlessly devastated those subtleties, such as the beauty of private expressions and acts, that can be gently dealt with solely through a delicate sensibility. There has emerged a kind of dissatisfaction when things are not shown openly, crudely, and urgently. This dissatisfaction is related to that "thirst for explanation" that derives from the influence of so-called rationalism; it is also due to a restless utilitarianism; and finally it is connected to a poisonous sensationalism. Even people with "good intentions" dare to perpetrate this crude offense.

This becomes clear, for example, when considering that noble acts on the battlefield are at once turned into journalism, radio, film, and music recitals. I am astonished by the excessive speed of this transmission. A noble act takes place, a group of photographers rushes in, the act is broadcast by radio, it appears in the newspapers, panegyrics are written, the act becomes a film, and then it is forgotten: this process occurs at great speed and entirely negates all the nuances and subtle lyricism immanent within the act itself. Only the act's external form is magnified and dwelled over at length in its monotone repetition.

For example, I felt rather apprehensive about the people's attitude regarding the nine war heroes lost at Pearl Harbor. One cannot believe that there is anything false in those hearts filled with exaltation, gratitude, and praise for such noble acts. Yet there are always those who take things to excess. Weren't the cameras shamelessly pointed at the bereaved, who amid all the pride and sorrow were privately praying for the souls of the departed? And didn't many writers and reporters rush off to the homes of these war heroes, forcing the bereaved to speak of their inexpressible emotions? Who becomes garrulous when their loved ones return home as fallen heroes? Have these people lost their consideration for others, so as to leave the bereaved alone in quiet privacy? I detest those who defile beauty and nobility through such fast-paced exposure. And I am disturbed by the fact that our emotions, having momentarily surged forth, soon sink into the depths of oblivion.

This tendency of exposure also gives rise to self-justification. People try to show how they serve the state by explaining all of their actions and statements. A kind of self-advertising has spread throughout the present age, which represents a grave concern in respect of our morality. People have forgotten the grief, joy, and sincerity that reside within silence and grown insensitive to the aching lamentations and hidden sacrifices that lie within the depths of men's hearts. Even if one realizes these things, however, they are still immediately exposed in view of the present situation. We have lost the ability to love and value that which is hidden as hidden. Must love of country be manifested as self-justification? Must love become an art of self-protection? It is under such conditions that emotion has disappeared from present discussion and the ways of expressing it ignored, resulting strictly in a flood of crude ideology that is apt to determine values.

I would like to cite the advancement of film and photography as further accelerating this decline of sensitivity. It remains a question as to whether these products of modern civilization have brought about positive or negative effects on human spirit. Literature, painting, and sculpture all have their own inherent limits, the minute determinations of which help form these arts. Film and photography, however, still lack these limits. Herein lies the trap into which nations that first incorporate the West's machine civilization invariably fall. These nations forget that machines are to be employed moderately. That is, as can often be seen in other regions as well, machines subjugate man rather than being subjugated by him, thereby making man their unwitting slave. Both film and photography wander about this danger zone.

People do not understand the gravity of this extremely innocent offense, which consists in photographing everything indiscriminately. The camera is at once trained on whatever is unusual, beautiful, or valuable. No distinction is made between what is suited to be photographed and what is not. For example, I am always doubtful about the filming of art objects and old Buddhist images of the Yamato period. Is it really normal to believe that the cinematic exposure and dissemination of these Buddhist images, whose glow emerges strictly from the darkness of old temples, will heighten our national sense of aesthetics? As in the case of language, this tendency toward vulgarization and standardization is quite remarkable. In their confidence that objects are accurately reproduced, spectators have lost sight of the astonishing inaccuracy resulting from the loss of those shaded emotions lying within the object's depths. This inaccuracy is concealed by the accuracy of the object's external form, which gives rise to the illusion that one has clearly seen something accurate—just as one is being entertained. Thus man's sensitivity has fallen into a state of utter paralysis.

IV. ON THE EFFECTS OF SPEED UPON SPIRIT

What kind of pressure has modern civilization, whose character consists in the sudden increase of speed through mechanical progress, exerted upon our spirit? Has it distorted this spirit? For example, the "narrow road to Oku" journey that for Bashō required months can now be completed in several days by train. We look with interest outside our windows at the scenery, villages, and people all rushing by at great speed. Yet how different this "looking" is from Bashō's "looking"! How much has the development of modern civilization sharpened our powers of observation? To be sure, we now have microscopes and telescopes. Perhaps our observations have become more precise and accurate in certain specialized fields, which are as divided up as capillary tubes. In terms of our total devotion to nature, however, has there been any progress in the depth of our love and emotion? Which has more greatly enriched man's image of the stars: those stars reflected in the naked eye of the ancient Greeks or those reflected in the telescope of contemporary scientists?

Bashō utterly devoted himself to every tree and blade of grass. Of course we too can shed tears of grief when lingering at scenic spots and places of historic interest, and we can devote ourselves to every tree and blade of grass. Yet we won't be so devoted as to entrust our weary flesh to the trees and plants, literally "weaving a pillow of the grasses." Our weary flesh is carried along by transportation. Man's energy for walking clearly seems to have declined in the modern era. But hasn't this decline also led to a waning of the spirit's walking ability? Although we are able to "look" at the trees and plants along the journey, we do not, like Bashō, die for them at the journey's end. Are there any accurate ways of knowing other than this "sacrificial dying"? For Bashō, "looking" was synonymous with "sacrificial dying."

It appears, moreover, that contemporary spirit moves in proportion to advancements in transportation. We are now able to access all the writings of both East and West quite easily. When the need arises, we speed-read both our own classics and the thought of European sages as if gazing out the window from an express train. Strictly speaking, a three-day roundtrip to the "narrow road to Oku" region is not a journey, or at least it does not correspond to this word's originally true meaning. Yet we call such trips "journeys," just as we call ourselves "travelers." The same can be said of today's reading and thinking. What is so conspicuous now is the absence of reading and thinking; instead there are merely fans of reading and thinking, as well as a host of other types of fans. I am troubled by the dearth of that enduring energy with which one spends ten long years reflecting upon a single book or passage.

These trends—the deplorable modern customs that began in the Meiji period with the opening of the country—are related to intensification. We had to introduce as much Western civilization as possible so as to swiftly arm ourselves. It was our fate to be forced to apply ourselves to the external trappings of modern civilization within a very brief period of time. These customs became second nature, and herein lies our spiritual crisis. We collected the fragments of Western thought and tried to erect an edifice of ideas, as adorned superficially with Western strength, trying despite everything to join the ranks of "world spirit." Such manner of intensification was also applied to Oriental and even Japanese civilization. Together with the appearance of the catchphrase "revival of the Japanese spirit," tea-ceremony rooms were added in the corner of buildings and simple dinnerware laid out as if actually serving Japanese food. This was done in part to secretly cater to the wishes of those Westerners interested in the Orient. Such is the tragedy through which we are living.

The danger, which is linked to utilitarianism, lies in the attitude of those sages who approve of this turn to intensification. These sages have displayed such toxic symptoms as unawareness and a restlessness to steadily increase the speed of things. Although clearly well intentioned, spirit has as if boarded an express train and is being rushed off by means of a fateful coercive force. To where is it rushing? I am occasionally touched by the foreboding that it is headed toward its own ruin.

V. ON THE DELUSIONS OF THE VICTOR

Externally, the war that we are currently fighting represents the overthrow of British and American power, while internally it represents the basic cure for the spiritual disease brought about by modern civilization. These are the two aspects of this holy war, and the war will be crippled if we neglect either of them. The struggle against the poison of civilization cannot be won in the brief span of even one hundred years. Fortunately, we are the military victors in East Asia. But there is nothing so dangerous as the conviction that this victory is at once a victory over that poison of civilization that is now our own. I would like to warn myself against falling into such delusion.

When an area is occupied, there are those who think at once of enjoying the profits without reflecting on the toil involved in long-standing construction. The same thing takes place in regard to thought. That is to say, we are overrun with opportunist ideas from our military victories. A countless number of naive people have come forth. Blind to the abyss beneath their feet, these people delude themselves by clinging to the legacy of the classics and disparaging everything, as if the recovery of spirit were fast approaching. The current danger lies in the presence of men who have been selfishly spoiled by victory. This danger, which, as I have stated, is related to the particular egoism of those who seek salvation, blindly guides spirit.

It is only natural that the spirit of our classics be considered as the most effective wonder drug against the poison of civilization. What is crucial here, however, is how this drug is administered. Without an accurate diagnosis for the diseased spirit, it should be clear based on my previous examples that even wonder drugs won't prevent this poison. Yet doesn't there exist the delusion that all diagnoses can be abandoned and salvation granted simply by groping for the classics? The classics ought to strengthen our spirit. If they weaken it, however, they must somewhere be gravely defective. The same can be said of faith. Degradation ultimately begins when one imagines that referring to the gods, Buddha, or the great men of old will win one even the slightest salvation. For the classics and sacred texts exist for the purpose of continuous struggle, not for the purpose of reassuring us. These texts are harsh ghosts that provide us with our final teaching, which is that we are condemned to eternal hell. Is there anyone who, in reading history, isn't filled with dark passions and resentful thoughts? Is there anyone aiming for faith who isn't aware of the suffering caused by gratuitous acts? These texts teach us that it is only through sacrifice that we can prove what the future will be like. There is nothing so foolish as the delusion that, without dirtying one's hands, the spirit of the classics will achieve something in the future entirely of its own accord.

Confronted with the pressures and mechanist ideology of civilization, which attacks through a virtually natural force of coercion, as well as all the resulting spiritual diseases and debilities and man's rampant disintegration, will spirit perish or be saved? These represent the stakes of that other war that lies hidden within the present world war. We must not daydream about the struggle against this abyss because of our victories in the war before our eyes. However, this struggle is glossed over by the delusion of "peace" that is frequently embraced by the victors. People have been losing this struggle because of the notion of "peace." It is noteworthy that, in modern Japan, "liberalism," "Communism," and "materialism," for example, all spread during times of "peace." The poison of civilization thrives under the guise of "peace."

Peace is even more frightening than war. A war waged for peace is nothing more than a joke. The present war represents a war on this abyss, and on this battlefield the nation's fate will be decided by the clarity that rejects all delusions as well as a fearless, steadfast faith. A king's war rather than a slave's peace! Such a victory does not exist within the notion of victory. There is only this heartfelt wish.

My Views on "Overcoming Modernity"

NISHITANI KEIJI

I. In general, what is called "modern" means European. Politically, economically, and culturally, modernity is situated at the end of the post-Renaissance, or *kinsei*, period, when the European world spread to the world as a whole. Modernity in Japan is also grounded upon European elements, as introduced following the Meiji Restoration. What is so striking about this introduction of European culture, however, is the fact that the various cultural fields were imported separately from one another, with virtually no contact between them. If we compare this with the introduction of Chinese culture following the age of Prince Shōtoku, for example, a marked difference seems to appear. Chinese culture was introduced in such a way that all of the fields were interrelated around Buddhism and Confucianism. This difference may perhaps be attributed to the fact that Western culture was already divided into various specialized fields, which made it a so-called advanced culture. In speaking of such a division, however, one might expect these specialized spheres to be interrelated. In which case, it would be Japan itself that adopted a fragmented manner of importing this interrelated Western culture. But it seems that the reason for this fragmentation lies at an even more fundamental level. That is to say, Western culture had already lost its interrelatedness in the West itself. Rather than merely speaking of a division into specialized spheres, therefore, the fact is that Western culture had no center with which to unify this division, that it had lost its unity as totality. Such a situation, moreover, already existed latently in the early post-Renaissance period. Although post-Renaissance Europe has often been described as bereft of any unified worldview, this period was even more fundamentally one that split or divided the foundation that would make any unified worldview possible. Culturally, it can be said that the post-Renaissance period decisively broke with the Middle Ages on the basis of three movements: the Reformation, the Renaissance, and the birth of natural science. These movements became the source of three major streams of thought that governed the West's spiritual culture throughout the entire post-Renaissance period and into modernity. Yet these streams of thought were not what might be called tributaries of one main current; rather, they were independent of one another and indeed fundamentally discordant. Each concealed its own entirely distinct course of worldview formation. If we define "worldview" here as that which allows man to grasp himself in and together with the world, then post-Renaissance man can be described as confronted with the fundamental difficulty of how to understand himself, as he was situated between three divided paths of worldview formation.

Simply stated, religion in the Reformation involved at bottom the absolute negation of the world and humanity, for it centered on God as absolutely other to world and man. Here man, whose essence was sin and death, could be saved only by faith and submission to God. According to the standpoint of natural science, however, the natural world was governed by mathematical and physical laws. Furthermore, man was grasped at the same level as other creatures (for example, the theory of evolution), and animate creatures were grasped at the same level as inanimate ones. Natural science thus harbored the tendency to grasp everything at the level of inanimate existence by reducing existence to its lowest rank. In contrast to humanity's absolute negation as set forth in the religion of the Reformation, natural science was indifferent to humanity. Third, the Renaissance and humanism represented the standpoint of humanity's absolute affirmation. This standpoint aimed at nurturing humanity—in the context of both the self and mankind in general—by advancing education in view of humanity's perfection as well as by harmoniously developing the faculties of man and his soul ("soul" in the broadest sense here, as including both sensibility and reason). Generally speaking, this standpoint became dominant during the post-Renaissance period in such spheres as culture, history, and ethics, just as the first standpoint became dominant in religion and the second standpoint in nature. These standpoints can also be described, respectively, as focusing on God, the world, and humanity or the soul. Splitting off from one another because of this difference in emphasis, they fell into an unmediated division between religion, science, and the humanities (culture, history, ethics, and so on). However, these three spheres are the pillars of human existence. Since ancient times, God, world, and soul have been the three basic concepts that formed the cornerstone of all worldviews or life views in the West, just as in the Orient there are the "three powers" of heaven, earth, and man. In the West of the Middle Ages, these three concepts formed an undivided harmony as united in Christianity. Despite the many disturbances throughout medieval intellectual history, it can be said that this foundation itself was solid. However, the loss in relationality between these three concepts resulted in the collapse of the medieval spirit along with the imposing structure of its worldview. We have now arrived at the claim that the three pillars each stand alone, as it were, and that each tries to independently support the whole structure. This marks the beginning of the post-Renaissance period.

Political problems centering on so-called liberalism were also involved here. If the basis of liberalism lies in the assertion of rights for the independent existence of individuals in the world, then this standpoint can be seen to join together individualism and cosmopolitanism. Here there emerged a pure radical individualism, a radical cosmopolitanism (or socialism), and, in opposition to these, a radical nationalism. Needless to say, there thus arose a profound confusion regarding the relation between individual, state, and world. I do not have time to explore the various difficulties that came about in the relation between those standpoints I have mentioned, that is, those of religion, science, and culture, and so forth and individual, state, and world. It is simply that Western culture, with all its discordant divisions, infiltrated throughout such places as post-Restoration Japan, thereby bringing about the danger of splitting apart the very foundation of the nation's unified worldview formation such that people would fall into confusion in their self-understanding. If therefore the basic problems of today consist in rebuilding the very foundation of worldview formation as well as initiating a new self-aware formation for man, then these problems are now shared throughout the world. Here I would like to try to consider how these things may be achieved. At stake is the question of how the standpoint of religion, from which the absolute is to be grasped in its demand that humanity be negatively transcended, can provide a space of free play to both the standpoint of the humanities (culture, history, ethics, and so on) in its total affirmation of humanity and the standpoint of science in its indifference to humanity, while at the same time unifying this free play. At stake, then, is the question of what such a religiosity must be that would make these things possible (for even today it seems that it is the standpoint of religion that must form the basis of the whole), as well as the issue of reestablishing an ethics to be grounded upon this religiosity. Such an ethics, moreover, must penetrate as one throughout the world, state, and individual, as these sustained complicated conflicts with one another and brought about confusion throughout the post-Renaissance period. What, then, should this religiosity and ethics be?

II. First of all, religiosity must open up an absolute transcendence vis-à-vis not only humanity and culture but even ethics. Without this, it would lack authenticity as religion and be unable to completely satisfy man's religious needs. For example, it would be unable to truly provide a way to overcome death. Yet such an absolute negation of humanity must at the same time involve a way to affirm humanity through that negation. The religiosity of the post-Renaissance West could not possess the force to unite the post-Renaissance spirit because it lacked the "absolute negation qua affirmation" of humanity. That religiosity sought to spread faith throughout secular life by stressing absolute faith in God as well as the contradiction between God and humanity, and yet it lacked the standpoint from which to change and unify that contradiction so as to focus on faith and culture as the same rather than opposite paths, as it were. As a result, culture and history became secularized and man could not free himself from faith. The religiosity to be sought now absolutely transcends even the standpoint of science, but at the same time it must not contain any dogma that would definitively alienate it from science. I believe that we must penetrate within our subjectivity in order to seek such a standpoint of religiosity. Does, then, this standpoint actually exist within us?

The shortcut that allows us to see such religiosity consists in looking within ourselves for what remains as subjectivity after first subtracting what is taken by science. First of all, our bodies are a suitable object for natural science. Just as men of old spoke of the harmony between the four elements of earth, water, fire, and wind, the body can be treated at the same level as all other things, such as dust, viruses, amoebae, and worms. Going slightly deeper "within" us, then, how about what is commonly called the "mind" or "soul"? These things yield phenomena that constitute the objects of cultural science. If by "mind" or "soul" we mean only what is commonly called "conscious" phenomena or the conscious "self," then these too could be treated scientifically by, for instance, psychology. But if we were to stop only at the stage of "consciousness," then strictly speaking such things as mind and soul would be excluded. In fact, as psychology became "scientific," it got to the point of eliminating all hypotheses regarding such substances as "mind" and "soul" and sought to regard conscious phenomena in purely functional terms. That is to say, psychology did away with such substantial "things"—that is, things that "are" in and of themselves—as the mind and soul, and along with this psychological phenomena came to be seen on the basis of their relation with physiological phenomena. It can be said that all kinds of phenomena at the level of consciousness disappear together with the disappearance of the body. Nothing would then remain of us when seen apart from the body as physical object and the conscious self commonly called "mind." It can be said that nothing actually remains. In this remainder-less site, however, something in fact does remain. Indeed, it is here that the standpoint of true subjectivity first appears within us as subjects, and this represents the one thing that cannot come into the view of science since it can never be objectified. We may call this the standpoint of subjective nothingness. Despite this name, however, it does not mean "nothing." Rather, it signifies that which cannot be objectively apprehended as "being" in the manner of things. For example, "life" already contains something that cannot be apprehended as being. Although living things are part of being, "life" contains that which cannot be fully determined as "being." It involves many more activities. Most essentially, these activities can be apprehended only by intuiting within one's own interiority the fact of "living." Even more profoundly than "life," man's subjectivity can be apprehended only by the fact of his self-interiority, which operates through his spontaneous freedom. When one penetrates within this subjectivity, which appears in free acts, it can in no sense be determined as being. Rather, it negates the ontic apprehension of the self and, in this sense, presents itself strictly as nothing. This subjectivity is neither thing (physical object) nor "mind," that is, the conscious self generally called "self." Thing and mind still belong to being. What is generally called "self" is still conceived as a substance, like things in their status as "being." True subjectivity goes beyond thing and mind, however, and appears as their negation, that is, as the "falling off of body and mind." This subjectivity appears as the negation of the conscious self, or as the so-called no-self or no-mind that destroys the ego. It is here that the true "mind" or "soul" appears, that is, the subject's true subjectivity. This subjectivity involves the absolute negation and transcendence of both the body and its natural world and the mind and its cultural world. Here there is the freedom of religiosity that is absolute freedom from the world. In saying that we actually exist, I mean that we always harbor at the basis of our existence as subjects this standpoint of subjective nothingness and its attendant freedom. It is simply that we are unaware of this. True subjectivity appears within all of our subjective actions, beginning with looking and listening. This subjectivity remains obstructed from our self-awareness, moreover, because we identify the true self as the conscious self, that is, the self that is "conceived" in substantialist fashion as "self." When we thus transcend this latter "self" and become aware of our true self, such awareness comes to us inseparably from both the body and its natural world and the mind and its cultural world. Conscious mental activities likewise remain unchanged here. It is simply that we become aware of these activities not as the working of the conscious self but rather as that of the subject as nothing. For the "falling off of body and mind" can also be described as "mind and body falling off."

This is why the absolute negation of everything, including culture and science, can at once turn to absolute affirmation. Although the subject who creates culture and engages in science is not yet at the standpoint of self-aware subjective nothingness, this standpoint in its transcendence nevertheless inheres within that subject as its true subjectivity. The true mind qua subjective nothingness absolutely negates both body and mind in their status as being, and yet at the same time it gives life to these in its unity with being. Freedom from the world can in and of itself turn to freedom within the world. True freedom opens upon both these aspects, that is, world transcendence and world immanence. As goes without saying, this standpoint of subjective nothingness is a feature of Oriental religiosity. Only Oriental religiosity resolves the difficulties of the relation between culture and science as contained in the religiosity of the post-Renaissance West. True liberalism can be realized only in this kind of freedom. This is Oriental liberalism.

III. Such self-awareness of the standpoint of subjective nothingness is of course exceedingly difficult. On the other hand, however, it is characterized by an extremely realistic path. That is to say, a path that can be assiduously trod even in one's daily life, or, more concretely, in each and every occupation. Realistically, we live our lives as individual citizens. Yet the state must suppress the arbitrary freedom of individuals. This is an inevitable requirement for the state to exist. In the post-Renaissance West, such a requirement gave rise to profound difficulties between the individual and state. Today the state is forced to be quite thoroughgoing in this requirement because of its emphasis on "self-annihilation in devotion to the nation." Each and every person must selflessly exert themselves in performing their work. "Self-annihilation" basically means extinguishing the arbitrary ego or egoistic self. As I shall show, selfless exertion and professional service can thus open up a path to profound religiosity. This path is like one in which the absolute negation of the ego can at once become the subjectivity of physical and mental activity in real life. Such a path is based on real life itself and can be persistently explored without isolating oneself from it. It can be practiced inseparably from each occupation, in the same way that one devotes oneself to mastering a work activity. First of all, the state requires of its citizens both mastery in one's work and self-sacrifice (or self-annihilation) in one's work activities. The demand for mastery is the most realistic and concrete in one's daily life and involves the most external action, whereas the demand for self-annihilation is the most internal of one's feelings and soul and involves the most interior aspect of one's daily life. The path of religiosity as subjective nothingness is able to directly penetrate both these aspects as one. It can be said that mastery belongs to the sphere of technology, broadly understood. In "liberalism," mastery is often employed for the pursuit of personal gain. But today this mastery must be penetrated by the most fundamental spirit of national ethics, as in the notion of "self-annihilation in devotion to the nation." This ethics is fundamentally tied to religion. Hence the standpoint of subjective nothingness is the path that runs through the three spheres of technology (in a broad sense), ethics, and religion and represents the religious standpoint that can be uncovered through a national ethics within real work activities.

To take matters a step further, then, why must the state demand of its citizens such self-annihilating service in their work? Needless to say, this is because the state must strengthen as much as possible its own internal unity. Such unity is necessary for it to concentrate its aggregate force as an individual totality and act with great energy. Moreover, this concentration of aggregate force would be fundamentally impossible without a profound ethicality, in which each and every citizen is reduced to the state qua totality by annihilating their selves. The great energy created by concentrating the state's aggregate force is at bottom an ethical spiritual force. That is to say, what furnishes this energy is strictly the concentration of the people's ethical spiritual force, which comes from each person striving to master their work in a self-sacrificing (or self-annihilating) manner. However, what internally unifies all citizens in each of their working lives is the core of state existence itself. This energy issues from the core that is the state's existence and is an expression of state life itself. In this sense, we can call this energy "moral energy." The state requires of each of its citizens efforts of self-sacrifice or self-annihilation, through which they become ethical—and through which, conversely, the state first becomes ethical qua this community of citizens. Moral energy emerges from within this living relation between citizens and the state. Moral energy, that is to say, is that which truly springs forth from within each citizen, and thus each citizen and their collective force are united internally with the state. Thus moral energy is state life itself, as strengthened and revealed by the core of the state's existence. The ethical essence of the state's existence is moral energy.

It can be said that moral energy is deeply rooted in the religiosity of subjective nothingness while penetrating the sphere of technology that lies on its surface. Religiosity must in and of itself exist strictly on the horizon of worldliness. It is related to the ultimate existence of individuals in the world. In order for this religiosity to become truly concrete and function within real life, however, it cannot stop simply at worldliness but must instead be mediated by ethics. Religiosity must in and of itself transcend the sphere of ethics while providing the basis for ethical spirit; it must also exist immanently within ethics and become the source of its life force. When this happens, religiosity actually becomes the deepest source of moral energy within the core of state life. The limits (or impasse) of Western religiosity during the post-Renaissance period can be found in the inability of religion's radical transcendence to become united with such radical immanence. It is only the Oriental religion of subjective nothingness that can provide a way out of this impasse. Here Oriental religiosity is of great significance for the future world and its world religion.

IV. In the foregoing we saw only a current slice, so to speak, of the unification or interpenetration between world religiosity and state ethicality, which is required as the basis for establishing a unified worldview and thus also for man's new self-aware formation, as these are the fundamental problems today.

Now it is impossible for this requirement to be directly realized just anywhere at any time. For in the context of historical reality, the present always carries with it the historical past, that is, tradition. The present of state life is fundamentally determined by its traditions, in other words, by that state spirit that, as tradition, runs throughout history within the ethnos, which constitutes in turn the substratum of the state. Hence, when I remarked that moral energy must manifest itself from the core of state life through the unification or interpenetration between world religiosity and state ethicality, a serious problem develops regarding what kind of traditional spirit is contained within state life. In fact, even in the Orient itself Japan is the sole country in which Oriental religiosity has been deeply linked to and grounding of state ethics and has become the driving force behind the state's energy. The Way of the gods, whose essence lies in the "pure and clear mind" and which constitutes our traditional state spirit, exists in profound harmony with this Oriental world religiosity. While the Way of the gods represents our state spirit, it seems to have originally possessed such dimensions as to enable it to contain the world religiosity of subjective nothingness. Since Prince Shōtoku, there have often been those within Japanese intellectual history who became aware of Japan's spirit at this level. For example, the *Jinnō shōtōki* [*Chronicle of Gods and Sovereigns*] basically reveals such an awareness of Japanese spirit in the manner I have described, despite the presence of various minor problems. The text reads: "The sun goddess Amaterasu Ōmikami had only honest intentions" (book 2). Referring to the divine mirror as a symbol of Amaterasu's intentions, we read: "The mirror transparently and selflessly illuminates all things in the world. . . . This is the source of honesty" (book 1). On the other hand, this transparent and selfless "pure and clear mind" forms the quintessence of state life and circulates in the traditions of ethnic history as the essence of the Way of the gods. In this sense, the text cites Yamato Hime no Mikoto: "Worship purely with a clear mind, not with a dark one." Further on, the text requires that the source of the Way of the gods be cleansed: "What is called 'source' means to have nothing in one's mind. Yet this does not mean that the mind is suspended within emptiness. Heaven and earth exist, as do rulers and ministers. Good and evil are repaid, just as light produces shadows and sound produces echoes. The way of virtue is clear and free from ignorance, like a mirror illuminating an object, in which one abandons desire and benefits others first." The text continues: "It is a principle that the beginning of heaven and earth begins today. In addition, rulers and ministers are not far removed from the gods" (book 2). Elsewhere we find such passages as "Awaken to the source of the mind and return to virtue" (book 3) and "Rulers and ministers are the descendants of the gods in both their bloodlines and in their just acceptance of the imperial command" (book 1). That is to say, the "pure and clear mind" is at once the source of the mind that appears when one extinguishes self-interest and that which circulates within state life as the intentions of the sun goddess Amaterasu Ōmikami, just as it flows within our blood in our status as the descendants of the gods. It can be said that the basis of the Way of the gods lies in actualizing the ethics of service while coming directly in touch with the gods' intentions and achieving creative freedom, as expressed in the notion that "the beginning of heaven and earth begins today." And this is done by each and every citizen, merely in their status as the people, negating their self-interest and returning to the source of their minds, for they possess within them a mind of purity and clarity that eradicates all self-interest. There is in the Way of the gods something that exists in profound harmony with this Oriental religiosity of subjective nothingness. Hence, Lord Chikafusa also wrote: "Confucian writings have spread since the reign of Emperor Ōjin and Buddhism has flourished since the reign of Prince Shōtoku. Both Ōjin and Shōtoku were sacred avatars and seem to have intended, following the intentions of the sun goddess Amaterasu Ōmikami, to expand and deepen the way of our country" (book 1). It is certainly not easy to expunge self-interest and allow the source of one's mind to present itself clearly, as opposed to theoretically elucidating the Way of the gods or being moved by the spirit of mythology. The religiosity of subjective nothingness is what teaches us to do so.

If, therefore, the religiosity of subjective nothingness can be generally understood as Oriental religiosity, then it was Japan's particular circumstances that allowed this religiosity to discover the way to permeate throughout real life and become unified with the people's sense of ethics. I see here the deepest aspect of Japanese spirit. And if the establishing of a unified worldview and man's new self-aware formation (the basic problems of today) must be based on life lived in accordance with the Way—which, from the source of subjective nothingness, penetrates the individual, state, and world as one—as well as grounded upon the unification or interpenetration of state ethicality and world religiosity (that is, a religiosity that preserves its transcendence qua religion while at the same time actively enveloping from within such standpoints of worldliness as culture and science along with individual free action in the world), then there is something at the deepest roots of Japan's traditional spirit that can provide a course of resolution to these present world problems.

In order to resolve these problems, of course, our nation's traditional spirit must face the new trends of contemporary world history with its new problems for the state and, through our very efforts in realizing these problems, arrive at a radically different self-awareness from that of the past. Or rather, it is precisely now that the Way of the gods must be developed and grasped in its original worldly aspect.

V. As goes without saying, the problems that our nation is now facing are those of founding a new world order and constructing Greater East Asia. The concentration of the state's aggregate force and above all a powerful moral energy are now required in order to realize these problems. However, the construction of Greater East Asia must of course not mean for our nation the acquisition of colonies, just as the founding of a new world order must be a just one. In a certain sense, this latter represents a world-historical necessity, but at the same time our nation is burdened with this necessity as its mission. For such historical necessity derives from the fact that we have developed into the only strong non-European nation and are thus pressed to confront Anglo-Saxon domination in Asia. Moreover, it is at bottom our strong state unity and the moral energy produced therefrom that have enabled us to develop into the only strong nation that has escaped Anglo-Saxon domination. This same energy has now become the driving force behind our activity of constructing Greater East Asia while fighting the United States and England. When I thus say that the world-historical trend toward a new order in both the world and Greater East Asia is historically necessary, this is necessarily of a piece with saying that our nation is burdened with this historical necessity as its mission. The linkage between these two things is based on the role that our moral energy has played and indeed is now playing in world history. In other words, this moral energy is also the source that has made us into a strong nation and so necessitated the shift in world history, just as it actually furnishes us with the strength to be a leading nation burdened with the mission of founding a new world order. (Here we can see the profound link between politics, history, and ethics). This moral energy has thus now come to signify the driving force for worldwide ethicality. It seems that here we can see a radical development over its previous meaning.

As I have stated, moral energy realizes a popular or national ethics by having each and every citizen serve the state and annihilate their selves in their work, while at the same time furnishing a high degree of concentrated energy to the state, which qua community of the people is itself made ethical. If moral energy worked in only these ways, however, it would be unrelated to that worldwide ethicality I have mentioned and could on occasion become linked to such injustices as the colonial exploitation of other races and states. Moral energy could then serve a kind of national self-interest. For our nation at present, however, moral energy as the driving force behind state ethics must at once be the driving force behind world ethics. That is to say, the state's energy exists for the purpose of realizing world ethics, and conversely world ethics can be realized only by the moral energy of those states burdened with this mission. This moral energy thus introduces a character of the state qua world and the world qua state. What, then, does this mean?

Previously I stated that moral energy is manifested from the core of state life. In saying that this energy introduces a character of unification between statehood and globality, then, I mean that state life has at its core opened up the horizon of that globality. This in turn seems to mean that the state's existence and significance have changed from within into something new. For if the globality of its existence merely signified something like the state's immediate self-expansion, this would be no different from the plan to found a world empire through conquest, as seen in the world history of the past. It would be nothing more than a reversion to a manner of world domination that is even older than Anglo-Saxon world domination. From the perspective of past state behavior, therefore, the globality revealed by state life today must signify the negation of that behavior. The state has gone beyond the standpoint of merely emphasizing itself alone and arrived at a self-awareness of the horizon of inter-national communality, as based on the nonduality of self and other. It has opened up a horizon in which self and other put an end to their selves so as to create a communal totality where both can live. In this sense, the state has necessarily revealed the aspect of what may be called "self-negativity" that lies at its root. Moreover, the state can today claim authority for itself as a leading state precisely because it bears such a spirit of communality. That is to say, it can practice a just self-affirmation because of its self-negativity. This also seems to explain why the idea of "the whole world under one roof" [*hakkō ichiu*] has today again come to be recognized as our national doctrine, for this is fundamentally different from world empire through conquest in that it allows each nation to take its own place. This doctrine was originally contained within our nation's state life and involves the negation of the standpoint of mere national self-interest, the revealing of communal spirit through that negation, and the claim of leadership as based on the self-awareness that this spirit was originally part of our tradition. It is here that Japan's current mission is also formed. As this doctrine of "the whole world under one roof" is today actually being achieved as our mission, it has for the first time acquired full self-sufficiency and manifestation. The spirit of "benefiting oneself in benefiting others" and "self-awareness that enlightens others" can thus be said to have appeared in the standpoint of the state.

VI. Previously I discussed the ethicality of moral energy, which runs throughout the individual, state, and world as grounded in the religion of subjective nothingness, as today's fundamental problem for overcoming the spirit of modernity. It is now the state itself that has revealed the aspect of globality, that is, the aspect of a kind of state self-negation marked by an inclusiveness that allows each nation to take its own place. The state's moral energy has actually introduced a character of the state qua global and global qua the state, and through this there has appeared within historical reality—and indeed, world-historical reality—an ethical path running throughout the individual, state, and world. In a word, the "pure and clear mind" that is the fountainhead of our state life has come to operate within world-historical reality. In thus saying that the state's moral energy is manifested by means of each individual serving the public and annihilating their selves in their work, this means that these individuals will not only acquire pure and clear minds in their efforts at professional mastery and self-annihilation; they will also merge with the fountainhead of state life that runs throughout national history as well as come in touch with that world ethics that lies at the bottom of world history (what the ancients called the "way of heaven"). For today our state life has flowed into world history and become its bloodline, so to speak, and together with this the fountainhead of state life and the ideals that run throughout its history have become the guiding ideals within world-historical reality. If individuals can become grounded in subjective nothingness and attain the source of their minds by devotedly practicing self-annihilation and deepening their grasp of the "pure and clear mind," they will pass through the deepest part of state life and come in touch with what Lord Chikafusa called "the intentions of the sun goddess Amaterasu Ōmikami," which "transparently illuminate all things." They will then become aware of the opening of the originally religious, or what must be called transhistorical, world out of the depths of the historical world. For self-awareness of subjective nothingness is at once an awareness of the standpoint of eternal life and the overcoming of death; it transcends both ethics and history. And yet, as I have stated, this self-awareness does not merely involve a separation from reality, as it represents a new subjectivity that inheres deeply within man and operates in ethics and history. It is a subjectivity of "life in death." The fact that "professional service" can actually signify this—in other words, that the work activities of each and every person directly involve a path that reaches down to the deepest levels of world religiosity and state ethicality—is due to our nation's traditional spirit, as created out of the secret harmony between Oriental religiosity and our own spiritual path. It is also due to the fact that, as I have remarked, this spirit has in its radical development today become part of world-historical reality. In this sense, it can perhaps be said that Japan's spirit may offer a profound course of direction for the ethicality of moral energy, which runs throughout the world, state, and individual as grounded in subjective nothingness, as this nothingness forms the foundation for the basic problems today, that is, the establishment of a unified worldview and man's new self-aware formation.

It seems that there are now incessant calls for the establishing of Japan's worldview. However, if the globality of Japan's spirit that underlies this project stops merely at something like the nation's direct self-expansion, as I explained earlier, then it will be unable to truly ground its worldview, just as it will in truth fail to deeply grasp what is Japanese. Japan today has revealed, at the basis of its own state existence, what may be called the profound standpoint of "self-negativity" and "benefiting oneself in benefiting others." Through this the national founding doctrine of "the whole world under one roof" has become the doctrine of historical, and indeed world-historical, reality. In this way Japan stands in self-affirmation, which consists in claiming authority for itself as a leading nation. Accordingly, the globality of Japanese spirit must in the context of present reality appear from its original basis in what may be called "self-negativity qua affirmation." Since these two conceptions of the globality of Japanese spirit may be easily confused with one another, it seems necessary to become all the more clearly aware of their difference. I have tried in the foregoing to simply consider what kind of basic structure Japan's worldview should possess on the basis of the latter standpoint.

From Our Standpoint

Reflections on Overcoming Modernity

MOROI SABURŌ

I have long aimed at conquering modern music and restoring music to its place as a spiritual art rather than an art of sensory stimulation, and this is precisely my topic today as well. Since we live in the present age, we are forcibly drawn to modern music and are inevitably exposed to it at least once. Given this fact, however, a person's future course is largely determined by how he deals with this exposure; simply put, does he unconditionally yield to such music or does he begin to seek out its essence based on his doubts and opposition to it? One of my doubts about the great composers of modern music concerns why their music doesn't develop as they mature, for their early work is comparatively greater. I have discovered many things while trying to clarify and study this question. My conclusion is that modern music contains fundamental errors, and that to correct these errors we must restore music to its place as a spiritual art. As a personal conviction, moreover, I have come to firmly believe that we must adopt this standpoint in order to make Japanese music into something genuine.

It is thus important to know modern music, and with this knowledge it is very natural for us today to explore music's essential issues. Modern music forms one wing of modern Western culture, and while it possesses its own particularity as music, its basic character is the same as modern culture in general. In studying the nature of modern music, however, one realizes that questions go beyond modern culture and must be traced back further and further into the past until one arrives at the origins of modernity in its opposition to the Middle Ages. But such discussion of modernity as a whole by returning to its origins is undertaken in other fields, which relieves one of the task of raising the present issue of music. I would simply like to note that modern culture is thoroughly European and that it is rooted in anthropocentrism.

In terms of music history, modern music or modernism in music appeared for several decades in the early twentieth century, which thereby distinguishes it from modernity in the sense of general cultural history. The history of Western music is extremely brief, as music came to be recognized as art in roughly the fifteenth century. If we understand modernity to mean post-Renaissance, then virtually all of music history is included within modernity. Even broadly understood, modernity from the perspective of music history appears after the eighteenth century; that is, it begins with classical music. Modernity in the broad sense thus contains classical, romantic, and modern music narrowly understood. In any case, any discussion of modernity in music must of course first consider European music. In the following, I will begin by conceiving of romanticism as the womb of modern music and then gradually proceed to modern music.

The essence of romanticism lies in introducing the individual as the highest principle through elevating subjectivity and burning up individuality. For romanticism, the highest art expresses the moment when the whole is known by the individual, whereupon individuality bursts into flames and sets off sparks. In this acute expression of anthropocentrism, the elevation of subjectivity accompanies a respect for or perhaps even overemphasis on individuality. Constrained by nothing, individuality always desires perfect freedom in a dignified manner. In romanticism, the highest idea is precisely this perfect freedom of individuality. The genius or master appears as the idol of this idea and feels powerful longings, fulfills ideals and dreams, and discovers the liberation of individuality. Given these characteristics, romantic music seeks to express dreams and fantasies, and this fantastic nature is one of its major features.

Essentially, fantasy is not a product of the intellect in its universality and objectivity; rather, it is a product of subjective and instinctive passion. It is passion that always guides and grounds romanticism and drags along the intellect. Indeed, fantasy becomes stronger and dreams more powerful the more intense passion becomes, as a result of which the dissociation from reality becomes extremely strong. The contradiction or dissociation between passion and reality does not cool passion but rather arouses and intensifies it all the more. Because this causal relation proceeds endlessly, subjectivism goes to extremes, and even the writer's personal life is influenced by this ideality: his real life is crushed, the value of life is sacrificed, and man becomes a medium who exists for art. It is from this contradiction between reality and passion that there also appear the major features of romantic music, such as tragedy, pessimism, and skepticism. Here art serves the role of acting as an escape from reality. Such negativity leads to the destruction and dissolution of all organic relations in human life. This characteristic of dissolution is extremely significant in both romantic and modernist music.

As goes without saying, throughout music history the division between periods of style cannot clarify the specific years in which styles begin and end.

The end of an old style overlaps with the beginning of a new style, and the former is always the womb of the latter. Although it is extremely common for new styles to take the form of a reaction against the old, the latter nevertheless influence and even foster the former. In music, modernism also arose as a reaction against romanticism, and this opposition was seen as a radical one at least at the time and for some years thereafter. Ardent supporters of modern music were thus convinced that a new style had been brilliantly created. Today, however, romanticism and modernism are seen as essentially no different, for modernism is considered to be the final stage of romanticism.

Modern music emerged at roughly the beginning of the twentieth century or very end of the nineteenth century and was at its peak from then until about the beginning of World War I. There are some cases in which modern music is generally seen as ending later, but even if one regards its dominance as continuing after the war, this music had slightly changed from its prewar peak and one could begin to sense a reaction against it, however weak. Here I would like to proceed in my study by determining modernity as ending in World War I and the present-day as beginning thereafter.

Having achieved its brilliant peak, romanticism began to collapse on account of its essential negativity. Its ideal synthesis dissolved, first gradually and then more radically. The massive forms created by later romanticists were not connected by powerfully organic bonds, as with the early romanticists of the eighteenth century, but rather by an extensive array of parts, such that only bright and dark emotions appeared with any strong contrast. To push this point a bit further, synthetic form dissolved into fragmentary parts, such that sensual elements rather than the synthetic nature of form came to occupy the central place in music. This dissolution of music's synthetic nature into elements represented the natural result of romanticism, which had placed the highest value on the moment when individual passion ignites, and yet this tendency toward dissolution reached its zenith in modernity. While it is true in this sense that modernity emerged as a reaction against romanticism, we must recognize that modernity is also essentially the final stage of romanticism its purest form. In studying modern music, we must begin by understanding the preceding points so as to then proceed to this music's features in its reaction against romanticism.

Modern music revealed its earliest and most perfect success in impressionism, which was centered in France. It is a well-known fact that impressionism in music was created on the basis of the profound influence of symbolism in literature and impressionism in painting. Impressionism sought to accomplish through music what symbolism had attempted in poetry. In its basic sense, symbolism regarded words as absolute signs, and it was in this internal world of signs that pure poetry was written. Applying this theory, music came to be written in the internal world of sounds or chords, such that each chord was separated from others as an absolutely distinct sign. This view destroyed the organic connection between chords so that they became dissociated from one another, as a result of which chords or sounds lost their functional value, which was replaced by the value of sensual color. The impressionist theory of "verticalism" sought purity in sounds and regarded the chord's sound as a symbol or sign of the world, such that the relation between one sound and the next was guaranteed only by subjective sensation, as it was unnecessary to form this relation objectively.

In thus completely individualizing content and negating both real objects and restricted and limited phenomena, impressionism reached a vague state of the absolute and mystical in which even the self was negated. The dissolution seen at the end of romanticism here reached its zenith, beyond which impressionism would fall into utter dissolution and decay. Impressionism pushed dissolution to its highest degree, and in its search for absolute purity, tried to fully negate all reality, passion, and limitations. Whereas romanticism waged a battle between reality and passion, both these things were negated in impressionism. That is, although essentially inheriting romanticism's most radical and purified characteristic of negativity, impressionism yet established its own original mark. French impressionism exerted its influence virtually throughout the world, and particularly in Russia, where this music announced its end by giving rise to mysticism.

In the end, the strong individualizing tendency as seen in impressionism first reached completion with the individual's destruction. Here was a world of extreme and pure negation in which the individual disintegrated as individual. Expressionism possessed this same individualizing tendency but viewed the individual as everything: everything existed for the individual and everything passed through it. Within this expressionist tendency, man's inner life became extremely important, and color, form, and matter were absorbed within the world picture as sketched by individual spirit. In other words, the world depended upon the individual. It is clear that this tendency was rooted in the romantic exaltation of the subject, and the contradiction between reality and passion was sublated within the interiority of human spirit. Although expressionism resembled Oriental philosophy in its basic theory, this music was based strictly on the intellectual aspects of human spirit, such that the individual was seen as an intellectual individual. While thus upholding the romantic principle of the individual, expressionism negated its passion in favor of the intellectual. The intellectual individual seeks to destroy all the restraints on itself of which it can theoretically conceive. He dismantles the organic relations between elements as previously existed in music, such that completely different relations are formed as based on the logic of the intellectual individual. In contrast to the impressionist attempt to know the world of absolute purity as instantaneously revealed to the individual, expressionism sought to discover this world within the theoretical structures created by the individual as based on his own logic.

In this sense, it is perfectly understandable why the former found its essential object in chords while the latter found it in counterpoint. These can be called pure chord and pure counterpoint.

Impressionism and expressionism are similar in terms of their subjectivism, individualism, and rejection of passion. In the former, each sound or chord is an absolutely distinct sign as formed strictly within the individual's subjectivity; moreover, the individual's own individuality will necessarily be fully negated when he most purely expresses this world of absolute purity. It is on the basis of this destruction of the individual that impressionism comes to take on the tendency of objectivism. In contrast to this, expressionism seeks to discover the world of absolute purity within the individual's own intellectual-logical structures. The individual thus always tries to be universal, and it is from this universalization that the same objectivist tendency appears. Although both impressionism and expressionism lean toward a respect for the intellect as based on their rejection of passion, the former certainly does not regard the intellect as essential in its reaction against the romantic overemphasis on passion. In other words, there is a difference in the status of the intellect between these two schools: in contrast to its limited function in impressionism, the intellect becomes the very essence of expressionism. Impressionism is purely and simply the final stage of romanticism and, in this sense, looks to the past, whereas expressionism in part looks to the future despite its similar grounding in romanticism. Although expressionism temporarily lacked the spectacular influence of impressionism, it nevertheless gradually prepared the way for a new transition.

In addition to their intellectual tendency, impressionism and expressionism both possess a strikingly sensual or sensitive tendency. What exactly is the pure and absolute world they sought by negating passion? In the final analysis, this world is merely a sensual image removed from real life that is fancifully drawn by man. This world is the otherworld painfully sought by man on the basis of spirit's despair vis-à-vis reality, and here man's spirit finally loses its bodily attachment to the world and simply clutches at pallid ghosts. Such people try to express their sensual image of these ghosts through a subtle intellect or keen sensibility and so come to possess both intellectual and sensual tendencies. Their music is to be understood with the mind rather than listened to with the heart, as it tends to stimulate one's senses or sensitivity. It thus falls into terrible decay upon losing its sincerity as art. Among the adherents of modern music, there are by no means few examples of this.

The bewildering changes in modern music gave rise to a method that might be called "primitivism," which represented a counterattack against the intellectual aspects of impressionism and expressionism. Primitivism was conceived for a time as a powerful reaction against impressionism, and people were overjoyed that it would enable them to recover their health. Primitivism employs folk elements as discovered in national music, but rather than deriving from any ethnic consciousness or elevation of ethnic spirit, it is grounded in an opportunism that most easily discovers in this music primitive or barbaric elements. Opposing the extremely primitive or barbaric to extremely advanced civilization is already decadent, like the American plays about beggars that always meet with great applause. The wish for extreme civilization and extreme barbarianism are both signs of an insatiable desire for sensory or sensual stimulation. Just as impressionism sought pure chords and expressionism pure counterpoint, primitivism sought pure rhythm. Pure rhythm is not rhythm in the true sense, that is, the heart's rhythm, but rather a mere shock that stimulates the senses or nerves. In primitivism, all the string and wind instruments turn into percussion instruments. In this way, the keenly skeptical intellect follows the path of decadence by becoming buried within the excitement of sensual stimulation. In this sense, modernism utterly lapsed into sensualism and aestheticism.

Such has been the state of modern music in the West. As Europe itself recognizes, this music has encountered serious transitional periods. These transitions are fundamental, like the transition from the Middle Ages to modernity rather than from the classical to romantic or romantic to modern periods. Although I will later refer to the efforts made by Western musicians in relation to these transitions, I must first look at the state of music in Japan. Since there exists a basic difference between Europe and Japan regarding the notion of modernity, I must first study this notion in particular.

The history of Japanese music began in earnest after the Heian period. Korean, Chinese, and Indian music as imported from the Asian continent during the Nara period were in full flourish during the early Heian period, but this era of imitation had passed by the latter part of this period with the emergence of our country's own music. This was the new system of *kagura* and the vocal music of *saibara*, recital chanting, and *imayō*. Music temporarily declined in the Kamakura period, but signs of new music appeared that prepared the way for the next era of prosperity. Thus, in the Ashikaga and Muromachi periods, Noh emerged and *biwa* music developed among the people. In the Edo period, an extremely rich and unique era of prosperity appeared for Japanese music, one that was even more flourishing than the Heian period. This music was suitable for all the people and not simply appropriated by the upper classes. That is to say, the court nobility of the upper classes were still playing Heian-style *gagaku*, Noh chants had become the personal music of the samurai, while among the townsmen and artisans there was such highly developed music as *jōruri*, *gidayūbushi*, *itchūbushi*, *katōbushi*, *tokiwazu*, *shinnai*, and *kiyomoto*. It is thus clear that Japanese music differs in every respect from Western music, as it achieved its own unique development fully in accordance with our own national conditions and national characteristics. With the importation of European music in the Meiji period, then, there was of course no such thing as modernism in music; rather, there was only the sudden appearance of this transplantation. Here there emerged the era of complete or blind imitation.

At that time Western civilization was being rapidly imported in every field, not only music. Having long been closed off from the world during the Tokugawa period, our Japan rapidly modernized in order to catch up to this civilization. Japanese modernity can thus be said to have begun in the late nineteenth century, which is very different compared to the situation in Europe. Western music first entered Japan in 1869, when soldiers from Satsuma learned it from British troops, and thereafter the importation of this music centered on performances. As a result, foreign teachers were invited over, who long assumed leading positions in the Japanese music world, and this situation continues in part today. Although there were some people of great talent among these foreign teachers and musicians who visited Japan, most could certainly not be considered first-rate artists. While quite skilled, the majority of these musicians were not such formidable artists, and they naturally had certain limitations in their attitude about Japan's musical culture. Western music was transplanted to Japan by such people, although the Japanese themselves later came to study abroad. As goes without saying, however, in both these cases the Japanese lacked sufficient ability and preparation to regard European music critically. They thus had no choice but to accept this music uncritically, and essentially the same situation prevailed in the case of Japanese studying abroad. In this way, the importation of Western music in our country was characterized by two points: this music was centered on performance, and its reception was entirely passive and uncritical. As a result, Japan came late to music composition and its musical culture was in disarray.

The initial focus on performance in the importation of Western music was itself certainly not mistaken but rather a natural course to follow. It would have been even more natural for these Japanese with only very slight familiarity with this tradition to write music freely. Yet the study of and interest in music composition was neglected for an excessively long time, and this imbalanced situation has brought about very unfortunate results. State music conservatories have introduced composition courses only in these past few years, and Japan's top symphony orchestras have only this season begun to seriously perform works by Japanese composers. Music composition was long left entirely in the hands of interested individuals, and needless to say this brought about poor results. Japan's tardiness in studying composition has not only produced an unfortunate imbalance in the development of its music culture; it has also been one of the unfortunate factors behind our inability to understand the essence of music. Although there has been considerable progress in performance techniques, critical studies of the essence of Western music have been scant, and everyone is forced to depend upon the musical views of foreigners as introduced in books. Since these views are quite diverse, however, confusion is inevitable. That is to say, Japan's tardiness in music composition has perpetuated our borrowing of Western music and created all kinds of confusion in our music culture. It has also produced an extremely dangerous absence in our understanding of the essence of Western music. People thus leap at classical music, romantic music, modern music, and medieval music without any proper links between them. Even in terms of performance, the various schools of Western music are randomly transplanted as based on individual circumstances, as it were. There has been a great inertia in the music criticism needed to put this situation in order, fill in the gaps, and link these schools together. Yet this disorder and borrowing from the West are to be found not only in music. Differences in degree notwithstanding, the same problem can be seen in Japanese culture as a whole.

In this way, we can understand how Japanese modernity essentially differs from European modernity. That is, modernity in our Japan is a cultural phenomenon with its own unique characteristics, as it is a jumble of good and bad. Japanese modernity is disorder itself, as it was brought about by imitating Western civilization in its random importation. It is unlike European modernity, which was created and developed as something intrinsically European and which, in its anthropocentric seizing of the world, is now in decline and faces a fundamental transitional period. This difference must of course be accounted for. In the case of the Japanese people, with our outstanding ability to create our own culture based on our particular strength in assimilating things, the time has now certainly come for a national awakening so as to conquer this disorder. Yet it is absolutely necessary that we first confront the disorder and clearly recognize that so-called Japanese modernity is fundamentally different from Western modernity.

Now if the meaning of our modernity is as I have described, then the meaning of our overcoming of modernity naturally differs from that of Europe. Nevertheless, since our modernity was formed under the powerful influence of Western culture, we cannot possibly be indifferent to the overcoming of modernity in Europe—and it would be a mistake to be so. This is similar to the fact that the present Greater East Asia War is always in a reciprocal relationship with the war in Europe. I would thus like to look at the way that overcoming modernity in the West has taken place in the field of music.

After World War I, a certain change gradually grew stronger in European music. This change aimed to directly eliminate modernism, but it is unknown whether this goal has actually been achieved, and even less can one say whether this change has expanded to eliminate European modernity as a whole. Yet it is a fact that this change has taken place, and it is certainly not useless to examine it. This change is called the "neoclassical trend," but I don't think that it desig-nates a fixed school, as historians often insist; rather, it should name an active tendency found in many schools and composers. The neoclassical trend did not suddenly appear after the war but instead flowed alongside impressionism, expressionism, and primitivism when these schools flourished before the war. This trend grew stronger after the war. As with the relationship between roman-tic and modern music, the neoclassical trend has opposed modern music and yet has discovered many hints within it.

First, the neoclassical trend has adopted a standpoint of objectivism in con-trast to subjectivism. As I stated, both impressionism and expressionism showed such an objectivist tendency in their latter stages. Although this ten-dency was negative, the objectivism of the neoclassical trend differs from these two doctrines in that it represents a positive departure point. The adoption of objectivism involves taking the beauty of order as created by sound as one's object of expression, rather than such things as the beauty derived at the instant when individuality burns, fantasy as depicted by passion, or the figure dis-tressed by the contradiction between reality and passion. The standard for objectivism was thus Bach and the art prior to him. Here intellectual activity occupies a leading position, melody and line as musical continuity are much more important than chords as musical instants, and contrapuntal structure is seen as essential. Even chords are dealt with on the basis of their continuity or horizontal sense rather than as disparate individual symbols.

Analysis is the principle of romanticism and modernism since these are both examples of chord music. In, for instance, the relation between theme and motif, the techniques of motif development, the principle of the sonata form, and the methods adopted from modern painting, it is the essence of chords that is ultimately at stake. Here everything was in the process of disintegrating into elementary chords. A new transition began by recovering sound's unity and continuity from this disintegration. This signified an organization of sound according to some principle, and thus there came about a revival of tonality and a search for principles that could replace tonality. Present-day music is tonally much more moderate than modern music, and there are many cases where partial use is made of atonality and multitonality. However, some new developments can be expected, as the question of sound's organizing principle cannot be resolved simply by a revival of tonality. But today the neoclassical trend remains at this negative stage.

Objectivism privileges form as that which unifies music. Rather than some concrete form, form means here a principle of formation. Although romantic music contains truly vast forms, to some degree a paradox emerged in that these forms are formless. Their form is not structural or three-dimensional but rather flat and flowing. While privileging form, the neoclassical trend aims at form's simplification or tightening, and yet it still seems to lack any noteworthy discoveries in this regard. The move toward simplification can also be seen in early romanticism, and this seems to have foreshadowed the new transition. Together with the simplification of form there has also appeared a simplifying of orchestration. The extensive use of orchestral music from romantic to modern music has changed to small-scale "chamber music," and this usage is being conventionalized. In the neoclassical trend, one can thus see such features as intellectual tendencies, musical continuity, contrapuntal structure, grasp of unity, a revival of tonality, and the simplification of form and expression. As of now, however, this trend remains strikingly reactionary and still shows no forceful positivity in its status as a new transition. It is yet unknown whether this trend will actually conquer modernism or expand to the point of conquering modernity as a whole.

Now even if we were to recognize within the neoclassical trend an attempt to overcome modernity—or, more accurately, modernism—in the context of European music, this would nevertheless not be directly equivalent to our own overcoming of modernity. Overcoming modernity in our sense also includes the conquering of modernism, and in this regard does touch upon the neoclassical trend. But this trend is only a partial problem for us, as there exists a more fundamental sense of overcoming modernity. This involves eliminating Japan's borrowed Western culture and righting our own cultural disorder. That is to say, this recovery will take place through a national reflection on and thoroughgoing criticism of Japanese modern culture. This represents an awakening from our blind imitation of Western culture.

In order to effect this awakening, we must first guard against any simple negation of the West. That is to say, the overcoming of the West can never take place by simply negating it. It is necessary for us to understand the essence of Western culture, and in order to do this, we must sharply and penetratingly perceive this culture with our own eyes and ears. In the case of music, we must not worry about or depend upon the views and value judgments of Westerners but rather listen with our own ears and judge with our own hearts. In this regard, the study of Western culture must henceforth become much deeper and even more systematic. It is also important that we absorb only what is truly necessary for us rather than leap randomly after various types of music, as we did in the past. Grasping the essence of Western culture by ourselves will be very helpful in directly understanding the nature of the disorder into which Japanese culture has fallen. This is precisely the first step in liberating ourselves from our credulity and blind imitation of Western culture. If we do not firmly liberate ourselves now, then in the future the West will still leave behind various remnants of itself within us and we will oppose only the nonessentials without conquering the West fundamentally. While we must not of course be credulous of Western culture, we must neither make light of it nor simply negate it.

The first step in overcoming modernity in our sense involves perceiving the essence of Western culture with our own eyes and thereby distinguishing between what of this culture must be truly adopted and what abandoned. That is to say, this involves adopting Western culture critically and systematically. Even in the field of music, there is much to put in order and yet still much to adopt, but these activities must be done critically and systematically. On the one hand, we must profoundly discern the essence of Western culture, while on the other we must understand the Japanese classics. If overcoming modernity in the Japanese sense were the same as overcoming Western culture, then it would be natural to reflect on and pursue the Japanese classics. However, the pursuit of the classics must not be simply retrospective. The notion that "things are good because they are old" is tantamount to antiquarianism; it is impossible to see any creativity here. In our pursuit of the classics, we should adopt the attitude of "restoration is renewal," for any simply reactionary or retrospective attitude must be thoroughly avoided. The notion that Japan's true spirit existed only in the past and is not present today is most dangerous and must not be the standpoint from which we pursue the classics. To seek the ancient means to think about the origins of things rather than to pursue past forms. In other words, for us to know the Japanese classics does not involve commenting on their forms; rather, this is to know what is fundamental about Japan, and such knowledge is thus of great spiritual significance. In music, for example, a true search for the classics in no way means simply modernizing *gagaku* or using Western instruments to play *naniwabushi*; rather, the first principle involves touching upon the spirit that has maintained Japanese music or the Japanese people's fundamental spirit that created this music. When, as now, we face a period of national reflection and attempt to overcome Japanese modernity, we must conduct our search for the classics all the more properly since this activity carries a crucial meaning for us. Among those today who comment on the tradition of Japanese music, we must be on our guard against the many people who ignore its spirit in their excessive focus on its formal and sensual aspects. This is precisely what it means to be cursed by the sensualism of Western modernity, and such pursuit or restoration of the classics must be thoroughly rejected along with our credulity toward European culture. Since music is art, it is of course natural to discuss form. Because form is always created by spirit, however, one would be utterly mistaken to forget its origin and discuss form alone.

I have explained that an overcoming of modernity requires both a knowledge of the essence of Western culture and a pursuit of the Japanese classics, but it is especially important in the case of music to abandon Western modernism and, above all, its tendency toward sensualism. I have already discussed the essence of modernism, but since that is temporally the closest to us, we must of course first pass through its influence. This influence is all the more deeply rooted given that modernism is considered the most revolutionary and progressive style to date. The sensualist tendency in modernism is very easily accepted, and it has corrupted both music's creators and audience with the extremely fair-seeming argument that "music must be interesting and enjoyable." As I have said, this same influence can be seen in the pursuit of the Japanese classics, where various foolish attempts are treated as if they were very creative and Japanese. In this way, the spirit of the classics has been all the more misunderstood while Japan's cultural disorder becomes all the more rampant. Although I don't believe that the conquering of modernism for the Japanese people directly corresponds with the neoclassical trend in Europe, I do think that the future development of Western music—and not only the neoclassical trend—will always touch us.

Integrating the preceding points, we see that overcoming modernity in the Japanese sense means nothing other than building up our own culture. Although the immediate meaning of this involves overcoming the West, the more constructive and positive sense is that of creating our own culture. Fundamental in this work is the recovery of spirit, which requires establishing its predominance while returning the sensual to its original place as means. This is the important work that has been assigned in particular to artists, as we must restore and create everything according to the spiritual order. Western music has already lost this spiritual order and follows the sensual order. However, I am very doubtful as to whether the neoclassical trend essentially opposes the sensual. Although placing spirit in a dominant position means putting all form in a subordinate position, this must nevertheless not be confused with making light of form. The point is to place form in its original position so as to establish its proper relation to spirit, which always creates it. Beethoven's remark that "there is no law that cannot be broken for the sake of beauty" is rich with implication. Spirit must always be the master of form and the sensual, not their slave. In this same sense, we must attend to the fundamental in our pursuit of the Japanese classics.

This thought blows new breath into all previous forms of expression. The art of the future will be extremely different, and although we may often think that it will be based on completely new forms and means, such wild leaps are impossible. Rather, the many words and forms that people have long developed will be revived by a new breath, rescued from sensual decadence, and appear once again as new. Although there will naturally appear more new things, the fundamental point is that everything will be reconsidered and restored in accordance with the spiritual order. The new, which in modernism was sought after as the highest value, will here change into truth, for it is truth alone that creates the truly new. In contrast to artistic themes that advance toward the individual, particular, and unlifelike, we must tell of the happiness and sadness that lie in all people's hearts. The universality and lifelike nature of themes must be returned as art to all people and made into food for spirit. Our future art will be created on the basis of this apparently commonplace truth. Art created in this way will perhaps come to possess the various artistic strengths of our classics. For us, the only important thing is to advance toward truth.

The Theological Grounds of Overcoming Modernity

How Can Modern Man Find God?

YOSHIMITSU YOSHIHIKO

INTRODUCTION: SICK MODERN MAN

There is no need to begin with precise definitions of the meaning of the modern spirit. Relying upon such useless definitions would certainly cause inconvenience, as they are either too broad or too narrow. It is best to study our quickly vanishing spiritual circumstances (which, like our flesh, condition our spirit), and to do so from the perspective of our spirit's new life task, by reflecting on our bitter fate.

I would like to directly take up the question of the modern spirit from the perspective of the basic fate of modern atheism. In fact, I began my own spiritual life when I bid farewell to modern man in my late twenties (modernity is always the object of internal critique, and so, strictly speaking, we are perhaps not "modern men"). Our generation embarked upon our spiritual lives in spiritual circumstances that somehow corresponded to those in Europe following World War I. Despite differences in topics as well as consciousness, we shared with Europeans the sense that modernity was at its end. Yet compared to modern man, who in his optimism remains unaware of his sickness, we have been allowed to all the more deeply grasp in its internal moment the origins, course of fate, and hopes for development of modernity since we had to struggle with modern man's self-consciousness as a problem of critical agony. For example, there is the problem of understanding Nietzsche and Dostoyevsky. These figures were not already expressions of the modern spirit; rather, they represented protests on the part of the titanic and heroic soul that sought to save human life from the deluge of this spirit by finding in its greatest depths all its possibilities in the struggle against it. Without such a grave counterattack on the part of the soul, I believe, there can be no true overcoming of modernity. What I think makes the modern spirit worthy of such spiritual suffering is not simply the fact that it is the typical ideology of a certain historical period; rather, it is because modernity represents a metaphysical test of the human spirit. In the spiritual history of mankind, these past 300 years of Western modernity have contained unparalleled problems. What has driven man's spirit through the violent whirlpools of modern society, from the Renaissance to the French Revolution and finally to Communism? Through modern theology (modernity has actually been the era of theology's disqualification), modern philosophy (which has actually been theology's unlicensed proxy), and modern literature (which has actually been charged with the task of living man's theological investigations, as it were, amid the signs of the ineffectiveness of theology and philosophy), was there not something that possessed or haunted man? Nietzsche knew that Europe was "sick," despite his misguided and hysterical views of mankind's spiritual history as a whole. In a word, Nietzsche's philosophy may be described as the "tragedy of a sick man's healthy will." Dostoyevsky had a more theological view of the soul and recognized modern society as "demons" (the possessed). However, now is not the time to speak of these men. First of all, it must be pointed out that, from a profound perspective, Europe's spiritual problems possess a *metaphysical and theological character* and thus cannot simply be categorized as social thought. In this sense, I shall examine the issue of modern spirit as a question of *modern atheism*. Taking up Dostoyevsky once again, he writes in *The Brothers Karamazov* that contemporary "socialism" is a problem of atheism rather than a mere social problem. I must of course explain that a certain view of cultural history is presupposed in the way I have set up this question. I must say that *historical and cultural problems* must ultimately be seen as *problems of religion and thought*, and that this is not an abstract notion but rather a broad view of mankind's cultural history. In any case, I would simply like to point out that the problem of the modern West's cultural and spiritual history is one of a properly fundamental or metaphysical spirituality, given that these issues of religion and thought have been most problematic in the context of, at least, Western modernity's spiritual character—that is, because it appears as if modern society, unlike classical and medieval societies, were a cultural society that is distinct and independent from religious issues. From the perspective of the fate and problems of Western culture's internal structural moment, I would like to consider what theological task this indicates in our creation of culture in the new century. Here I am not trying to predict the future of culture, for our will to action internally demands that culture be created less as a vague prediction than as the essential logic of human spirit. For those who ask, What should we do? rather than, What will happen? *the question of action* is always *the question of truth*.

Proceeding from my standpoint, which contains many issues that should already be clarified, the modern spirit is inevitably determined on the basis of its relation to the medieval spirit. If a certain view states that the modern spirit negates the Middle Ages by returning prior to them, then we would have to reexamine whether the relations between antiquity, the Middle Ages, and modernity can truly be grasped by popular common sense. If, moreover, this view speaks of a "new Middle Ages" in relation to the new century that represents modernity's negation, then we would have to discuss how this "new Middle Ages" is grasped in terms of its character. Rather than treat these historical questions here directly from the standpoint of a historian, I would like to propose a response to them on the basis of my own theological concerns.

THE FATE OF MODERN ATHEISM

Some explanation is perhaps necessary in speaking of modernity as the age of atheism. Indeed, the modern spirit is at times thought to have liberated the inner piety of man's spirit from the formalism of medieval ecclesiasticism, since this modern spirit conceives of modern piety as existing in the subject's inner freedom and spiritualization, rather than placing the holy and divine in mundane or external space. In Hegel's *Philosophy of History*, the crusade to restore the Holy Land in this sense understood the following at Christ's tomb: "Why seek ye the living among the dead? He is not here, but is risen" (Luke 24:5–6). Hegel remarks here that "the West bade an eternal farewell to the East at the Holy Sepulchre, and gained a comprehension of its own principle of subjective infinite Freedom," and yet immediately in the next line he writes, "Christendom never appeared again on the scene of history as *one* body." In fact, modern inner piety lapsed into the spirit of anthropocentric rationalism and liberalism and led to the self-dissolution of both the unified idea of an external spiritual kingdom and inner religiosity itself. Precisely for this reason, Kierkegaard saw in Hegelian or modern human piety the faithlessness of the secular spirit and protested against Luther by ordering him to "return to his monastery." Like a prophet, Kierkegaard appealed to the *need to reintroduce Christianity to so-called Christendom*. I am not overlooking the fact that, in its fundamental opposition to so-called Renaissance humanism, the eschatological piety of fideism on the part of the so-called *Reformator* formed a critical moment intermittently throughout modernity. Rather, I am saying that this piety's original will to faith is indebted to the legacy of faith from primitive Christianity through medieval Catholicism and that, with regard to its distinctly modern characteristics, it is possible to directly point out—in the direction that Hegel rightly described as Lutheran—the fate that traced historical logic toward secularized and rationalized faithlessness. Later I must point out the modern spirit's just claims and problems of truth in relation to both the Middle Ages and the new era, but first I shall discuss this spirit's distinctly negative aspects.

Just as the Middle Ages cannot be sweepingly determined as an age of faith in the Christian sense (in other words, just as the Middle Ages also involved constant spiritual battles between various kinds of spirit), the modern spirit's atheistic character did not sweepingly determine public society, at least until the modern sixteenth and seventeenth centuries. In this regard, it was reasonable for such people as Ernst Troeltsch to ask, "What is modernity?" and to assert that a distinctive modernity cannot be found before the completion of the Enlightenment rationalism and modern civil society of the eighteenth century. In terms of philosophical and scientific thought, moreover, the tradition from Descartes to Kant and Hegel is essentially an extension of the medieval metaphysics of spirit. Feuerbach's attempt to point out the true form of Hegelian philosophy as a mere secularization of medieval theology was true, as is Alain's remark today that Hegel is still in the midst of an eternally endless Middle Ages (with the exception that Hegel, in his mistakenly blind faith in progress, regarded the Middle Ages and antiquity as past). However, even if I recognize that the modern spirit in no way emerges *ex abrupto* but rather refers back to modernity's sources, such that the Renaissance, rational-intellectual inquiry, free inner spirituality, and so forth are actually rooted in and first begin to bloom in the Middle Ages, one is nevertheless fully justified in pointing out this modern spirit in Luther and Descartes. Frankly speaking, I can find only coldness and indecency in a kind of anthropocentric cultural sensibility which is that of the *honnête homme* of the sixteenth and seventeenth centuries and a certain spiritual naturalism of what is essentially Christian faith. Thus, while I of course feel as most people do about the life force of artistic power and form of Renaissance art in general, such art is nevertheless completely different in charm from the simple and inspiring spiritual beauty of medieval piety or the spiritual sympathy evoked by the striking force of Byzantine mystic symbolism. Although I by no means dislike art, unlike some reactionary people of faith who abhor even Michelangelo and Leonardo, I cannot but sense a metaphysical emptiness of spirit in the work of these artists, despite their human and creative genius. In this regard, I fully understand Pascal's sentiments when he remarked, "I cannot forgive Descartes. . . . He would have been quite willing to dispense with God"—although I don't think that Pascal's critique of Descartes signifies a true resolution in the sense that these men were extreme opposites of the same modern spirit. Between the slogan "Modernity is the era of humanity's liberation" and the confession "Modernity is the era of the loss of humanity" there exists a difference between dream and reality. In this regard, we must consider that only recently has the European intellect confronted the mass of specious common sense that proclaims, like a dramatic political speech, that free humanity created the wonders of scientific civilization and social culture upon its liberation from ecclesiastic oppression and truly began to ask, What is man? As Karl Adam points out in his signature work *The Spirit of Catholicism*, an actual dialectic in Western spiritual history appears in the inevitable logic that leads from the sixteenth century's "separation from the church" to the seventeenth and eighteenth centuries' "separation from Christ" (deism) to the "separation from God" (atheism) that can be seen since the nineteenth century, and this directly calls forth Berdyayev's remark that "he who kills God kills man." If I may point out another dialectic of modern atheism in the manner of Jacques Maritain, one can find a severe dialectic of modern anthropocentric humanism from Descartes' notion of God (where He is seen as the guarantor, or *garant*, of man's rational domination of the world in his backing of man's demiurgic [*demiurgos*] activities, thus leading to a methodologically dualistic separation of God from humanity) to Hegel's notion of God (where He dissolves into monism in being absorbed within man's idea of reason as a limit concept, and presently becomes the suspension of life of man himself in a civilizational climate of materialist atheism and humanity's technologist determinations). Here I am not ignoring the many readers who are able to remain at one moment in this dialectical process. But one must consider that the reality of history is both crueler and more logical than that. Finally, we must recognize that when Nietzsche, the son of a Lutheran pastor and who rebelled against what he perceived as an enervated Christianity in the context of modern Protestantism, stated in the interest of life's possibilities that "God is dead" (note that Nietzsche said that God is *dead*, not merely that He doesn't exist), he was driven to the tragic conclusion as uttered by Kirilov in Dostoyevsky's *Demons*: "Hence I must commit suicide once and for all." In any case, with the awakening of humanity's anxiety from the acute self-consciousness of atheism, the question, What is man? had begun to be asked anew of the optimistic, liberal secular spirit of Western humanism. It was under these circumstances that the work of eliminating modernity was performed from the nineteenth to twentieth centuries.

This work involved the following perspectives: (1) a kind of *mythologism* that attempts to essentially restore society and humanity through the divinization and maintenance of some God substitute or "order" upon which an ancient humanity might have been able to live but which was lost in its Godless beginnings; (2) an antihumanist (*humanitätswidrig*) and reactive faithism, such as so-called dialectical theology, that basically eliminates humanity's value order in its essentialization of such Godless beginnings; and (3) an *integral humanism*, as it were, that rediscovers humanity by finding God and seeks integral development for a healthy humanity as based on the first condition of human existence. As can at once be understood, the first standpoint here is theologically nothing other than the heroism of the modern spirit's self-consciousness. The following all belong to this category, even if they appear to be nothing but symptoms of modern humanity's critical problems: the sociological conservatism that, as based on Comte's *myth of rationalism* in its worship of humanity, aims in its historical methods to restore "society" and "order" as lost by modern, abstract individualism and rationalism; the *materialist myth of salvation* that places its hopes in the salvation of class revolution by negating in one stroke both the selfish bourgeois society of modern individualism and the monasticism of ancient feudal society; a heroism that, amid the ruins of a humanity laid waste to by these myths, *holds to the desperate self-consciousness of a fateful humanity*, and in which people think about the following (even if these appear to be nothing but symptoms of modern humanity's critical problems): "The Night-Song" (*Zarathustra*) that mankind has yet to hear as well as humanity's elegy of "*amor fati*"; the new *myth of the intellect* on the part of such "Godless mystics" as Alain and Valéry, who, in their desperate faith of self-reliance, try like Ulysses to save themselves from drowning by resolutely throwing themselves into an ocean of despair; and the mythologism of Stefan George, who, from his poetic to political myths, tries to establish himself as a kind of heretical Catholic priest. In contrast to this first standpoint, the second standpoint can become a prophetic warning against the third standpoint insofar as its negative character signifies a "corrective" (*Korrektiv*) or "conversion" to the negative. Hence, this second standpoint is actually one of anxiety that becomes an "escape from spirituality" rather than the "predominance of spirituality," while either lapsing into self-righteous idealism or leading to dualistic and hypocritical distinctions. From this "corrective" standpoint, Kierkegaard sought to be himself before God when facing those who despaired of modernity, and advised these men who did not try to find themselves before God to "seek possibilities," while also asking himself, "*How can man become a Christian?*" Before I speak of the possibilities of the third standpoint, I must first determine the historical character of modernity, for in fact therein lies the uniqueness of the spirit of the modern West in the context of world spiritual history, and this relates to what I have to say here.

THE INTERNAL RELATION BETWEEN THE MIDDLE AGES AND MODERNITY

How and why did modernity emerge from the Middle Ages? As is generally stated, both Renaissance humanism and Cartesian *séparatisme* inevitably arose out of the self-dissolution of the unified cultural principle of medieval traditional society as the desire and accomplishment of man's autonomy in regard to his individuality and rational intellect. In this sense, the Middle Ages can be interrogated in terms of its causal responsibility for modernity, which is its prodigal son. On the other hand, however, modernity can be described as the continued development of the serious test posed by those problems that could not be resolved in the Middle Ages, such that the problems of Western modernity remain the spiritual issues of Europe's Middle Ages. The notion of a "*new Middle Ages*" must be both understood and criticized in this sense. I have discussed this situation in my essay "Ideas of Medieval Spiritual History" [Chūsei seishinshi no rinen], as contained in the volume *Lectures on the Spiritual History of the World* [*Sekai seishinshi kōza*], published by Risōsha. The notion of a "new Middle Ages" carries great significance, particularly when one thinks of the Christian Middle Ages. For those who contemplate problems of spiritual history from the historical standpoint of Christian theology, Christianity is not an issue of the medieval past but rather the most concrete and world-historical real issue of today—and indeed, of tomorrow. Yet we must understand that this notion differs widely from the contempt reserved for Christianity in the intellectual circles of Japan, where the West first came to be known only upon modernity's collapse, for Japan never acquired a historical position from which to truly understand Christianity.

Modernity is often described as the negation of the Middle Ages or the rebirth of the free, natural humanity of antiquity. After the collapse of the ancient world and its people and culture, however, the cultural, political, and intellectual formation of Europeans as a people newly established itself as the formative process of what Hegel called the "Christian-Germanic world." Unlike the transition from antiquity to the medieval world, contemporary Western man and culture bear the same ethnic cultures and social traditions as those from the Middle Ages. This Christian-Germanic world is determined by the mutual interplay of the three elements of *politics*, *religion*, and *culture*, that is, the social ethos of ancient peoples, the religiosity of a newly emerging Christianity, and the mission and accomplishment of Christian education together with the logos-based culture of classical humanism as mediated by that education. In brief, the medieval world in its public aspects since at least the time of Charlemagne (despite the constant tension between the Christian church and the political order of the state, or rather precisely because such tension produced the aim of ideal unity) was one in which both the principle and reality of universal unity among these three elements were strenuously preserved, whereas the modern world has lost this principle and reality of unity. Although the mutual relation among these elements continues in terms of their respective aim for autonomous rule, the modern world nevertheless constantly suffers from the tragic oppositions contained within it. Thus, while there came about such new and intense developments as the demand for a modern, autonomous "reason of state" (*ragione di stato*), the consciousness of a rebirth of pagan classical culture, and the aim of freedom in subjective personal piety, these developments nevertheless always drifted through medieval society, where they pressed like questions for true and deeply internal answers. When the previous principle of universal holistic unity was replaced by a universal revelation of individual autonomy, there could of course be found a truly fitting social necessity and a corresponding division between the distinct characteristics of the spirit of the times. The modern spirit did not simply oppose the medieval spirit as its negation but rather emerged as a result of the medieval world's spiritual self-dissolution, thereby signifying the self-development of a single people. Even if modernity is commonly described as a rebirth of antiquity or a "revival of the gods," this does not mean that one has directly adopted the pagan world of concrete antiquity, which is no longer innocent and healthy but sick and in need of salvation. The notion of an ideal and logos-based free humanity, as dreamed of and idealized by modern man, is a mere glorification and an object of reactive nostalgia. The concrete world of antiquity was rather a kind of Adventist humanism (*adventistischer Humanismus*), which both required and anticipated salvation. Saint Augustine, who stood at the collapse of antiquity in its transition to the medieval Christian world, personally witnessed and confessed as much, but this point is also made by such contemporary thinkers as Theodor Haecker, who finds it in Virgil, the "father of the West." Classical man fell sick in seeking salvation and thus was a *religious man who prayed before the limits of fate*, just as he was a man of a sound and natural moral character, as based on *pietas* (love of homeland), *amor*, and *labor*. The humane values of classical humanism in this sense exist less in an oppositional relation with the supernatural religiosity of the Middle Ages than in an anticipatory relation regarding salvation (in at least the essential sense of this relation). What must be pointed out in modernity's intent to "revive the gods," however, is a kind of negative, reactive, and apostatic indifference (this, too, is something for which the Middle Ages are not without responsibility).

In any case, the European world is unique in world intellectual history in that, throughout both the Middle Ages and modernity and the formation of Europeans as a single people, this world always bore the question of the unity and division between the truth of Christian religious existence and humanistic logos-based culture. This is due to the fact that Christianity represents the *truth of the formation of a supernatural community of the soul* that endeavors to be the creative spirit behind all culture. On the one hand, Christianity is endowed with absolute characteristics that transcend culture and the people, since it is based on an utterly new revelation of grace as the logos-based spiritual truth of supernatural reality. On the other hand, precisely because it is the life and truth of religious reality, Christianity is *linked to all of the most internal possibilities of ethical life in the life of a people*. Christianity bore this supernatural spiritual truth as it moved west through the Mediterranean world, but in the social formation of a new people on the European peninsula, a tragic imbalance between this truth and the people became a great world-historical test in Western spiritual history. In the history of the idea from Saint Augustine to Saint Thomas, the medieval world held fast to one metaphysical and logos-based value system for human life in the context of the supremacy of theological existence. (In the practical order of this theological idea, one finds the most symbolic expression of the Christian Middle Ages in, for example, the "evangelical heroism" of Saint Francis). Both culture and religion and the intellect and spirituality appeared to breathe as one life within the systematic universality of Thomistic unity and order, but thereafter an imbalance was widely exposed in the Western Christian world between the truth of Christianity and those who bear this truth. This imbalance was caused neither by scientific culture with its Saracen origins nor by the fascination with Hellenic beauty. Nor was it made inevitable by the failure of the Crusades, the collapse of the Holy Roman Empire, or the newly emerging civil society. Rather, this decisive dissolution was prompted by Western society itself, which had once knelt before Christianity—indeed, such dissolution was prompted by the internal and external faithlessness of the Christian church. We lack the time here to discuss how the modern spirit originated in the medieval spiritual world's own internal crisis, as well as how this modern spirit became a kind of "faithlessness of autonomy"—separating from its union with the living community of faith, such that the abstract individual became separated from its ground in the traditional life of the whole community, thus causing the self-dissolution of individualist liberalism and rationalism. We also lack the time to discuss the process by which the modern spirit, following the collapse of a sound theological and metaphysical intellect, led first to skeptical nominalism and then to agnostic nihilism. Such discussions would require a separate description. Next we will examine the meaning of the new questions about the medieval spirit in the context of the modern spirit as well as their answer in the form of contemporary man's demand for a "new Middle Ages." In order to avoid repeating modernity's stumbling blocks, or rather the possibility of new stumbling blocks, we will also seek the theological grounds for a "new order."

THE NEW ORDER OF INTELLECT AND SPIRIT

If, as Dilthey points out, the Middle Ages represented the working of the metaphysical intellect in its relation to "God and the soul"—that is, spirit's ultimate objects—then it was the most glorious and grand period in the spiritual history of the world. Yet even if this intellect was, like a Gothic cathedral, something majestic and strong that rose high in the metaphysical sky of the angelic intellect, as it were, the Middle Ages were not a period of knowledge about the "world and nature," as manifested in modern science. There is no need for us to discuss here whether a *problem of the modern scientific intellect* is to be characterized in terms of pragmatic social and technological factors, as in the manner of some sociologists of knowledge (for example, Scheler), or as based on the logos-centered essence of the self-consciousness that was part of the absolute, free intellect of the Greeks, as in the manner of other sociologists of knowledge (for example, Essertier). For both standpoints recognize that these characterizations are joined together in regard to their form of high intellect (that is, not

primitive or simple), which can be called something like the logos-based technology of the modern scientific intellect, just as they allow us to discern here a
crisis of modern spirituality, since the modern scientific intellect gradually isolated the logos from the metaphysical intellect of spirit. In this sense, we consider Bergson to be of profound significance, as this twentieth-century philosopher surveyed the Cape of Good Hope from modern science to metaphysics
with the aim of establishing new links between the mechanic and the mystic at
the end of modernity. Nevertheless, we believe that the misery of the modern
intellect stretches from the grandeur of the scientific intellect's technological
domination of knowledge about the world and nature (including man) to the
misery that is the *poverty of metaphysical speculations on spirituality*. We must
unite at the level of logos the grandeur of the Middle Ages and the grandeur of
modernity as intellectual projects that both seek the truth. It is a separate question as to whether this unity can be rightfully promised in such thinkers as
Bergson. A similar issue can be pointed out in terms of the *problem of ethical
culture*. With the self-collapse of medieval feudal society, there flooded forth
the *Declaration of the Rights of Man*, which represents modern man's values,
and the self-conscious demands for freedom and personhood, and these came
to generally dominate the cultural consciousness of both modern civil society
and modern humanism. However, this phenomenon must be described along
the lines of the secular consciousness of the medieval Christian notion of personality rather than as the ancient Greek notions of individuality and freedom.
It was Christianity that, in contrast to all ancient societies, gave a final, deter-
minative expression to this supernatural spiritual essence in the "Gospels"
through the dignity of human personhood as "children of God." The Middle
Ages may be described as the period that strove to realize (under medieval historical conditions) an old social reality of this "new man." In this sense as well,
what had existed in the living *total unity* of the Middle Ages (such unity was
rooted in the ethos and living nature of the simple society of the people and
corresponded to its social reality) lost its ground of original life in modernity,
insofar as this was an atomistic or atomistic-collective consciousness of the *isolated and abstract individual*. Thus, with the inhuman application of the technological intellect, modern Western society followed its fateful path toward the
"slave society" of capitalist self-interest, or rather plutocratic rule. This can also
be described as the fate of a one-dimensional and isolated manifestation of
those elements that were all grounded in, for example, the Thomistic metaphysical principle of unity and order to which I referred earlier, whereby an
"establishment of order" exists in the ultimate ordering of the "autonomous
value functions" of the natural intellect and social ethics in supernatural spirituality. In this sense, it is not insignificant that such people as the philosopher
of medieval culture Alois Dempf refers to Saint Thomas as the "father of
modernity" in finding the path of modern man's autonomous culture precisely

in the completed expressions of the Middle Ages. This is not the place for us to consider the Thomistic worldview and view of culture. Nevertheless, this view is related to our own proposal, as it is directly linked to the third standpoint— that is, that which reaches the conclusion of modernity's corrective—and which still remains for me to discuss.

Although the modern spirit's autonomous intellect and social ethos signify the development of that which originated in the Middle Ages, this notion of "autonomous man" gradually became removed from its original ground, leading to its abstract dehumanization. Western rationalism and liberalism (in the broad sense of these terms, which comprehensively includes relativist skepticism, in its rejection of all absolutes, and egocentric pragmatism. Western rationalism and liberalism may be social ideologies, but they are also linked to the metaphysical question of the knowledge of truth. Consider how today's political totalitarianism is, in fact, metaphysically characterized by relativism and agnosticism!) thereupon eroded all traditional values and truth throughout not only the Western world but also the entire planet. Awareness of the "crisis of the West" is nothing but the immediate awareness of the crisis of humanity, sociality, truth, and ethos that has spread analogously throughout thought in general and now covers the entire planet. Standing within the nihilist storm that represents the fateful ruin and suffering of man in his draining autonomy, Dostoyevsky expressed with great intuition the basic character of atheism in the autonomous spirit, declaring that the modern spirit is represented by man's "revolt against God." Since the early nineteenth century, however, this modern spirit has been expressed in the form of many prophetic warnings to the European intellectual world. These warnings extend from Joseph de Maistre, who, in the midst of the French Revolution, observed and reflected on the false superstitions of the modern era, to Donoso Cortés, who predicted the Spanish Revolution and the heroism of contemporary nationalism. Indeed, the poet-hero Charles Péguy, who, through his heroic struggles, made the most fundamental critique of the modern world, also issued such warnings. As Bergson writes, "I long suspected that Péguy would survive when we extricated ourselves from the fallen path that is our present dark century." Péguy bitterly pointed out the plutocracy and soullessness of the modern world: "There has been no era like modernity in which the temporal (the contemporary human) was so protected from the spiritual. Never has there been an era in which the spiritual was so unprotected from the temporal." For Péguy, political and economic questions as well as all social questions were matters of the soul. Pascal's plea for grace in his basic objection to the Cartesian spirit—"[Descartes] would have been quite willing to dispense with God," as he wrote— becomes here a passionate cry for the salvation of all civilization and society, as well as an objection to modernity as a whole. By returning to the origins of modernity's error, such an objection orients itself toward the Middle Ages as a time of faith in the context of curing modernity of its faithlessness. This objection to modernity may generally be determined as a move toward what Berdyayev called a "new Middle Ages."

As I have already stated, however, the notion of a *"new Middle Ages"* must not simply involve an elementary return to a ground in the Middle Ages, nor a reactionary negation of modernity as its polar opposite. Thus, if the current demand for a "new Middle Ages" signifies a return to a pre-Christian or pre-Christian-Germanic *ground of life of the people*, it would save man from the lifelessness of modern abstract rationality insofar as it represents a return to sound natural life—in fact, such a return to life would not simply be planned but rather involve a dialectic of the instinctive activity that is nature's self-defense as a reaction of natural life. It must be pointed out, however, that if this demand for a "new Middle Ages" signifies an *apostatic idolatry* of a new pagan myth as a conscious transformation of modern Godlessness, then this would be less a salvation from modernity than modernity's own pathological self-tragedy. The modern intellect and personality must themselves be revived within a higher unity through the idea of metaphysical order. In every sense, *an order of value cannot be formed by placing the "will to truth" in a subordinate position.* In this regard, the Nietzschean path of *amor fati* represents, together with the path of "Faust," the flight of desperate men. The correct goal, that is, the search for "the eternal" or "life," must be secured by a recovery of love that begins with a humble repentance of the intellect. More precisely, the "new Middle Ages" must be sought less in the individual moments of the Middle Ages than in the more internal and subjective form of a *"new order,"* whereby the idea of metaphysical unity as sought but unrealized during the Middle Ages comes to be discussed and explored as a task of the new era. It is not to be found in any impossible and meaningless return to the historic Middle Ages.

Even though the abstract nature of modern autonomous man is false, we who live in modern society must seek a more internal path of salvation and sanctification, one that corresponds to the reflective mode of modern self-consciousness. The public institutions and objective forms that linked spirituality and the political in medieval society, insofar as these do not now become self-conscious in their linking and fail to permeate the individual's total interiority, are merely the old, mistaken masks of monasticism, worthy of the antipathy shown them by both the French Revolution and Marxism. I have already pointed out the nature of the theological atheism that lies at the basis of the French Revolution and Communism. There exist children of this century who still restlessly seek in these godless paths the salvation of a new society and civilization, as enjoined upon them by modern society. Yet anyone who casually entrusts to the world man's liberation—which is only possible in God and grace—can only be a heartless believer who merely looks on at the suffering of the Redeemer, as found "amid suffering until the end of the world." I must say that such people are themselves responsible for causing the world to stumble before God and the church. In the new era, new mistakes are to be found just as new truths are revealed; or rather, we are charged with new *tasks of truth and love*. From his standpoint of Christian culture and philosophy, Maritain writes that modernity is that period of civilization that has reached the "age of reflection" (*l'âge de réflexe*) and that the medieval order, as characterized by the "supremacy of spirituality," realizes an analogous historical life in the new forms and self-awareness of modernity. Herein lies the significance of Maritain's insistence on the "sanctification of the profane" (*sanctification du profane*) as what is truly needed to resolve today's crisis of spirit and society, as caused by the dualistic and hypocritical separation in modernity between the holy and profane. This notion approaches the heart of Péguy, who called for a fundamental spiritual revolution against modernity.

This path of modernity's salvation or overcoming is not a path of religiosity that leads to an antihumanism diametrically opposed to modern, anthropocentric humanism, a radical negation of human culture; rather, it is the religiosity of Catholicism as represented by a God-centered humanism—or what Maritain calls "integral humanism" (*humanisme intégral*)—which signifies a different path of affirming humanity as the complete revival and ordering of man's spiritual potential and demands in the context of his concrete totality. In contrast to modern humanism, this integral humanism points out the abstract lifelessness of such separatist anthropocentrism and seeks a living structure oriented to a properly supernatural life of grace. Unlike the claims for a modern, abstract humanity, integral humanism recognizes the need for what we saw Haecker refer to as "Adventist humanity" in the human expressions of a sound natural morality and intellect in the classical world. What is expressed here is the central notion of Thomistic theology's worldview, "Grace does not destroy nature (humanity) but anticipates and perfects it." It is this very principle that represents Catholicism's worldview and view of culture, as expressed in the Thomistic "metaphysics of order." This principle encompasses infinite content and can be infinitely applied, but we must realize that the deep respect for nature as expressed in this theological notion cannot be compared with the naturalist and merely subjective love of nature in romanticism. We must also realize that the theological and metaphysical "reverence for reality" as God's creation, the "reverence for humanity," and "a love for human virtue and the logos" are here expressed, precisely, as a summoning to supernatural eternal life, or rather as a confession of thanks and praise. Together with Saint Francis's "Song of the Sun," Saint Thomas's theological affirmation of nature is an expression of praise for God, since the entire universe is His creation. Such a *return to original nature* signifies, first of all, modern man's repentance. Modern man's ultimate salvation lies in this advice not to despair in exploring possibilities for the religiosity of supernatural grace, that is, the eternal blessing of what

Kierkegaard called "man standing before God," as well as in opening himself up to the "revealed world" of supernatural spirituality.

CONCLUSION: OUR TASK

For us Orientals or non-Westerners as well, this insight indicates both the glory and poverty of those modern elements existing within us, and allows us to understand the metaphysical significance of returning to our original nature or ground of life and of opening our eyes more widely to the natural moral and spiritual activities of classical man. Insofar as this notion signifies a sound truth of the logos-based intellect, it also reveals a possibility for achieving at a higher level the unity between the modern scientific intellect and the classical metaphysical intellect, regardless of past or present, East or West. We believe that, with our repentance of Western modernity, a new East Asian spiritual civilization must and will be rebuilt through a sound metaphysical and logos-based intellect. We must not lose hope in mankind. Yet those who rely only upon themselves will certainly be disappointed. We know that faith and hope come when we constantly strive to forget ourselves and serve truth, love, and our homeland. Isn't it the case that modern, autonomous man has lost sight of the truth and love that he must serve, and in the end always seeks refuge in the myth of despair while putting his ego ahead of God? Above all, overcoming the modern spirit must signify a liberation from the modern ego that exists within us. If, as I have said, *the first condition for overcoming modernity is the penitence of the soul*, then this matter must begin with the soul of each and every individual. I have also thought about how the basis for resolving this question of overcoming modernity through the theological principle of "nature and grace" can be applied to today's concrete problem of the cultural spirit of "East and West," or more directly, how it could be applied to the problem of the metaphysical foundation of our East Asian order of spiritual civilization. However, I would simply like to repeat here that this spiritual matter of modernity's overcoming or salvation is neither someone else's problem nor a problem of total history. As a matter of the soul, it is ultimately our own problem as well. Here let me simply recall the passage from the Gospels: "Blessed are the pure in heart, for they shall see God."

Two Additional Remarks

1. As part of the task of "overcoming modernity," I have attempted a kind of direct theological critique of the standpoint of world spiritual history as characteristic of Western modernity. It is not necessary to state explicitly here that,

from this author's standpoint, Western problems are at once those of our own culture and spirit and that, purely from a spiritual and metaphysical perspective rather than one of Eurocentric world history, the universal problems of modern Western spiritual history are viewed as a major test of the "truth of man's spirit." Hence, for this author, the problem of the West as a mere "culture" of human society located on the European peninsula is, apart from its religious and metaphysical significance, a matter of indifference, regardless of its intrinsic value. Just as, before God, both East and West face the *one source of love and truth*, so too are they given their own *immediate existential tasks*. With the utmost earnestness, we must live the path of man—that is, the path to God— within the spiritual history and tradition of our homeland. Yet this standpoint does not, as some believe, lead to a kind of humanism or relativism of the truth, since *existence*, which is concretely grasped and realized as a single *truth* (logos), is determined *providentially*, as it were, in each of its historic and social forms. Morality and love live as such concretely existential tasks. My standpoint here is not based on geographic or external considerations of world history but rather on geological or internal-existential, so to speak, considerations of history.

2. If the task of "overcoming modernity" is seen from a viewpoint that is critical of modern individualism and liberalism (in the sense that both of these are, broadly speaking, cultural ideologies), then some people may believe that I am being unnecessarily rash in taking up these matters directly in terms of the problem of atheism. I would like to say, however, that if we understand—not simply as an objective problem of "culture" but rather as a question of the *existential subject that makes possible* culture—that the *individual* essentially lives as part of the living community that is the historical whole and that its *free* creativity becomes truly valuable within the promise of *order* and *tradition*, then the "question of the soul," that is, the question of spirit, must be considered prior to that of culture. Considered theologically, the "question of spirit" with regard to the natural, sound life of human society and culture can tentatively be conceived as distinct from that of innate religiosity as an issue of the supernatural salvation of the soul. However, if we consider that the ultimate metaphysical meaning of man as historical, concrete, and ethical existence leads to the question of supernatural religiosity, then we will understand that all cultural and social questions assume an internal and vital relation with the "question of God and the soul." I would like to think that everyone who happened to be gathered here for this symposium seemed to recognize, in their respective ways, that the problem of overcoming modernity is ultimately one of *"how modern man can find God."* Let me close this addendum with a verse from the Gospels: "But seek ye first the kingdom of God, and his righteousness; and all these things shall be added unto you." (October 17)

The Heart of Imperial Loyalty

HAYASHI FUSAO

I

The heart of imperial loyalty is not mere patriotism, nor is it allegiance to one's feudal lord or shogun. It differs from both the Chinese notion of devotion and the Western notion of loyalty.

Of course the heart of imperial loyalty corresponds to these things. For there can be no imperial loyalty without patriotism, just as there can be none without allegiance.

The foregoing lines are rather scholarly in style, but I will not try to define here the heart of imperial loyalty. Rather, as one of the emperor's people—and, moreover, as an intellectual with a particular background—I would like to offer a confession about the sense of imperial loyalty that budded all too belatedly within my own heart.

I was born in the thirty-sixth year of Meiji [1903]. The Russo-Japanese War took place when I was two to three years old. I passed my childhood in the final upsurge of Meiji patriotism. The Meiji period ended when I was ten. I was in my third year of primary school when the Meiji emperor passed away.

The ceremony for worshipping the imperial funeral took place at night in our schoolyard. I remember attending this ceremony as the representative of my third-grade class. The bonfires were burning, the sky was dark, and the sea roared from beyond the pine forest next to the schoolyard. Wearing a crested kimono and *hakama*, I lined up in back as a lower-grade student and bowed long and respectfully at the principal's command. I can recall even now how my eyes smarted from the indigo scent of the crested *haori* coat worn by the student in front of me.

I wonder if at that time I possessed a heart of imperial loyalty. The answer is not so easy as it may seem. If I were asked then whether I was already a little traitor, I would have firmly said no. But if I were asked whether I understood the heart of imperial loyalty, I would not have been able to give a ready answer. I had already learned the tragic tone of the poem "Twilight sweeps across the village of Sakurai, where the greenery grows thickly." Yet I did not cry at that ceremony. Although I felt the ceremony's grief, I did not understand the depth of its meaning. The same was true later when I heard the news of General Nogi's self-immolation. I felt only shock but didn't understand the depth of its meaning.

Now then, was I born without a heart of imperial loyalty?

It would be easy to respond here, "That would be impossible. The heart of imperial loyalty lies in the blood of the Japanese people. I, too, am Japanese. It is simply that, as a child, I wasn't aware of such loyalty." This response is perhaps not wholly false. In searching every corner of my heart, I can find no proof that I was then an unpatriotic traitor who felt no loyalty to the emperor.

I can only say this: whether internally or externally, there was nothing at all in the efforts or education of my childhood (including my primary school years) that was able to actively awaken and make conscious the sense of imperial loyalty that ran in my blood. In reflecting upon this now, I can only say that I had a truly strange childhood.

During primary school ceremonies, we always sang "Kimi ga yo" and read the *Imperial Rescript.* On the three grand national holidays, we also worshipped the emperor's portrait. The teachers were very respectful at such times, and the children were on their best behavior. These were always impressive ceremonies, replete in both solemnity and silence. After these ceremonies were over, however, no flame remained burning in our hearts.

It was not as if the teachers were unpatriotic or lacking in allegiance. Rather, there was no way for them to transmit the flame burning in their hearts to us children. The era was one of utter assurance. The nation prospered following our victory over Russia. The era was one of utter assurance, all desire for the gods was forgotten, and the ceremonies designed to communicate with the gods had become mere rituals.

At home, there was an image of the Meiji emperor on the altar. This image was displayed in the homes of all our neighbors. I lived in an old harbor town next to a village that subsisted through fishing and agriculture. Here the emperor's image could be seen in the alcoves of shops, on the black lintels of farmhouses, and on the cracked walls of fishermen's huts.

I was born and raised on the far side of Kyushu in the town of Ōita, which still cherished memories of Ōtomo Sōrin from long ago. Despite the presence of the remains of the castle that once belonged to Lord Ogyū of the Funai domain, the memory of the town's former glory had dimmed, the white walls marking the samurai's paths had cracked, railways had opened up and spinning mills built, political party branches were set up, and vulgar political battles swirled about. . . . Along with everywhere else in Japan then, Ōita was already becoming a small city attracting different types of people. To borrow the terms of geography books, our town was nothing more than the "seat of a prefectural government with a railway junction and produce-distributing center." The townsmen of Ōita spoke only of promotions: the promotion of industry, the promotion of traffic, the promotion of the prefectural government and public hall, the promotion of the theater, cinema, cafés, and so on. The dream of the municipal leaders who met in the prefectural assembly hall was to someday travel to Hibiya and stand in the Diet.

Petty ambitions and pleasures, moneymaking, and political strife buried the town like seasonal dust, and with this dust the houses grew old and decayed. The emperor's image that was always displayed in the alcoves and on the lintels and walls faded like frescoes from the distant past. I have not forgotten that image. Yet the flame that burned in the heart of my father as he displayed this image did not spread to his son. The thousands of children who grew up in this town were blessed with a prosperous reign and sense of utter assurance, and because of this we forgot the tears and the poetry and did not understand the intensity of the flame that burned in our fathers' hearts. This story is not limited to my town alone but is rather part of the sad history then shared by hundreds of other large and small cities in Japan.

Although each year the teachers took us junior high school students to the prefectural shrine, where we stood in line in the courtyard during the memorial service for the fallen troops, there were nevertheless always some who laughed when hearing the Shinto priest's prayers.

The gods had been lost. For those students, the solemn and pious words of prayer and praise to the gods of Japan were like an utterly foreign language and sounded like a parody of Buddhist scriptures that provoked only laughter. The teachers scolded these students, and there was always one old teacher wiping the sweat from his face whose veins bulged in heartfelt anger. Despite their rebukes, however, most teachers had to stifle their own laughter under their whiskers.

Ours was a truly strange era, or rather a supremely vulgar one. Who is to blame, the students or teachers? We cannot blame either. If anything, it was that very era in Japan that produced these teachers and raised these students that should be denounced.

As junior high school students, we spent long hours studying English. We put an enormous amount of effort into this task. I am not saying that, in hindsight, studying English was wrong. But why wasn't even one-tenth of that time used to teach us Japan's ancient language? It would not have taken us even that long to learn the meanings of words used by our mothers and fathers long ago and to become familiar with the serene and classical grace of that style!

Walking up and down the hill leading to our school, our torn shoes treading along the red clay, we unfortunate students memorized our English flash cards. We read these cards back and front, memorizing "I am an Englishman" while gazing up at the sky like little birds drinking water. In my first year, a young teacher who had graduated from a Tokyo mission school had us perform an English speech as a class exercise. This was the speech in which Antony grieves over the death of Caesar. We sat in the first row and giggled, "Julius Caesar was an honorable man"—*an onara*-[fart] *buru man*! This was just too much. We very nearly suffocated trying not to burst out laughing.

By the time we were in our third and fourth years, however, we no longer found English speeches or even this *onara buru man* phrase so amusing.

Yet we still laughed. We laughed at the language of our mothers and fathers from long ago.

> By the command of Sumemutsukamurogi and Kamuromi,
> Who are enshrined in Takama no Hara,
> Eight million gods gathered for discussion.
> Sumemimanomikoto ordered that the realm of Toyoashihara no Mizuho
> Be peacefully ruled as a tranquil land.

One doesn't need five years of classes at ten hours a week in order to understand the severity, depth, and beauty of these lines. One doesn't even need a tenth of that time. Granted, our national language textbooks did contain a chapter of one or two pages on Shinto prayer, a chapter on the *Kojiki* [*Records of Ancient Matters*], and excerpts from the *Man'yōshū* [*Collection of Ten Thousand Leaves*]. Yet the teachers presented these materials in a very general way that omitted much, and the students simply listened and forgot. The teachers didn't demand or the students supply even a fraction of the effort involved in looking in dictionaries, making flash cards, and trudging up and down the red clay path to school.

> Your basket, with your pretty basket
> Your trowel, with your little trowel
> Maiden, picking herbs on this hillside
> I would ask you: Where is your home?
> Will you not tell me your name?
> Over the spacious Land of Yamato
> It is I who reign so wide and far
> It is I who rule so wide and far
> I myself, as your lord, will tell you
> Of my home, and my name.

What is so difficult or amusing about this imperial poem? We were never taught it and so never learned it.

We thus entered high school laughing at our mother tongue but not laughing at a foreign language. What awaited us in high school? What kind of education could we expect there?

However, let me proceed slowly here and dwell a bit more on my junior high school days. I do not wish to attribute the late budding in my heart of a sense of imperial loyalty solely to the faults of my education and environment. As a means of blaming myself, let me reexamine my own footprints.

I read a great deal of literature when I was in junior high school. I didn't, or rather couldn't, read any classical Japanese literature. I could read in English without great difficulty *Peter Parley's Universal History, on the Basis of Geography* and *Fifty Famous Stories*, but even passages from the *Heike monogatari* [*The Tale of the Heike*] and *Tsurezuregusa* [*Essays in Idleness*] were as difficult for me as a foreign language—and I didn't even try to get hold of the *Kojiki* and *Man'yōshū*. I could get by without reading them. Nobody chastised me for this. A perfect score in English made one a star pupil. Yet it was difficult for me to read even the Chinese-style writing of the Meiji period—strictly speaking, I couldn't read it. Even if I read it, I couldn't understand it. I devoted myself only to the "contemporary fiction" of the time and the literature in translation.

In the Taishō period, what kind of literature was represented by Japanese contemporary fiction and translated works? I must now reconsider this. But I would first like to make a digression.

II

In the winter of the fifth year of Ansei [1858], Saigō Takamori tried to drown himself in Satsuma Bay together with Gesshō. Saigō alone survived and subsequently came to be exiled to Ōshima, where his alias was "Kikuchi Gengo."

It seems that this alias was of great significance. The documents state that Saigō changed his name upon orders from the domain authorities, but apparently this does not mean that the name was given to him by clan officials. One can surmise that either Saigō himself had long used a similar alias or that he chose it on his own initiative during his period of exile, after which it appeared in the records of the domain authorities.

At this time, it seems that Saigō was using the Buddhist name Shisui [still water], as in the phrase *shisui meikyō*, or "serene frame of mind." This name reveals the influence of the Wang Yangming school, but it is also redolent of Zen Buddhism.

Upon returning from exile in Ōshima, Saigō assumed the name Ōshima Sanzaemon, which signified quite literally his three years of exile. This story is well known, and there is no need for me to repeat it here. However, the name "Kikuchi Gengo" appears not to have received much attention.

It is said that one of the ancestors of the Saigō clan was Kikuchi Takemitsu, who was a loyal retainer of the Southern Dynasty.

In the Kikuchi genealogy, there are many people with the surname of Saigō. In the first generation there was Kikuchi Noritaka, who was the feudal lord of the Kikuchi district in the realm of Higo. In the second generation, Masataka was the younger brother of Tsunetaka and bore the name Saigō Tarō. Later there was Kikuchi Takamasa, who was called Saigō Saburō, and Kikuchi Taka- mori, who was called Saigō Yasaburō.

It is said that the branches of the Kikuchi clan took the surname of Saigō because their birthplace was Saigō, located in the Takagi district of Hizen (although the birthplace of one branch was the Saigō of the village section of Kamogawa in the Kikuchi district of Higo). The character *taka* was often used by the Kikuchi clan, thus explaining why our own Saigō Kichinosuke also bears the names Takamizu and Takamori.

There still remains the nameplate Saigō used when he was thirty-eight years old in the first year of Genji [1864], bearing the name "Saigō Kichinosuke Takeo." Here the characters for Saigō Kichinosuke appear smaller, while those for Takeo appear larger, or perhaps this latter name meant something else. But if Takeo was a name used long ago by this samurai, it would seem that he was related by name to the kinsmen of the Kikuchi clan who were loyal to the emperor, as for example Kikuchi Taketoki, Kikuchi Takeshige, Kikuchi Take- toshi, and Kikuchi Takemitsu. Thus, while the existence of the name "Kikuchi Gengo Takeo" is theoretically possible, I am now unfortunately unable to locate the source of this name Gengo.

Now the reason for such an inquiry derives from my wish to consider the birth of this heart of imperial loyalty in Saigō Takamori, that is, I would like to con- sider his reflections on his ancestors and his awakening to his lineage.

In my opinion, Kichinosuke had in his youth repeatedly been told by his parents and grandfather about the Saigō clan's lineage and genealogy. However, I could also imagine that the opposite was true, that is, that the young Kichino- suke had never been told of such things. I have frequently encountered the argument that, since the genealogy of the Saigō clan (like that of heroes, accom- plished retainers, and men of wealth) is not so much a fabrication as a mere subsequent discovery on the part of biographers, it is sufficient to recognize Saigō Takamori's greatness without regard to his lineage.

For me, however, such an argument represents the common sense of mod- ernism in its destruction of tradition, and is utterly unrealistic. With the advent of "civilization and enlightenment," the Japanese people forgot the value of tradition and lineage. We forgot Japanese tradition when the people began to regard as common sense Fukuzawa Yukichi's individualist notion of "independence and self-respect" as well as the belief of the Freedom and Popular Rights Movement that "no man is above another." Granted, these notions may have been linked to Japanese tradition upon their inception. Yet, when they became part of the people's common sense in its arrogant belief that it could eliminate the "abuses of feudalism," they highlighted the worst function of such "common sense." The Japanese people were thus transformed into vulgar utilitarians who also eliminated the "fine customs of feudalism" and forgot their own history and lineage. The argument that "Saigō was great regardless of his lineage" is akin to the notion that "might makes right" and is the father of the merchant's notion that "wealth means victory at whatever cost."

We were born at a time of triumph of such common sense. According to this common sense, a poor samurai family from Satsuma, who were more or less foot soldiers lacking the means for their next meal, would not have thought about their own lineage, and the notion that the Kikuchi clan were ancestors of the Saigō family was, if not a falsehood, then a mere subsequent discovery on the part of biographers.

Yet Japan's feudal era cannot be judged or evaluated on the basis of such decadent common sense. In that era, there was great respect for lineage and tradition. I believe that Saigō's parents and grandfather spoke proudly of their family line's purity in this setting where, lacking the means for their next meal, they could barely put food on the table. No records state that Kichinosuke's lullaby song as an infant was the tragic ballad about the Kikuchi clan dying like falling blossoms on the banks of the Chikugo River. Nevertheless, one can realistically imagine that the young Kichinosuke was told that his ancestor was Kikuchi Takemitsu, the third son of Kikuchi Taketoki.

However, the documents note that Saigō Takamori assumed the name Kikuchi Gengo in November of the fifth year of Ansei, when he was thirty-two years old.

That was certainly late. If I were asked whether Saigō's recollection of history and awakening to his lineage did not take place very late in his life, I would have no materials with which to refute that view.

The history of imperial loyalty in the Satsuma domain is a long one. The evidence regarding Shimazu Nariakira's imperial loyalty conforms to this tradition, as he lacked any ambition to "attend to Kyoto," that is, act as a tool to use the imperial court, as some historians believe. The same is true of Nariaki, a senior noble from Mito, who was also said to "attend to Kyoto." It is only because historians don't understand Mito tradition that they interpret this situation as evidence of Nariaki's own ambitions. Such an argument forgets to take into account Mitsukuni from Mito. There can be no interpretation of Nariaki if one forgets this builder of the "Tomb of the Loyal Retainer Nanshi—alas!" and the editor of *Dai Nihon shi* [*The History of Great Japan*].

However, I lack the materials to confirm that, even prior to Shimazu Naria-kira, Saigō Kichinosuke was a patriot of imperial loyalty.

In Satsuma during the second year of Kasui [1849], a domestic incident took place known as "Takasaki's ruin" or "Yura's ruin." Kichinosuke was then twenty-three years old.

This matter has generally been interpreted as a common domestic incident that occurred in the household of a daimyo at the time. This daimyo, Narioki, had a concubine named O-Yura, with whom he bore a child named Hisamitsu. An evil retainer intervened in this situation and tried to remove Nariakira as the daimyo's heir. Such righteous samurai as Takasaki Gorōuemon, Yamada Ichirōuemon, and Akayama Yukie then formed a group to rid the court of all corrupt elements, but their efforts were thwarted and they were executed. Saigō Kichinosuke and Ōkubo Ichizō were also implicated in this affair, albeit indirectly, but this gave them the chance to harden their sense of resolve.

I, too, believed that this was how events took place, but upon further study I gradually came to realize my mistake.

"Takasaki's ruin" was in no way a mere domestic incident.

Though I disappear from the world
With my aim unrealized,
My heart remains as white as this morning's snow.
—TAKASAKI GORŌUEMON

Even I think that I will disappear from the world
Like the white snow.
Shine, moon, in the cloudless sky!
—KONDŌ RYŪZAEMON

There are other poems about white snow written by the men who were forced to commit suicide because of this incident. It snowed in Kagoshima on the day of their execution, which was very unusual. These poems were not composed in an arranged manner, since the men were forbidden to see each other. Rather, it was the southern snow, which sometimes falls and accumulates only to then suddenly vanish, that encouraged them to write in such a manner. Behind these works there must lay the same scholarly mantle. I am unfamiliar with the art of poetry and know only that these poems are not written in the *Man'yōshū* style.

Research shows that the Keien and Hirata schools of National Learning were active in Satsuma. Keien, the mainstream school, was directly affiliated with

Kyoto. Yamada Ichirōuemon, one of the central figures in "Takasaki's ruin," was an official who lived in the Satsuma palace in Kyoto. Well known as a poet, Yamada became close with such loyal court nobles as Konoe Tadahiro and Sanjō Sanekata and was at times rebuked by the *bakufu* for going beyond his own samurai status in his friendship with those at court. This is perhaps revealed by the fact that Yamada Ichirōuemon's letter as given to a Kyoto towns- man constitutes an important document in the case surrounding "Takasaki's ruin."

Yamada had a servant named Umeda, whose son was Umeda Genjirō. It seems that Genjirō was a favorite of Yamada and that as a youth he had served in Satsuma. This Genjirō would later be known as Umeda Unbin, the Confu- cian imperial loyalist.

In this same incident, there were four men in Satsuma who had fled their own domains and settled in Chikuzen, where they were protected by Shimazu Nariakira's great-uncle, Kuroda Narihiro. These four men were Takeuchi Ban'uemon (Kazuraki Hikoichi), Kimura Nakanojō (Hōjō Umon), Inoue Izu- minokami (Kudō Samon), and Iwasaki Senkichi (Murayama Matsune).

Takeuchi Ban'uemon was the disciple of Hirata Atsutane during the latter's lifetime. Atsutane had many disciples after his death but few during his life- time. When Takeuchi was eighteen years old in the fifth year of Tenpō [1834], he moved to Edo and was deeply moved by his reading of Atsutane's *Tama no mihashira* [*The True Pillar of Spirit*]. At twenty-one, in the eighth year of Tenpō, Takeuchi resolved to travel east, where he became Atsutane's disciple.

There is only one imperial way,
Do you neglect this, people,
And take the false path of the enemy?

Shine, the way of the jeweled sword,
On the faces of those who are ashamed
Of this world where blowflies fly about in the air.

These poems were written by Atsutane himself for Takeuchi Ban'uemon, who always displayed them at his side and recited them day and night. Together with Hirata Tetsutane, Takeuchi edited and published Atsutane's posthumous work *Sango kokuhon kō* [*A Study of the Thirty-five Foundations of the Country*], to which he also wrote the introduction. In the incident of "Takasaki's ruin," Takeuchi and his fellow samurai Iwasaki Senkichi tried to kill the evil retainer and were forced to flee and travel in disguise to Edo.

Kimura Nakanojō took refuge in Chikuzen, where in Ōshima (in Genkai) he met and then educated a youth named Kogane Maru-something, who later came to be known as Hirano Kuniomi. Kimura's National Learning and spirit of imperial loyalty truly opened the eyes of the young Hirano. This fact is known by anyone who has read *Hirano Kuniomi den* [*The Life of Hirano Kuniomi*].

A full discussion of these events would be quite long. In short, as can be seen from the simple explanation above, National Learning and the spirit of imperial loyalty lie nobly in the spirit of those patriots involved in the incident of "Takasaki's ruin."

However, it is unclear whether Saigō Kichinosuke was aware of such things in the second year of Kasui, when he was twenty-three years old. No one refers to Saigō then as a patriot of imperial loyalty. In my opinion, his blood still lay dormant within his body. Although "Takasaki's ruin" may have awakened Saigō's blood, the facts suggest that he regarded this as a mere domestic incident.

Saigō still had to wait for the violent and harsh year of Ansei—when, according to documents, he was thirty-two years old—in order to consciously and resolutely assume the name Kikuchi Gengo Takeo.

Saigō Kichinosuke was Japanese. Although he was born with a heart of imperial loyalty, it still lay within his blood. Historical recollection and a realization of his lineage were required in order for this blood to awaken and revive, thus becoming the force of a living spirit. Indeed, Kichinosuke needed thirty harsh years for this to take place. Was it the 500 years of shogun government since the Kamakura period that had hardened his thoughts and delayed such recollection and realization?

In the absence of historical recollection and a realization of one's lineage, there can be no "living Japanese" or "Japanese as creator of history," even though one might be Japanese in the ethnological sense. Sadly, some people come to such recollection and realization earlier and some later. Also, some eras are earlier and some later in this regard. Masatsura realized his lineage quite early, having witnessed his father, Masashige's, desperate act, whereas Saigō Kichinosuke may have realized it later, having listened long ago to a lullaby about the Kikuchi clan's unselfish loyalty.

One must also consider the fact that the youths studying in the private academy of Shōkason under the direct tutelage of Yoshida Shōin realized their lineage quite early, whereas Taishō and Shōwa era university students realize this very late. Yet our children of today should find comfort in the fact that such lateness in one's historical recollection and realization of lineage is not necessarily cause for regret. Imperial loyalty is the same, whether one awakens to it early or late. There are no two hearts of imperial loyalty.

Taishō and Shōwa era intellectuals had to wait for the Manchurian Incident in order to awaken to their heart of imperial loyalty. These intellectuals first had to learn about the blood shed by many pioneers. There are also those like myself who finally came to understand the heart of imperial loyalty at age forty. Such lateness is a great misfortune. Yet our happiness is perhaps far greater than those who are merely "Japanese in the ethnological sense," without ever awakening to their national lineage.

Arima Shinshichi's posthumous work, *Taigi mondō* [*Dialogue on Great Doubt*], is believed to have been written during the Ansei era [1854–1860] for the purpose of instructing youths, and it contains questions and answers about imperial loyalty. The first question in this text is: "Or perhaps the following is asked: 'I am afraid to mention that the court now faces a serious crisis. At present, there seems to be a view that states that it is just to have one's domain retinue travel with all haste to the imperial court and serve with complete loyalty. Under the current condition in which each domain has its own master, however, having the hereditary retainers of these masters abandon their domains and leave behind their masters simply on account of their service to court seems to be an act that uselessly purifies their own names alone, and cannot therefore be called great loyalty. What are your thoughts?'"

In response to this question, Arima begins by patiently expounding the cardinal principles of the national polity: "Now, if one's master is weak and ignorant, remains idly indifferent to serious crises at court, and possesses no imperial loyalty, one must then devote oneself with all one's strength and ability to admonishing him and guiding him at all cost to such loyalty. If he fails to heed these admonishments and there is no other way to persuade him, then one has no recourse but to travel in all haste to court, even if this means making the journey alone and dying a loyal death. Such action truly expresses what is just, and only such retainers can be called loyal." As can be seen here, the problem of "the imperial court or *han* domain" was a question and source of distress shared by all the young patriots at the time. The era immediately preceding the Meiji Restoration was one of great wickedness. All types of evil things influenced the hearts of young people, thus blinding them. These youths fought intense inner battles in order to remove those blindfolds. I believe that Saigō Kichinosuke may have felt this distress the most deeply. It is highly significant that, in the midst of such distress and confusion, Saigō assumed the name Kikuchi Gengo Takeo. It was then that he went from being the Saigō of Satsuma to the Saigō of Japan, and even perhaps our "great countryman of the south." This was his "rebirth" or "revival."

Many so-called new historians interpret Saigō Takamori's life from their perspective of him as "a reactionary who was unable to go beyond the framework of the *han* domain" or as "the last feudal man who died in the tenth year of Meiji [1877]." They thus understand nothing. Their misunderstanding begins already from the fact that Saigō tried to drown himself in Satsuma Bay.

Gesshō was privileged in terms of his background and environment and never learned about the framework of the *han* domain. This monk who was loyal to the emperor possessed the same views and temperament as Saigō Kichinosuke, participated in the same secret pact, and finally tried to drown himself in Satsuma Bay together with him. The bond between these two men cannot be explained simply by the fact that Kichinosuke was a great man or that he was extremely kind. Rather, what united them was the sense of imperial loyalty that burned in their hearts.

Saigō died in the tenth year of Meiji, but his spirit informed the first Sino-Japanese War, the Russo-Japanese War, and the second Sino-Japanese War, and lives on even today. I can only discuss this marvelous figure who was our "great countryman of the south" from the perspective of his "heart of imperial loyalty."

Having included this section as a supplement to the first part of my essay, I would now like to proceed to a discussion of contemporary literature.

III

There exists the word *bunjaku*, or "effete." This word no doubt came over from China, but even in our own country the people have long been severely warned against such effeteness.

The Fujiwara, Taira, and Hōjō clans were all ruined by the effeteness of their sons, who were raised in luxury. It is also said that the long decline of imperial authority from the medieval period was due to the effeteness of the court nobility, just as it is said that the emperor Meiji, seeking to restore such authority at the end of the Tokugawa regime, banned the reading of such texts as *Ise monogatari* [*The Tales of Ise*] in his efforts to curb the nobility's effeteness.

Must literature always be accompanied by indolence and lead to the weakening of both individual and country? Perhaps so, as there is no lack of such examples in the histories of East and West.

However, there are examples to the contrary. Looking only at our country, there are not a few literary texts that have helped revive the country. Literature that revives the country is written by those with such an aim in mind, that is, this is a literature of patriots. When the country was in crisis, such texts as the *Kojiki* and *Jinnō shōtōki* [*Chronicle of Gods and Sovereigns*] were written with such a patriotic aim. The elegies of the former emperor Gotoba did not weaken the hearts of readers. Beginning with the *Kojiki den* [*Commentary on the "Kojiki"*], the efforts on the part of scholars of National Learning also represented a literature for the country's revival. The poetry of those patriots raised under the influence of the Wang Yangming and Mito schools lacked any effeminacy of style as well. With all due respect, not one of the 1,687 poems included in the *Meiji tennō gyoseishū* [*Collected Poetry of the Emperor Meiji*] contains even a hint of effeminacy. These superb poems in the emperor's voice helped make us into a great country.

There is both weak and strong literature. There is literature that weakens the individual and country, and there is literature that rouses the individual and brings glory to the country.

Now then, to which of these categories belongs the literature of the late Meiji and Taishō periods that we grew up reading?

Let me return once again to my time as a junior high school student up on that hill. What kind of literature engrossed me then, unknown to my teachers and others? This was the "pure literature" of the time. Such literature appeared in the form of novels published every month, the fiction sections of general magazines, and the translated literature published in fancy new covers.

The "famous passages" in the works of such writers as Ōgai, Sōseki, and Futabatei were already excerpted in our textbooks. There were also such rising novelists as Tanizaki Jun'ichirō, Akutagawa Ryūnosuke, Satō Haruo, and Kikuchi Kan. Works like *Baien* [*Smoke*], *Futon* [*The Futon*], and *Wakareta tsuma he okuru tegami* [*Letter to My Former Wife*] sold briskly in book form. I was also able to read *Kōyō zenshū* [*The Complete Works of Ozaki Kōyō*] and *Kyōka zenshū* [*The Complete Works of Izumi Kyōka*] by borrowing them from my class library. There were also countless translated novels to be found pell-mell on the library shelves: the Werther series, Dostoyevsky, Tolstoy, Gorky, *Wagner's Complete Works*, *The Triumph of Death*, *The Twilight of the Gods*, *The Blue Bird*, *Spring Awakening*, *Sanin*, and *Virgin Soil*.

There is no system or order to the reading of junior high school students, who simply read whatever is on hand. I read randomly, guided by the advertisements in the new publications. The teachers warned against such aimless reading, but they didn't actively guide me. Also, these teachers were raised in such a way that they either randomly read such contemporary fiction or didn't read at all. One language teacher who loved literature kept hidden in his bookshelf the book *Gendai jōwa meisaku sen* [*Selections from Famous Contemporary Love Stories*], which included such writers as Nagata Mikihiko, Chikamatsu Shūkō, and Tanizaki Jun'ichirō. Those teachers who did not read, read nothing at all, neither contemporary nor classical literature. Even the national language teachers knew nothing about literature other than what was in their textbooks. For them, the national language meant the Japanese language, in contrast to English, and national literature meant the literature of the nation, primarily the pre–Edo period works. It is best to read at some time the texts of classical literature as part of one's common knowledge as a junior high school student of the nation.

As junior high school students with a strong desire to read, we galloped like blind horses in whatever direction was advertised by Shun'yōdō and Shinchōsha, *Chūō kōron* [*Central Forum*] and *Bunshō sekai* [*The Writing World*]. We read books and then promptly forgot them. We would have been little influenced by these books had they been completely forgotten, but the dark waters of literature find their way into a reader's heart—and even if these waters suddenly recede, some kind of sediment always remains. There would have been little sediment had we read only 1 or 2 books, but we read 10 books a month, which turned into 100 books a year and then 500 books in five years. As impressionable youths with a strong capacity to absorb things, our hearts thus came to be filled with this sediment, and our spiritual constitution was sometimes changed as a result.

Readers of the past had only a small selection of texts, which they read closely and deeply. Since publishing became a profitable enterprise, however, readers must now read 100 bad books for every 1 good book. Even bad books leave behind a sediment in one's heart. As junior high school students who loved literature, our hearts were like pots overflowing with rust.

Later, as a university student, I was charged with violating the Peace Preservation Law. When questioned by the prosecutor as to my motives for embracing left-wing ideas, I replied, "It was the influence of literature." This was not an evasive answer. Alone in my cell, I calmly searched my heart for the answer to this question, and this was what I found. Yet my response had many complex meanings.

Asano Akira writes in one of his works that he was never unpatriotic but that at some time or another even he had lost his sense of imperial loyalty and become a leftist, and that this seemed to be the result of the literary influence he received as a youth. Asano confesses that, from the time he read Morita Sōhei's *Baien*, the foundation for his leftist turn was laid and he unwittingly became unpatriotic. I fully understand Asano's sentiment here. I grew up in the same cultural environment and traveled the same course. Of course such unpatriotism is not caused by *Baien*, which is just one of many similar books. Rather, it was the literature and literary trends of the time that turned most of us intellectuals in our forties into a settlement race that forgot both country and emperor.

Following Tayama Katai's *Futon*, *Baien* was one of the monuments of naturalism. Japanese naturalism learned from Zola, but it left Zola's strong social criticisms to the socialist movement. In its mere status as "pure literature," naturalism developed with a strong sense of hedonism while degenerating into egocentrism and a belief in man's bestiality. Rejecting all that was sacred, naturalism advocated the absolute quality of the ego while depicting man as a beast and challenged the divine with its weapons of positivism and rationalism. This trend reigned triumphant in Japan's literary circles when we were junior high school students. Although it seemed as if Tanizaki Jun'ichirō, Satō Haruo, Akutagawa Ryūnosuke, and Kikuchi Kan had emerged in opposition to naturalism, they were in fact its progeny. These writers divided up the various qualities of naturalism as their inheritance and were unable to break out of its framework. Although they made gestures toward combating naturalism, they were unable to establish a prominent literature that could rival it.

We drank in this literature like water and breathed it like air. Even if we hadn't read *Baien*, the general literary trends of the time would still have turned us into petty egoists, rationalists, and hedonists who forgot emperor, country, and the gods.

Left-wing literature is a descendant of naturalism. This literature began battling the literary establishment when I was in high school. Even without such battles, however, left-wing literature had already laid its foundation for victory in the literary establishment of the time, as the petty rationalists and materialists who had been reared on such "literature" were already filling up Japan's towns and countryside.

Asano and I were not alone in responding to the prosecutor's question that it was the "influence of literature" that caused us to turn to the Left. It seems to me that, had statistics been gathered on the basis of the written evidence, more than half the defendants would have said as much. However, I am not necessarily referring here to the influence of leftist literature. Since leftist literature did not exist at the beginning of the leftist movement, it was the "pure literature" of the time that lay the foundation for turning young people to the Left.

From the late Meiji to the Taishō and Shōwa periods, Japanese literature has certainly not revived the country; rather it has made the individual forget his country. Such a tendency may be traced back to the merchant literature of the Edo period and even the court literature of the Heian period. In Meiji, the source of effete literature may be found in the direction indicated by Kōyō's "Society of Friends of the Inkstone" movement, or in Shōyō's *Shōsetsu shinzui* [*Essence of the Novel*]. Asano Akira begins by rejecting contemporary literature and attacks even Sōseki and Ōgai. Here we can see a just expression of revenge against the modern Japanese literature that caused us youths to forget our country. Such revenge also burns in my own heart. This revenge is at once a holy war of atonement. Japan would lose nothing if all the works of post-Meiji literature that gave birth to naturalism and leftist literature were to be consigned to the flames.

To even look at the third generation of contemporary literature is to defile the eyes. Our path lies only in breaking with and struggling against this literature.

This struggle has already begun, but the following question must be clarified in order to advance even further: why have young people jostled with each other to read such literature? These works were read not only by budding writers, for even those with no literary ambitions jostled to read them. Most of these young readers were healthy and earnest, and yet they came to lose their spiritual health by reading such literature.

This phenomenon cannot be explained by such phrases as the "allure of novels." There was undoubtedly something else that actively captivated the hearts of young people. I would like to discover what this is.

IV

The spirit of literature lies in the desire for purity.

Impurity and vulgarity, utility and hypocrisy, convenience and compromise, flattery and servility, cowardice and baseness, greed and self-interest: all such defilements are the enemy of literature.

There can be no literature where there is no desire for purity. Such desire represents the ideal of literature, and it is because of this ideal that the heart of literature carries an eternal charm.

At its inception, even naturalism had not yet lost this ideal. Naturalism sought to fight against society's hypocrisy by depicting man's beastliness and tried to overthrow the reign of the vulgar by rejecting all divinity. This attitude is one with a desire for purity when society is full of hypocrisy and the vulgar with their financial power reign supreme.

Following the middle years of Meiji, monetary power gradually corrupted Japanese society, and the ideal of a pure national polity, as restored by the Meiji Restoration, became tarnished. Society came to be ruled by shameless hypocrites, money-grubbing philistines, and ingratiating sycophants. People saw themselves as advocating civilization and enlightenment when in fact they were kowtowing to Western trends, and the country seemed intent on becoming a semicolony of the West.

Once colonized, a country loses its beauty. People lose their confidence and pride when their country becomes a foreign settlement. More than anyone else, writers have sensitively grasped and struggled against this deplorable tendency.

Koizumi Yakumo warned against the dangers of Japan's westernization as an outsider, while Okakura Tenshin fought such westernization from within in his books *Nihon no kakusei* [*The Awakening of Japan*] and *Tōyō no risō* [*Ideals of the East*], and Uchimura Kanzō tried to stop the spread of corruption in Japan through a revival of Bushido from within Christianity.

All these efforts were in vain, however, as society was already given over to the pervasive rule of money and the domination of the vulgar. Many writers committed suicide upon losing this battle. There were writers who, unable to escape society and find refuge in "beauty and solitude," died miserable deaths in the gutter. There were others who, in their quest for purity amid the corruption and emptiness, ended up destroying themselves. Some men despaired of literature itself and sought their path in politics, but then were silenced by their shock at political corruption and left. Still others searched for spiritual asylum in the "New Village," but this proved futile.

This sad history of Japanese literature represents the struggle and defeat of Japanese intellectuals. The strong attraction to literature on the part of Meiji and Taishō youths is above all due to the fact that literature served as their mouthpiece. During this horrible time, it was perhaps only literature that deplored and struggled against Japan's vulgarization and loss of purity. Although this struggle was weak, it is a fact that literature fought this fight desperately. Without knowing why, young people were thus attracted to it. It was through literature that they tried to guard their own spiritual purity.

Unfortunately, however, the corruption of literature that accompanied society's corruption took place rapidly. Or rather, this deadly poison was already inherent in naturalist literature from the beginning. Man's bestiality, the rejection of the gods, rationalism, egoism, individualism: all of these were its banners. The various literary schools that subsequently appeared took on at least one of these elements. What is even more unfortunate is that these schools used Western spirit as their weapon. They unwittingly used Western principles and schools to struggle against Japan's vulgarization. There was no one who abandoned these Western principles and struggled against the evil in Japan on the basis of a spiritual return to Japan itself. These people were like passengers heading to Tokyo who boarded a train leaving from Tokyo: the further they advanced, the greater their distance from the imperial capital.

The most conspicuous example of this was proletarian literature. At its inception, this literature did not lack a kind of patriotic intent. It emerged alongside the left-wing movement at a time when people were convinced of the country's imminent ruin: the ills of capitalism had reached their peak, political parties and financial cliques were appropriating the country's resources, the "imperial organ" theory had gained tacit acceptance, foreign powers were scheming to neutralize Japan's military preparedness, and the working class in both the city and countryside had fallen into extreme poverty. Apart from the professional left-wing activists, many naive youths who participated in this movement unquestionably believed that they had thus found a way to save the country.

Yet what were their weapons? Needless to say, they were all completely borrowed from abroad. These youths turned to Kropotkin, Bakunin, Marx, Engels, and finally Lenin and Stalin. The weapons they chose to save the country were, from the beginning, those that ruined the country. The errors and harm perpetrated here were even more flagrant than those of naturalism. In naturalism and the other literary schools at that time, few writers openly rejected Japan's national polity. Some naturalist writers even advocated Japanism. From the beginning, however, leftists rejected the national polity. Such an error and serious crime cannot be forgiven.

I, too, was one of these leftists. As I write these lines now, I shudder to think of the gravity of my crime. In looking back at my spiritual history and reflecting on what caused me to turn to the Left, I can only conclude that it was the literature that appeared after the mid-Meiji period.

A path that leads to the rejection of the gods, the bestiality of man, rationalism, egoism, and individualism naturally represents the rejection of "Japan, the land of the gods." This path was traveled by contemporary Japanese writers either consciously or unconsciously. We writers thus misled the youth and the country. How can this wrong be atoned? How can amends be made?

Death is perhaps the only way to deal with the guilty. Yet the gods of Japan have not condemned us to die for this crime.

Rather, they commanded those who fell into this hell of vice and filth to return and be reborn, so that we may purify ourselves in the limpid stream of our country's traditions.

When, heeding this auspicious voice, we kneel before the gods and the emperor and realize the depth of our sins, new reeds will gently sprout up in our breast, bowels, and every part of our body. This, then, is the heart of imperial loyalty.

This heart is pure and clear, like spring water that bubbles forth between the rocks; it is intense and all consuming, like the fire that burns at the earth's core. The heart of imperial loyalty understands the great truth that there is neither self nor other, but only the gods and emperor.

This heart is neither simply patriotism nor love of country. Without understanding the heart of imperial loyalty, patriots and those who love their country can at any time turn into traitors.

The heart of imperial loyalty emerges when we come to understand the depth of our sins and, abandoning all individuality and sense of self, kneel before the gods of Japan. Only this heart can create true patriots and lovers of their country.

The revival of literature must also follow this path. Mere purity, solitude, and an uncompromising nature are not the way to save literature. This is not the way to restore literature to its proper form.

Japan's "pure literature" fought against literature's vulgarization, but the utter deformity to which it has now fallen can only be explained by the fact that it lacks the heart of imperial loyalty. The writers of this "pure literature" were pure, aloof, and uncompromising. As a result of their lack of imperial loyalty, however, they were unable to radically fight against society's vulgarization: some of these writers went only halfway before succumbing to the power of money and becoming authors of popular fiction, some became Russian or French, some became whining authors who sold books filled with idle complaints, while others became authors of national policy books who were patronized by the government. Literary purity has completely disappeared, and along with it the sense of confidence of these writers. This is the era of effeteness. It is an era in which a literature set on ruining the country has poisoned our youths and robbed the people of their self-confidence.

"Japanese literature, return to your true nature! You are the progeny of the country. You are the valiant son who, born from your country, can now exalt it. You must succeed to the proper lineage and genealogy of Japanese literature. Reject all the filth of contemporary literature! The true purity sought by literature can be found in the heart of imperial loyalty. You must cultivate only this sense of imperial loyalty as lies within your own heart! Do not look anywhere else; just walk straight on the path as revealed by this loyalty."

This, then, is my prayer. I beseech you, gods of Japan, to hear my humble prayer.

The Course of Overcoming Modernity

SHIMOMURA TORATARŌ

WHAT WE CALL "modernity" originates in Europe, and it is precisely this "modernity" whose overcoming is today, at least, under consideration. If, therefore, the overcoming of modernity can become a problem *for us*, then this must concretely mean a confrontation with European modernity. Hence, modernity's problematic status and course of overcoming for us are not necessarily identical with those in Europe. What is required here is an independent grasp of the problem.

For us at present, however, Europe is no longer a mere other. Like our predecessors, we have *in fact* tried to learn about the modern West, through which we have grown. Today we reflect upon and criticize what, how, and how much we have received from the modern West. This represents the crux of what is strictly our problem of overcoming modernity.

Regardless of modernity's origins in Europe, the fact that we ourselves could and indeed have become modern derives from the global nature of modernity. Regardless of the motives and manner of this reception, it must be said that European modernity could become our modernity because of that globality, even though we possess an entirely different historical ground. If this has resulted in our developing the same abnormal symptoms as in Europe, then we must also criticize ourselves rather than simply criticize them. Modernity is us, and the overcoming of modernity is the overcoming of ourselves. It would be easy if the overcoming of modernity were simply a question of criticizing others.

If we are to approach this problem strictly independently, then we must reconsider the overcoming of modernity *as such*. If we were to criticize modernity as foolish without living up to that criticism ourselves, then this is nothing but shameless garrulity. If modernity is to be negated, then we must be prepared for what this *actually* means and take full responsibility for the consequences. We must once again take as our departure point the question, Can we negate modernity?

As has often been repeated, one of the main incentives behind Europe's discourse of overcoming modernity lies in the degeneration of post-Renaissance culture into an external machine civilization. If that is the case, however, was the time preceding the post-Renaissance period strictly spiritual and the people focused strictly on their interiority? Can one really say this without some kind of idealization? Even if we were to grant this point, wouldn't such "spirituality" or "interiority" be *merely* spiritual or interior, such that its exteriority would be exposed in allowing a nonspiritual or noninternal "modernity" to arise from within itself? Isn't it true that the interiority and spirituality of the Middle Ages were not a true sublation of exteriority and nature but rather a mere opposition to these, a negation through force (*Gewalt*) that thus rendered itself someday subject to another negation through force? Wasn't the post-Renaissance period really a fall *of* rather than *from* the Middle Ages? Or rather, wasn't this period the *development* of something that was implied within the Middle Ages and yet neglected and negated then? Wasn't the post-Renaissance period the development of the Middle Ages themselves?

It has also become a cliché to say that the building of machines during the post-Renaissance period actually enslaved man to them, as if man's enslavement began at this time. Yet wasn't man subjected to different, and indeed more extensive, kinds of slavery even prior to the invention of machines? Machines originally functioned to liberate man from his enslavement to labor. We are today not at the end but rather still at the beginning of this liberation. Furthermore, man's enslavement to machines is of course not the responsibility of the machines themselves; rather, the responsibility lies with the organizations and institutions that operate these machines, and ultimately it lies with spirit. The machines themselves are the products of spirit itself, just as the very building of machines signifies spirit's victory. Indeed, isn't it a question of simply driving home this victory to its final point? This is above all a spiritual question, that is, it is a question of spirit. Why can't spirit keep up with machinery? Can our present difficulties be resolved by destroying machines? Dare we wish for such destruction?

It will be said, however, that machines have brought about only external "civilization" rather than an internal "culture." No doubt. Yet is a merely internal culture unmediated by civilization really possible? Can civilization be negated without compromise and inconsistency? Isn't the problem rather one of culture actively overtaking civilization so as to dominate it? In this sense, the crisis of the post-Renaissance period lies in the imbalance between the physical sciences and mental sciences. But was this crisis due to culture advancing too far ahead of civilization or lagging too far behind it?

These reflections are of course not intended to affirm "modernity" as is. Their purpose is strictly to conceive of sublating modernity after having recognized its positive aspects, rather than focusing solely on the negative ones. For it is dishonest in respect of our own actuality to describe modernity as simply a bad or useless period.

It is upon this premise that "spirit" first becomes an issue. In contrast to the necessity of nature, the essence of spirit is freedom. Spirit's axiom consists in its superiority to nature, and this represents a transcendental postulate without which it lacks the meaning of "spirit." However, the problem lies in the character of this freedom. The ancient sages sought freedom in training the soul to obey nature. This must be called subjective freedom. Modern philosophy has formed "objective idealism." Yet the transformation of this "objective idealism" into a true "idealism of objective freedom" represents the culmination of the self-awareness of modern spirit, which originally formed modern science. The experimental method of modern science originally sought to reveal that which does not exist naturally, or in nature, and it shared this spirit with magic. The aim of this knowledge is not the intuition of essential forms but rather the development of nature's potential. Modern machinery is a product of this method. This represents the reconstruction or remaking of nature, as opposed to its mere application or utilization. What comes into being in this building of modern machines is not merely a subjective independence or freedom from nature but rather a truly *objective* freedom and independence. Must it not be said that objective idealism only here first acquires the ground for its concrete realization? In terms of its genealogy in intellectual history, modern science must be traced back not to materialism but rather to such idealism. For idealism represents the spirit that recognizes not the immediacy of existence but rather that all existence is mediated by the subject.

As goes without saying, the question here concerns the notion of the soul. One of the characteristics of Christian thought lies in its understanding of the soul as strictly internal. It is only in respect of this traditional notion of the soul that the new spirit is external. The ancient soul was opposed to the flesh. Today, however, the *mere* flesh no longer actually exists. Today the body is an organism that in some fashion uses machines as its own organs. The tragedy of modernity is that the old soul cannot keep up with this "new body." For what this new body-mind requires is a new metaphysics. Today the body is at once massive and delicate. It cannot be measured by such ancient methods of psychology as inner resolve and personal discipline. Rather, it requires political, social, and even national methods. Indeed, it requires a new theology.

Regarding the considerable difficulties in spiritual improvement or reform, it is noteworthy that culture, in contrast to civilization, does not necessarily advance. "Human nature" remains virtually unchanged from ancient times, which makes improvement close to impossible. But the question here is what methods have been applied for such improvement. Isn't it true that the only methods used thus far have been such things as introspection, persuasion, asceticism, and discipline? Isn't it true that these presuppose a fixed interpretation of spirit, one that limits the methods of improvement?

Isn't it true that the methods for overcoming modernity must be discovered through a new self-awareness of the notion of spirit? And isn't it the case that treatises on the emendation of the intellect are already being *experimented with* on a large scale, a scale that is surely unprecedented in human history?

Our task consists in newly reflecting upon our intellect. Isn't it true that our intellect has at least shown a tendency to be vegetative, given that it is receptive, flexible, delicate, and yet strong? All of these traits reflect this vegetative character. In every field, there is no people that can make "flowers" bloom as beautifully as we can.

Even today, the knowledge of our intellectuals is strictly literary, not scientific. This, too, must be described as part of our vegetative nature.

As a classical or traditional problem, must not philosophers today also conceive of a "Treatise on the Emendation of the Intellect"? Of course such conceptions must be on a contemporary scale, in respect of contemporary intelligence.

What Is to Be Destroyed?

TSUMURA HIDEO

A: European culture may be described as the center of present-day culture, but when we consider how Europe has been able to maintain its status as a world culture for so long, it seems to me that, in addition to its cultural traditions, its very universal power of expression is what has enabled this culture to spread throughout the world. Europe's defense and dissemination of this universal power of cultural expression can be attributed to its old political order with its accompanying military and economic force. Following the establishment of the Versailles structure, England and France in particular assumed military and economic control, which was reinforced through cooperation with the United States. Now it is a very complex and difficult question as to what will become of European culture after the collapse of its old order in the present world war. While it may be said that a new European culture is in fact already being born through the efforts of Germany and Italy, it might be better to say that European culture in the true sense awaits the completion of a new European order; that is, this culture will emerge only after the completion of a new European life sphere in the political sense. In other words, Europe's old culture as represented by England and France must in any case be crushed. However, France is a special case. Even though it is difficult to imagine how to rebuild a defeated France as a state, France and its neighboring Germany must work all the more closely together in the new order. I am most interested in the contact between these two cultures. From the nineteenth to twentieth centuries, these countries have long been extremely hostile to each other. In perusing past history, however, one sees that German culture both admired and was vastly influenced by French culture not only during the rococo age, of course, but even during Goethe's eighteenth century. French culture today is violated by democratic and Communist ideas, and its wounds have still not fully healed. Although France thus remains as irreconcilable with Nazi Germany as oil and water, how will

Germany guide and nurture French culture in the future? Nazi Germany still admires traditional French culture, but the question of how the French today regard Nazi Germany is not so simple. In other words, it is not unimaginable that France's very defeat will determine which cultural spirit is harmful to the state and should be abandoned. That is, such defeat would mark the return of a pure French culture. But I suspect that this forecast is actually a bit naive. Despite its defeat, present-day French culture will not so easily embark upon a new life but will remain for some time in a state of chaos. Many small countries have experienced tragedy in the present world war, but none of these tragedies can compare with that of France. In considering the disaster of Toulon and the betrayal of the homeland on the part of such leaders as François Darlan, it is doubtful whether France can ever rebuild itself as an independent state. Above all, France is now in need of food, and this situation will likely continue for a long time to come. No countries remain to supply it with food other than Germany, which has gained control of the Ukraine. Despite its defeat, France's unoccupied territories had managed for some time to subsist through American aid, but German-Soviet aggressions as well as Germany's great strength in the Mediterranean later made that utterly impossible. France has finally severed diplomatic ties with the United States, which means that it now has no choice but to depend upon Germany. If Germany comes in the future to supply France with sufficient food, then the Axis power over it will become that much greater, and there might come a time when France's recovery of its industrial and economic power will completely depend upon Axis aid. I would like to see how this situation would actually influence French culture. In fact, France's film industry has been destroyed, and its major artists have fled to the United States and elsewhere. At present, French film culture would completely die out if it were not aligned with the German film industry. Hence, this film culture in its need for industrial capital must suddenly be managed by Nazi Germany. Such changes cannot be overlooked. While collaboration between German and French film artists has become increasingly frequent, the French film art that, before the war, ruled global cinema has now all but collapsed. Even at the time of France's victory in World War I, its cinema was undergoing a period of chaos due to the inroads made by American film capital, and this took ten years to rebuild.

Now I have said that the first task of a new European culture is the exchange and cooperation between, above all, German and French culture, as well as future changes in French culture. The next task concerns the subjugation of the Soviet Union's Communist ideas. Even if the Soviet Union is crushed militarily, these ideas will not so easily disappear from Europe, which means that they must be thoroughly combated for the sake of Europe's new culture. Communist culture is much newer than the traditional cultures of England and France, but its international universality and permeability are strong. In my opinion, England's turn toward Communism—or at least toward high-level socialism—will certainly become more pronounced with its defeat, regardless of when this actually takes place. As concluded in June, the new British-Soviet military alliance treaty rules out any separate peace and seems to fix these countries' postwar spheres of influence, and yet it is no small matter for us that this global capitalist state and Communist state have entered into a life-and-death pledge. Although the treaty proviso to provide military support to the Soviet Union was not especially strengthened, this was no small matter for us in regard to the future of British politics and culture. A U.S.-Soviet pact was also concluded, but this seems to be noticeably less influential. Thus, although traditional British culture appears to be already in decline due to the country's war fatigue and the pressures from socialism, we must be cautious about what will happen later.

B: I would make a small objection. There is a question as to whether Europe's new culture can be discussed and whether we can forecast this new culture apart from the upheavals in world culture. There is of course also the question of American culture, but even beyond this, we can naturally look forward to the birth of an East Asian cultural sphere, whose relations with Europe's new culture will be of the utmost importance. To be sure, Europe's life sphere is centered on the continent and already extends, thanks to Germany and Italy, at least from northern and central Europe to the Balkans. One can of course conceive of a new culture as founded upon this life sphere once it is more firmly realized and grows to include the European part of Russia, and it is imaginable that this culture might overcome that overripened spirit of modernity that saw its best days in the late nineteenth century. However, I would like to focus on the relation between the cultural spheres of Europe and East Asia. Do these spheres share anything in common? I think they must. In this sense, culture in the context of the modern spirit differs from those cultures that already exist and are now struggling. In fact, the will that is operating in both East and West in the attempt to create a new world order is precisely the present-day cultural will, and I see culture in terms of the forces of this will. I cannot agree with the view that culture can be discovered only in the fruits of such completed forms as that old European culture that saw its best days in the late nineteenth century. There exists today something common among these forces of will that are engaged in armed combat, and so a common will must naturally live in the cultures to be nurtured in the future life spheres of Europe and East Asia. Only by giving life to this common will can we develop and accomplish a true new world order.

A: I certainly agree that a common and interrelated cultural will exists in the East and West life spheres as well as in the cultural spheres that are now being founded on their basis. But in order to discuss European culture in its most powerful global influence as well as the modern spirit that it created, I naturally first focused on the rebirth of Europe itself as a departure point for our discussion.

c: Even if the construction of Europe's new culture is centered in Germany, it is actually now taking place. In terms of the East Asian cultural sphere, however, Japan must bear responsibility. Thus, the issue here concerns the relations between Germany and Japan's new cultures. Even if these countries possess the same cultural will, aren't there excessively large gaps in religion, traditional spirit, ethnicity, and language? As such, it is not altogether meaningless to focus discussion strictly on the rebirth of European culture as a first step. As B stated, however, it is vital as an issue for Japan to consider the relations and cooperation between these East and West cultural spheres, for Japanese culture has lived without losing its own traditional spirit while absorbing abundant amounts of both American material civilization and an old European culture imbued with the modern spirit. Even now the word "culture" [bunka] is used very cheaply and in strange ways: in the Taishō period a "new-style [bunka] house" still meant something positive, while such phrases as "new-style rice dish," "new-style shorts," and "new-style kitchen range" were quite popular. Even here it is clear how Japan was negatively influenced by American material civilization. I see this as the influence of Americanism and wish to cite the most familiar examples as possible. The question of culture does not begin by twirling by the neck such lofty issues as scholarship, art, thought, and invention. In addition to "new-style shorts," I am also very interested in popular phenomena that incorporate the word "culture," such as the currently fashionable X or Y cultural societies. I also take seriously the former custom of urban female students who frantically ran about trying to obtain the signatures of Filipino and other foreign athletes. For the sake of Japanese culture, I take seriously the fact that nobody thinks it strange that photographs of Deanna Durbin and Tyrone Power still conspicuously adorn the walls of cafés and beauty parlors in present-day Tokyo. I take seriously the masses who are crazy about the female sword-fighting shows in Asakusa, the popularity of wild attractions of pure Americanism such as the Shocking Boys [Akireta bōizu] and the crowds of young men and women who become fascinated and frenzied when watching such cheap films as Genealogy of a Woman [Onna keizu], as if they had understood Izumi Kyōka. Although the blues have taken the record world by storm, does everyone know that the loathsome blues pop song "Lakeside Lodgings" [Kohan no yado] is still a big hit? In short, the problem lies in the way today's *men of culture* discuss Japanese culture while closing their eyes to all such vulgarity. *I would rather like to discuss these men of culture themselves as an issue of present-day Japanese culture.* I will now summarize the foregoing. Since the Meiji period, Japan has absorbed substantial amounts of

Europe's modern spirit and modern culture. There can be no doubt of this. Following the Taishō period, however, Japan has at the same time actually absorbed large amounts of Americanism. Americanism is indeed valued as something that must be absorbed as present-day civilization, as is also the case for lamps, radios, film, and the wireless. Following the Taishō period, however, Japan imported a way of life to accompany these modern conveniences, which gradually came to infect the country's life and customs. To take an example from the arts, while Tolstoy, Strindberg, and Dostoyevsky might indeed have been freely absorbed as part of the modern spirit, most students of the Shōwa period are no longer captivated by this spirit. Rather, they are captivated by Western cinema. A frivolous situation has come about in which a great many youths watch the American films *Crime and Punishment* and *Resurrection* with the intention of understanding Tolstoy and Dostoyevsky. In other words, I maintain that present-day cultural critics must take the influence of Americanism slightly more seriously while also considering the invisible obstacles it poses to the future construction of an East Asian cultural sphere. In terms of this cultural sphere, how much European culture really lives on today in (apart from French Indochina) Thailand, Malaya, East India, the Philippines, of course, and even mainland China? How much of the so-called modern spirit lives on there? We must not, of course, overlook the influence of the religious and educational policies of British culture in Hong Kong and among the second and third generation of overseas Chinese in Malaya (both Hong Kong and Malaya have been reared on British culture), and in Thailand and Burma among certain intellectuals, but it is nevertheless Americanism that has mostly swept through East Asia. It should be recalled that, beginning with the Philippines but also in such places as Malaya, Java, and Burma, American film occupies approximately 75 percent of all imports. The same can of course be said of Shanghai and Hong Kong, which were the cultural centers of mainland China. In these cities as well as in other areas throughout East Asia, there was once substantial British economic organization and pressure. Yet the frightening thing about American material civilization is that it has produced a way of life that accommodates the present day. It is in these areas that the masses have been influenced or tainted by Americanism. One would be wrong to think that only the ignorant masses rather than intellectuals have received such influence. This is a bad habit into which Japanese cultural critics easily fall. Such an idea is as naive as that which regards culture as existing separately from war. I don't say this because I am not a philosopher, but I take at least as seriously the contagion of the American way of life as I do philosophy. When one considers man's life today, the force of this Americanism is frightening. Such modern conveniences as the radio are part of Americanism, but how has Nazi Germany put the radio to use? That is, the question becomes *how one has struggled against the radio.* Globally, the United States is the country that has most fully developed the radio, but Germany is second. Nazi Germany put the radio to use in the service of certain ideas precisely when the German people showed their resolve in the face of death, and so its goals were completely different from those of the United States. Likewise, the United States and Nazi Germany's ways of employing certain kinds of Americanist films are also completely different. This represents a struggle on the part of spirit to oppose modern conveniences, for present-day man would be consumed by these things and disappear were he to stop struggling. Yes, the word "consumed" is suitable here. It seems that even the United States has been substantially consumed by the many modern conveniences it created. The modern convenience film is itself indispensable to the present day, and as part of man's way of life as created by the United States, is, together with radio, of considerable importance. If we take one false step in our plan to incorporate film into the life of the people or nation, however, then we will be sharply duped by the drug of Americanism. Throughout the world there are countries that have been seriously duped in this way, examples of which can be found among England and Holland's former East Asian colonies. This is due to the fact that American film swept over those places that were not permeated by the native country's true cultural force, given its former colonial status. American film spreads American customs, embracing countries in a longing for the American way of life. With its jazz, eroticism, and optimism, American film spreads both its powerful toxins and *considerable charm* to people in England, France, and even the smaller European nations, as all these countries were exhausted from World War I. Jazz can be said to have swept through Europe. Why aren't these things taken seriously? Germany and Italy were, of course, also once influenced by Americanism, but realizing the dangers, placed limits on its importation and then completely barred it several years before World War II. Since this influence was such as to have substantially appeared even in their domestic films, however, clearly their national customs had more or less been infected. Unlike the Communist films of the Soviet Union, American films appear as good and innocent, which makes them all the more treacherous. With no traditional culture as their background, these films are all the easier to understand and possess a sense of universality. Like the U.S. auto industry, moreover, the massive industrial and commercial strength of American film constitutes a major part of the country's industry. In regard to the advances of its film science, the United States reveals an immense force that surpasses that of Germany. Hence, its world supremacy in film is not altogether unreasonable. It is also not unreasonable that the United States has contributed most to the development of the global art of film.

In regard to the founding of a new East Asian cultural sphere, I have warned against making light of Americanism, but this issue can also be understood as involving a new Europe. Although the modern spirit must also be overcome in order to create a new culture, we cannot disregard the overcoming of Americanism and the force of its material civilization. If the founding of a new European cultural sphere is related or shares something in common with that of a new East Asian cultural sphere, then an important part of this involves the question of how to conquer Americanism.

It seems that A regards Americanism too lightly with respect to present-day European culture. England's film industry is actually in decline, and its film culture subsists largely by relying on the United States. In its heart, traditional English culture may well scorn Americanism, but in fact it is duped in this way.

D: The world order of the past can be described as built and maintained by the dollar and pound. If these are not crushed, then in effect the roots of democracy cannot be destroyed. Nevertheless, the currency war seems to be the most difficult to wage. Although the pound dominates the globe and the dollar reveals its force primarily in East Asia and on the American continent, world financial circles took the opportunity of the war debt issue during the twenty years after World War I to become centered in the United States. This testifies to the dollar's global strength. It is true, as C just stated, that American film spread throughout Europe with terrific force after World War I, and I agree that the presence of Americanism in Europe cannot be downplayed. This presence is in no way limited to film, however. As I just remarked, it consists partly in how American resources and the dollar's strength have played a major role in Europe. In this sense, there are of course many firmer grounds than film upon which to Americanize Europe. Now World War II is gradually destroying the value of the pound and dollar in both East and West. The new European life sphere as founded by Germany and Italy has already driven out 80 percent of the pound, with Portugal, Turkey, and Africa as the chief places yet remaining. The Greater East Asia War has driven the pound and dollar out of East Asia. It goes without saying that a global trend is now under way to replace the currency economy with an economy based on commodities, and yet the strength of the pound and dollar is still formidable. However, I do have one reservation about the projection of a global commodities shortage, that is, the shift to a world of commodities, toward which many people are now proceeding. Precisely because of the major trend involved in this shift, the new culture of the future harbors a serious danger if spiritual life is not even more fully reinforced. It is dangerous if people do not alter their view of commodities. As is of course true during the war but also after the war, it is inevitable that this situation will cause a global shipping shortage, thus making unavoidable the global maldistribution of resources. In this era, with Germany and Italy's founding of a European life sphere and the founding of a Greater East Asian life sphere under Japanese leadership, it will be crucial for us to pursue both industrial development and trade in our joint struggle for existence with regard to commodities. Even if it is difficult to perceive whether any systems will reorganize global financial circles, the point is to destroy Jewish finance capital's international dominance as well as the virus of material civilization on which it is based. In effect, a more natural and healthier life for mankind will be possible, but we will still have to combat Americanism even in its decline. This is a battle against the artificialization of human life and the spell of machine civilization. Although we must overcome the modern spirit that is Europe's legacy (Americanism seems to both draw upon this spirit and set forth a kind of opposition to it), I believe that there is still much sustenance to be inherited from this culture—assuming that the modern spirit is another name for nineteenth-century culture. On the other hand, I don't see anything of value to be inherited from Americanism. Yet this Americanism is precisely the more treacherous in the ease with which it infects people, its inevitability, and its type of familiarity. Above all, we must be vigilant against the danger posed by the fact that such infection is greatest in the occupied areas of both East and West, otherwise it will be difficult to treat the past infections there. I agree with B that the very force to wage this world war represents both the practice and process for Japan, Germany, and Italy to create a new culture. Such practice must fiercely continue even after the war, otherwise we won't be able to complete this war of culture. It is precisely then that the main stage for this war must be increasingly expanded. The war will first realize the life sphere and form the ground for a new cultural sphere. We will then be able to plan the creation of this new culture. Although the war of culture has already very much begun alongside the present war, what remains central is nevertheless the armed warfare that accompanies the battle for resources. In this regard, I believe that even after the war a major theme for us will be the question of how to combat the spell of American film, which, as the leading star in the American war of culture, has spread throughout the world for over three decades now. While the American film industry is currently declining, it remains unimaginable that it would receive the serious blow of losing all of the European and East Asian markets. According to the foreign news, one will not receive permission to make a film in Hollywood if the costs exceed $10,000. However, this seems rather dubious to me. Incredible as it may seem, one can make only newsreels for that amount, although I suppose that dramas using new prints of old works could also be made. Even if such news is false, however, the American film industry is truly in crisis from the perspective of trade relations. Yet even if this industry is in decline, I certainly don't believe that it will be ruined forever. It would be safe to say that American film will one day surely go back on the attack. In Europe's cultural sphere, German cinema leads and reigns over the other national cinemas and will do its utmost even in the postwar to prevent American film from making inroads. In the East Asian cultural sphere, however, can Japanese cinema really accomplish this great task? That is my first question. What must be done in order to carry out such a task?

As for my second question, it goes without saying that cinema is an art form that began with the end of modernity. Although this art form's essence can thus be said to contain something that opposes the modern spirit, is this really the case with films today? In surveying world cinema, one can discern four outstanding examples: Germany, France, the United States, and the Soviet Union. Among these, France ranks highest in terms of dramas, keeping in mind here the considerable weight of the tradition of its modern spirit as well as the fatigue of its postwar sickness. The United States opposes the modern spirit even in its content, which is simply to say that jazz and wild dance styles oppose this spirit, for it is the frivolity of its bubbly hedonism that is most responsible. Such opposition to the modern spirit differs from its overcoming. I have found this overcoming only in such German documentary films as *Olympia Part One: Festival of the Nations*, *The History of Victory*, and *Triumph of the Will*. In effect, one can look only to German and Italian cinema, and particularly documentaries, for the film art of the future. Dramas of the past generally turned to literature for their subject matter, but we cannot overlook the fact that they were unable to create truly original film art, since many of these works—as in the case of France—still drew their breath particularly from the tradition of the modern spirit. My point is that this explains why there have been few true cineastes, such as René Clair, who write their own screenplays. American cinema has produced many screenwriters, but, regrettably, as I mentioned, many of them have not even been exposed to the modern spirit, for which reason alone they may safely be described as opposed to this spirit. In other words, while there may be people in the United States who rebel against the modern spirit, there is still nobody who can surpass or equal it. One cannot explain this fact merely by the brevity of film history. It is difficult to understand if one does not ultimately focus on the connection between the U.S. film industry and American national character. I am doubtful as to how much American cinema has really progressed as film art, even if it has not confronted the present world war. Although it is true that this cinema stands conspicuously at the forefront of world cinema in terms of its industrial forms and film science (in color film and so forth), its development as film culture is negligible when one considers American national character and the decadence of its morality and customs. Yet American cinema will continue to be fiercely productive in the future.

B: It is extremely difficult to define the modern spirit. While scholars have set forth various theories about it, there can be no question that this spirit is relentless, full of anguish and doubt. Although I cannot wholly agree with such conclusions that the modern spirit is individualist or decadent, we must in the end take into account the global situation and man's life conditions at the time this spirit emerged. Nevertheless, World War II is essentially different from World War I, as can be seen when one compares both the main reasons for starting these wars and the means of settling them (that is, Wilson's naïveté). While the remote cause of the present world war was the settlement of World War I, leftists foolishly view these wars in a formulaic manner, as a first and second stage. In Germany today, both the House of Hohenzollern and the kaiser have disappeared and no longer exist; Hitler is backed only by the loyal German people. The present Axis ideals, which represent both a cultural struggle and war of life spheres, were completely absent in the German empire of World War I—as they were of course profoundly absent in the United States and England. It is common knowledge that the League of Nations thus appeared as the childish plan to settle the war. An altogether unspeakable situation arose when the United States, having entered the war "on account of man's enemies," as it cried, created this toy that was the League of Nations and forced each nation of the world to join while it alone backed out. Even if one regards this ridiculous outcome as a sign of American egoism and roguery, it also proves how hollow the union was then between England, the United States, and France. Even in the current mutually congratulatory relations among England, the United States, the Soviet Union, and Chongqing, one can detect a strange opportunism that will not last. Yet what is essentially different about the present world war is the idealism of their Axis enemy. I would not hesitate to call the present will to fight on the part of Japan, Germany, and Italy a world-historical idealism. Idealism is not necessarily an adjective prefixing literature or philosophy. Some decadent scenes had already appeared in which lukewarm steps on the part of thought and art proved unable to realize man's idealism. I think that it was their confrontation with this wretched and base global situation that roused Japan, Germany, and Italy to action in the form of this unprecedented war of idealism. In considering the immense sacrifices these countries have endured and the lofty aspirations they cherish for a new world formation, what else can the present hostilities be called if not a war of idealism? The will of these three countries is certainly unlike the lukewarm posing by England and the United States when they sought to clear up World

War I through war debts and the League of Nations. Even if armed hostilities are concluded in ten years, it would take at least another ninety years to form a new world by destroying both the Anglo-American global sphere of influence, which took several hundred years to build, and the Communist ideas that are part of the nineteenth-century tradition. Great perseverance will be required after the war in order to crush both the influence of the dollar and pound and English-language culture. Since it will take all of ninety years to wage this economic and cultural war, the present hostilities might come to be known as the hundred-year war. For me, this is in no way a rhetorical flourish. To return to my original point, given my position on the war, I find unappealing the mere phrase "overcoming the modern spirit." When one considers the world in its present state, it is natural that the modern spirit that flourished primarily on the basis of the nineteenth-century world would not be worth the crises of today and tomorrow. For example, Marx is also an example of nineteenth-century thought that may be subsumed within the modern spirit, but it goes without saying that this Jewish thought and spirit are now outdated. Moreover, the materialist view of history and Western rationalist philosophy in general are today of course quite conventional. In order to avoid misunderstanding, however, let me just state that in Japan today there is a danger that such Western notions as the materialist view of history are not always seen as antiquated, and this, too, is one of Japan's crises. It is not always easy to undo the knot in the minds of intellectuals who are imbued with rationalism. Some Japanese would not hesitate to respond to this point by asking, "But are there any brilliantly systematic scientific ideas to replace the materialist view of history?" but such manner of thinking and living is itself excellent proof of a nervous breakdown. I suspect that even today these mental patients remain influential among scholars, cultural critics, and young people. It is somewhat difficult to cure such patients. While this secret fear of mine of late is entirely unrelated to the Greater East Asia War, I am nevertheless actually hoping that this war will tacitly prescribe a course of treatment for the patients. Such treatment must at all costs take place at this opportunity. Now, as I have stated, if the issue here is one of overcoming the modern spirit, then the matter is quite clear and simple; that is, we must recover the Japanese people's ideas and principles of life. I would slightly change perspective, however, and say that we need to both overcome the modern spirit and free ourselves from the present-day spirit. What is the present-day spirit? I regard it as even more decadent than the modern spirit. The emergence of such decadence seems to be due to Americanism, our greatest enemy, which can roughly be seen even in the several references C just made to the current global situation. Striking at the heart of this issue, the proposition then becomes how the human spirit should fight against advances in material and machine civilization. At bottom, this also relates to so-called American-style individualism and hedonism. Furthermore, the great advances in this material and machine civilization eventually provide an excellent stage for finance capitalists and the uncontrolled activity of capital. The problem here is how to combat this frightening trend and regulate human and state life. On this point, I am virtually of the same opinion as C. Thus, what must tentatively be called the present-day spirit emerged after the modern spirit (more or less between World War I and World War II), and it is even more decadent and superficial. I believe that this modern spirit still has much about it that we should respect and inherit. I believe that we must inherit the Japanese classical spirit and its tradition in accordance with our national physiology as Japanese (thought requires its own physiology) while, at the same time, in no way disdain the West's modern spirit, as seen, for example, in Nietzsche, Dostoyevsky, and Tolstoy. It is quite dubious how well such figures as Nietzsche are understood in Japan. Can anyone swear that such shocking distortions as found in the statement, "Dostoyevsky humanism is already old-fashioned" cannot still frequently be found today among the Japanese people's ideas?

It may indeed be true that the riches of the scientific spirit as inherited from modernity are to be found even within the present-day spirit. However, it is a tricky matter for the word "spirit" to be attached to "scientific." These two words in combination represent the serious look of spirit and may, while floating about society, commit a great crime before anyone realizes it. That is to say, these two words offer a hypnotic suggestion to the blind populace that acts as an all-powerful panacea. The marvelous advances of natural and applied science are indeed characteristic of the present day, and yet caution is required when one considers that these are also the breeding grounds of material and machine civilization. In the repeated calls of "scientific spirit," "scientific spirit," is there not a fear that such spirit will become linked with a certain kind of Western rationalist philosophy and grow even more distant from the human spirit's home? We must be cautious here. I have remarked that the present world war is one in which the three Axis nations have risen up as a final measure against the decadence of the global situation. At least as far as the Greater East Asia War is concerned, however, I would be happy to see Japan reveal its great spiritual strength in dominating science rather than being consumed by it. For example, even the manifest truth of the lives (that is, deaths) of the nine war heroes amply accounts for this fact. Is it the case that these men were able to transcend their noble lives precisely because they savored and could rely upon *books about wonderfully systematic scientific ideas*? It should be properly understood that human life cannot be lived so easily. Foreigners seem to regard this Japanese way of living as mysterious, as can often be seen in the foreign press. For us, however, there is nothing mysterious or inscrutable about it. These reasons are understood in the heart, but isn't it the case that our great inner pride and confidence defy such things as scholarship and the scientific? With due respect, this concludes my remarks.

A Brief Account

MIYOSHI TATSUJI

REFLECTIONS ON THE JAPANESE SPIRIT AND THE CREATION OF THE JAPANESE SPIRIT

A. Today one of the most eagerly researched fields consists of the discovery—or rediscovery—of the Japanese spirit through the study, exegesis, and commentary on such ancient texts as the *Kojiki* [*Records of Ancient Matters*], *Nihon shoki* [*Chronicles of Japan*], and *Man'yōshū* [*Collection of Ten Thousand Leaves*]. However, some reflection may be needed as to whether this field is now approaching the discovery of something that is *fully* sufficient to embolden us for the future.

B. Does the Japanese spirit (and its properties) as discovered—or rediscovered—in these ancient texts represent a historical reality that actually existed in the past, or does it rather represent the creative values being sought today?

C. The methods employed in the overall analysis, exegesis, and commentary on the ancient texts have been partly scientific and partly creative. Given that the creative half has necessarily been pent up within the limited sphere of these texts, must this partly scientific, partly creative work be subject to such extreme limitations?

D. Scholars of these ancient texts have not been entirely rigorous in their scientific attitude, and yet doesn't this contradict the current impetus for accurate science and the promotion of a scientific spirit, both regarded as matters of the utmost urgency? Regarding the question of spiritual (or moral) culture, hasn't this become a mere temporary remedy that has for some time now ignored the long-promoted scientific spirit?

E. Reflection on the insufficiencies and limitations of the work that has sought to reflectively and retrospectively discover the Japanese spirit from the world of the past.

F. Isn't the Japanese spirit that is truly required by us today something new that must advance as we create and form it at every moment for tomorrow? If so, then what must be the relation between the creation of this spirit and those reflections upon it?

ONE FURTHER POINT

It is only natural that such terms as "Japanism" and "Japanese spirit" occasionally become household words, and that it becomes a matter of vital importance to examine and reflect upon them everywhere and at all times. What appears rather dubious to a simple and commonsensical man like myself, however, is that the intellectuals who search for these things are all doing so in a strictly retrospective and reflective manner, as if Japanism and the Japanese spirit existed only in remote antiquity. It is extremely rare to encounter the view that sees these things as properly sought in the future, as something to be discovered, created, improved upon, and perfected by us.

I would like to briefly offer my own humble opinion on this matter.

Needless to say, the efforts to search in the past for the site of Japanism and the Japanese spirit represent an extremely valid and vital form of research, as expressed in the phrase "knowing the new by exploring the old." However, the past is ultimately but one reference point or imperfect entity, something that is incomplete even in and of itself. I would like to ensure that this point is deeply brought home and never forgotten.

In terms of this phrase "knowing the new by exploring the old," we must in the end rely primarily upon the documents, namely, the research on classical texts. Based on all the classical research (which is now at its peak) and the statements and writings of these classical scholars that I have encountered, however, I must ask why there is such a basic lack of appeal in both the claims and the prose of this work—to say nothing of the fact that we have so few original views, as it were, that should guide our era.

Even at the *Bungakkai* [*Literary World*] roundtable discussion the other day, it seemed that there were not a few participants who held such views. Writers like us who have reached our forties each in our own way feel a strong attachment to the classical literature of our native country, and because of both the current political situation and our age, we finally share a deep understanding and sympathy for classical literature and art. We have reached a time in which we think about the classics with the sense of returning home. What, then, is the hidden reason why I, as someone who shares this tendency, first of all feel such dissatisfaction when deferring to the leading specialists in this field and listening to their valuable opinions?

It is not for us to meddle in the classical research and exegetical studies of specialists, so I will leave that aside. Rather, I would like to offer my humble opinion on the *commentaries* on Japanism and the Japanese spirit as set forth by scholars of the classics and Japanese literature.

All would agree that classical literature and the ancient texts are by right the spiritual inheritance left us by our ancestors, that they are the greatest mementos we have. In the first place, all of these writings came into the world with the objective of being intrinsically *of their own time*, and it is no exaggeration to claim that virtually none was produced and bequeathed with posterity in mind. For us, the classics are an inheritance that was (extremely naturally) left behind to us without taking us and later ages into account. We must not read too much of ourselves into these texts or fall into far-fetched interpretations when these texts were not saying such things to us. Since the classics were not intended to speak to us, we must not forget that they are always *incomplete*, even in their most perfect form, nor must we lack the fancy and imagination necessary to read them in a creative and supplementary fashion.

Exegetics may essentially be a scientifically genuine discipline, but it is nonetheless utterly insufficient for the reading and elucidation of the classics to be merely scientific, in the particular scientific sense of exegetics (although, of course, this criterion is also necessary). Indeed, we must not forget that the reading and elucidation of the classics are both scientific and a synthetic and *human* operation that requires an ultrascientific (rather than unscientific, which would be problematic) creative addition. Although one might think that there is of course no one so foolish as to forget such an obvious point, it nevertheless seems that the first reaction of all good-natured public scholars is to tuck up their kimonos and dash off when pressed by urgent business, like today. The fact is that vital secrets are related to the serious question of the talent and hard work required of the scholar's creativity.

I say this in all sincerity, although it may be my own prejudice, but it appears that today's classical research and investigations of the Japanese spirit are entirely unnatural, restrained, and insipid, as if someone were forced to row a small boat toward an all too obvious destination with only one thought in mind.

Classical research must of course be grounded upon the guiding principles of exegetics, and I would hope that, as a general rule, it remain as faithful as possible to those affiliated branches of study that support it, such as history, archaeology, folklore, and mythology. While I place the greatest value on scholars' creativity and imagination, with all due precision and pertinence, a scholarship that distorts the truth and caters to the public in all its transparent designs and unscientific absurdities is really injurious to public morality and does much to damage the glory of the Japanese spirit.

The various judgments and conclusions on the part of Japanese literature and classics scholars who seek the Japanese spirit only in ancient texts are unwittingly trite, narrow, crude, and unnatural—and these are presented under the guise of an all the more firm and fiery determination.

The Japanese spirit, like the history of the Japanese nation and the lives of the Japanese people, must in fact begin in the past, realize itself at every moment in the present, and still continue to develop every day for the future. We must be able to faintly imagine the ideal form this spirit will take in the distant future.

I believe that, when this clear and obvious principle is truly understood, the interpretation and elucidation of the classics will be performed in the light of the desired world of the future all the more calmly and accurately in a field and manner that most befit them.

What is the nature of this unsophisticated and pitiable intellectual tendency that insists on so gravely interpreting those gloomy aspects of our classical literature, that discerns unparalleled grandeur in very trivial figures of speech, and attributes mystical significance to simple local customs—that merely links our private hopes and desires for the future to the petty and imperfect world of the past (which thus becomes the very world of fantasy) as the site where those hopes were realized?

This morbidly zealous tendency of the so-called Japanists fully runs the risk of hindering the future of the Japanese spirit. The fervor and effort with which the nation as a whole is trying to advance toward the future are matched only by the Japanists in their advance toward the past. For them, the past has in fact become their future. From the perspective of sound common sense, this can only be seen as an illusory reversal. As I have stated, classical research must not be merely scientific but rather ultrascientific and creative. Nevertheless, to judge Matsuo Bashō a God-fearing patriot who reveres the emperor, as Dr. So-and-so has done, drives away all ultrascientific creativity and obviously contravenes our commonsense judgment. After reading such work, one must presently recognize that one is witnessing the display of a remarkably unscientific mind.

Such a remark as this clearly represents a neglect of the scientific spirit and results in making such unconscious claims as expressing contempt for that science that comes from the world beyond science. Those authorities who so fervently advocate the modern scientific spirit must not foolishly overlook such subtle points.

On the Overcoming of Science

KIKUCHI SEISHI

DURING THE ROUNDTABLE discussion, I was specifically asked by Mr. Yoshimitsu whether an "explanation of the relationship between science and divinity or spirituality" were not one way to overcome modernity. Since I was unable to provide a satisfactory response then, I would like here to make some humble suggestions in the form of a brief note. These remarks thus do not represent anything like an essay.

Regarding this question, the notion of a "machine-producing spirit" was raised in the middle of the discussion. In contrast to Mr. Shimomura's remark on the problems of such a notion, both Mr. Kobayashi and Mr. Kawakami of the literature camp stressed that machines are not frightening, with Kawakami going so far as to say that they should be left in the care of Charlie Chaplin and Don Quixote! I believe that this represents a misunderstanding caused by the inadvisable use of the phrase "machine-producing spirit." To put it plainly, I think that this phrase refers to the spirit of materialism. We must all recognize that such a spirit represents one of the banes of modernity. I suspect that even Mr. Yoshimitsu's remarks ultimately come down to an overcoming of this spirit of materialism. Mr. Kamei laments that the gods have become lost to the modern Japanese people, but this, too, may be one of the curses of the materialist spirit.

If modern scientific thought has fully negated everything divine or spiritual, then this is a very serious problem that cannot be left in the care of such figures as Chaplin and Don Quixote. Perhaps, however, Mr. Kawakami made this remark lightly in his belief that scientific thought is not all that bold. But for those of us who specialize in science, such things cannot be treated so lightly. Mr. Hayashi even said at the roundtable discussion that he did not believe in the theory of evolution, but we scientists cannot hold such views. We must believe in this theory just as we must not doubt the possibility that all life can be explained in terms of matter. Hence, it is only natural that life can be artificially produced in test tubes. Also, since it is in principle not at all strange that human beings qua living things are comparable to other living things, it is in principle not at all surprising that they be created in test tubes. Thus, insofar as we remain faithful to science and do not yield, there becomes increasingly less room for spirituality and divinity. Even without reference to these things, all traces of spirit now vanish. Doubt even comes to be cast on such things as free will and moral value.

Such thinking of course derives from the simple spirit of materialism. This would not be a problem if we could only understand that the world as grasped scientifically is but one section of the larger world. Yet it seems that those who are ignorant of science rather easily think in this materialist manner, whereas sufficient knowledge of science reveals that things are not so easy. We are everywhere dogged by the materialist way of thinking. Even without regard to scientists, I think that ordinary citizens who don't think too much about things ultimately occupy a similar standpoint. This would be the standpoint of so-called naive realism. I suspect that there may be only a few people who could truly oppose the materialist claims of scientists (even if these claims are not actively made) without resorting to such vague theories as mind-matter dualism. These scientists and the masses may well be compared to Chaplin and Don Quixote, and so maybe Kawakami is right in a way. As a result, the remark that "machines are not frightening" would be correct, and the absence of a world outside of such a scientific worldview would mean the disappearance of both the Japanese spirit and the concept of national polity. This would be horrible, but the facts fully reveal that such a scientific worldview would be abandoned by those materialist-based scientists if need be.

It is now especially important to consider these issues more seriously. We scientists feel particularly strongly about this. It is now not without reason that the calls to promote science can be heard alongside reactions against scientific thought.

A critique of scientific methods would be one way to solve this question. This is a task for philosophy, but scientists must fully reflect upon it as well. Recently scientists have actively set forth a critique of science, which I think can be attributed to the real need for a basic understanding of scientific methods in order to truly understand recent theories on the structure of matter, such as so-called quantum mechanics. In any case, a close examination of scientific methods clearly reveals that such notions of matter as atoms and electrons are not easily reconciled with materialist notions of matter, that, in other words, scientists are becoming more idealist. I suspect that extreme materialism may have sprung from physiology or psychology, which lack sufficient understanding of the methods of physics. Yet such an understanding is central given that materialist physiology and psychology are based on physical laws. As I have just stated, the notion of physical quantity is in no way materialist, as it is much more redolent of idealism. Of course many issues remain here that I have yet to resolve, but these are more philosophical than scientific in nature.

In regard to Mr. Yoshimitsu's remark on the relation between divinity, spirituality, and science, these former have no direct relation with science since they do not of course exist when seen from the aspect of the scientific worldview. Although it might be fine to philosophically explain the relation between science and the "real world" as well as the nature of those other aspects that are more accommodating of spirituality and divinity, I myself cannot place such trust in philosophy. Naturally I recognize its great value in overthrowing the dogmatism of both science and religion, but philosophy can in no way provide solutions; an X always remains.

I would like to ask everyone's opinion on this question, but it seems to me that neither God nor Buddha can be attained through the rationalist method of philosophy. It is unlikely that God can be found in the debate over whether He exists. I believe that, now as ever, the only remaining path to God and Buddha is that of the leap of mysticism. Of course "leap" here does not imply a neglect of science or philosophy, and it goes without saying that any leap that eludes science loses all value. But it seems that even today, when science and philosophy are so advanced, modern man bumps up against an iron wall in his awareness that a space yet remains for this kind of leap. The question, then, is whether one clears this wall or gives up trying.

Mr. Nishitani brings out the notion of "nothingness," as this has long been a feature of Oriental religion. Although it might appear that Nishitani is explaining the philosophy of "nothingness" in his essay, there is in fact no such "logic of nothingness" or "philosophy of nothingness," since his many years of practicing Zen reveal that he is merely using professional language to describe the path of his own leap. I share Mr. Yoshimitsu's dissatisfaction with the logic of "nothingness," for such nothingness already involves a considerable leap.

In any case, I think it is certainly possible to leap over that iron wall. We must in a single breath plunge into a world that exists beyond all philosophy and science, where there is neither thought nor discernment. Without this plunge, life itself has no value. Yet a reckless and self-satisfied leap will turn the world into something like an insane asylum, which is to say that leaps can be either genuine or false.

As to such questions as where this path lies or how one finds it, these must depend upon the efforts and resources of each individual. Yet men do not take these things seriously today. It is strictly on this basis that one understands the much-needed concept of national polity as well as a host of other ideas that will henceforth emerge. Thus, we must never neglect the efforts required of us in order to confront the present state of affairs and survive as true Japanese.

In terms of resolving this problem, we have not yet reached the point of making any grand claims. Speaking strictly from the standpoint of my present feeling, however, I am, like Mr. Nishitani, most drawn to the Oriental spirit of Mahayana Buddhism. All of our past thinking has centered on the Western notion of "self." We have taken a kind of pride in our awareness of this "self," but ultimately this renders any leap impossible. Now is the time that the Japanese people must seriously consider the traditional Oriental notion of "self-extinction." This is no superficial problem of simply curbing one's selfishness or changing individualist ideas; rather, it involves fundamentally overturning the way we look at things. Zen master Bankei's notion that "everything is as it should be in the Unborn" contains infinite meaning. Nishitani writes in detail about the relation between such Oriental religiosity, present-day conditions, and our everyday lives, and I largely agree with his views. As for myself, I have already stated that I am not at the point of making any public pronouncements.

While I have strayed rather far here from the notion of overcoming science, these remarks will be seen to be closely related to that topic if read as expressing part of my feelings as a scientist.

Doubts Regarding "Modernity"

NAKAMURA MITSUO

"OVERCOMING MODERNITY": ISN'T there something ambiguous about this topic, as if we somehow both understand and do not understand it? Even if we are generally able to grasp its meaning as a concept, what real meaning does this phrase have for us? In other words, how is its substance related to our actual reflections? I suspect that such questions well up in the hearts of anyone who encounters this phrase, which at least in our country is new and unfamiliar.

Matters are simple if, as has hitherto been done in our country, one conceives of the term "modern" as identical in meaning to that of "Western" and frames this issue of overcoming modernity in terms of Europe's decline and Japan's self-awakening. If the intent here is to settle this question through such crude notions, however, then there is no need whatsoever to introduce this new phrase. The borrowing of this Western concept to negate the West is itself already a disgraceful contradiction, for in fact it was certain contemporary European thinkers who expressed the task of contemporary culture through the phrase "overcoming modernity."

What worries me most of all is the ideality of our views on this topic. Does the phrase "overcoming modernity" echo in our hearts with the same powerful sense and clarity of content as it undoubtedly does in the hearts of present-day Europeans?

If we regard the Renaissance as the time in which the seeds of Europe's modern spirit were first clearly formed, then at least five centuries passed before this spirit reached its ripe maturity in the nineteenth century. All the cultural phenomena that characterize modern history—whether the Reformation, the French Revolution, or the Industrial Revolution—are the result of spiritual tendencies inherent to Europeans, for whom such phenomena are part of an experiment of one human spirit as conducted on a massive social scale. Whatever its outcome, this experiment is in a true sense a matter of reaping what they sow. Regardless of how bitterly disillusioned Europeans may be by the results of modernity, then, it is an undeniable fact that they have actually lived through this period. When Europeans reject the human spiritual order (or disorder) that is modernity, this rejection is premised upon their conviction that they have already lived through this order (or disorder) to its end. When they declare that nothing can any longer be expected from modernity, their despair stands alongside their sense of confidence that they have done virtually everything that modernity could offer.

From a different perspective, however, is it possible for us to possess such a healthy sense of despair and confidence in relation to "modernity," one that is rooted in everyday life itself? Has modernity been such a worthy experiment for our spirit? I, for one, cannot but think about such questions.

Apart from those who consider the Edo period as a unique type of modern society, isn't it the case that the particular feature of all of our country's so-called modern cultural phenomena since the Meiji period consists, above all, in their status as superficial borrowings. For many historians, it is a matter of common sense that the post-Meiji modernization of our country took place through Western influence. Given that this so-called modernity is a hasty foreign transplant, however, it already differs in character from European modernity. Whereas modernity is at the very least a kind of European domestic product, in our country it is above all an import. Isn't it true that this imported character is the most significant feature of our country's "modernity"? Isn't it the case that, in our country since the Meiji period, all the various kinds of modern cultural phenomena that appeared so hastily are idealistic in substance and superficial in regard to their social influence? Let us put aside for the moment the question of whether we should regard this as an advantage or disadvantage. If this is the major feature of all of our country's so-called modern culture, then for us, at least, it is no more than a meaningless and idealistic game to neglect our own "modern" character and speak of "overcoming modernity." Given that in our country "modernity" itself is already an imported product, this question of overcoming modernity is generally inseparable from that of imported culture. More concretely, in what ways have we incorporated Western culture since the Meiji period? How have both our everyday lives and spirit changed through the violent introduction of this foreign culture? Aren't these the kind of complex and difficult questions that we, at least, must truly reflect on, even if we are unable to resolve them?

For these are precisely the events that we alone in the world have encountered; these are the questions that we are actually living through.

The question of the merits and demerits that Western civilization has brought to our country is now much discussed. Just as the shallow discourse of idolizing the West once thrived in the past, so now the facile discourse of rejecting it seems to have caught the attention of the masses. Yet is the question of Western influence as received in this country since the Meiji period really so simple as to be settled merely by declaring our rejection of it? In a certain sense, this influence has become so deeply rooted as to affect the foundations of our way of life. Today the West's influence can be detected in our everyday affairs to such a degree that we are no longer conscious of it.

I am now writing these words using a fountain pen under an electric lamp: when I think about it, both these objects came from the West. It goes without saying that shoes and Western-style clothing are made by Western technology, and even the rayon and artificial silk used to make kimonos today are of course made by this technology, as are the machine-made silk, cotton, and dyes that allow us to freely color these kimonos.

When we thus consider the ideas, materials, and manufacturing processes of many of the goods that we casually use today, it is in fact difficult to find any that have not been influenced by the West.

This is the case not simply for goods. Even such activities as sea bathing, which has been so popular this year, became a custom because of the West's influence. In any event, such sights as young women clad only in swimsuits strutting along the sand did not exist long ago in Japan.

In addition, such indispensable elements of social life as streetcars, trains, automobiles, telegraphs, telephones, and the postal service are all Western imports. When one thinks about it, even the shape of the coins that we always pass about comes from the West, as does the conversion system of our banknotes.

In writing these lines, I imagine people might respond as follows: "Indeed, it is true that these things were originally imported from the West, but they have now become Japanized to such an extent that no one considers them to be Western. Since the people have now grown sufficiently familiar with these things, there is no longer any need to look into their background."

On the contrary, however, I believe that our current failure to realize that these things are Western reveals how deeply this influence has permeated our lives. That is to say, the fact that contemporary social life is inconceivable without such things as trains, telephones, and the postal system is proof of the fundamental changes that they have wrought upon our lives.

In any case, the everyday life of the present-day Japanese people lost its pre-Meiji form, whether politically, economically, culturally, or with respect to customs. Isn't the most remarkable feature of our country's so-called modernity the fact that this astonishing revolution in our way of life was achieved in the mere eighty years following the Meiji Restoration and its opening of the country, a span of time that is even briefer than the life of an aged man? Of all the nations in the world, which country has ever experienced such a violent and frenzied change? In this respect, even though this change took place through the influence of the West, it has no precedent even in the West itself. It is hardly the case that the West changes by imitating itself. As I have already said, modernity was fully created within the womb of the West's own spirit.

Such rapid absorption of foreign civilization was of course absolutely necessary for our country's survival from the Meiji period. Our country's striking development today is such that it would be inconceivable to ignore the efforts made by our predecessors. Although filled with racial pride, Europeans themselves have not hesitated to praise as miraculous our country's rapid rise to power through our skillful adoption of Western civilization. In regard to our current national strength, moreover, we are the equal of any foreign country.

I daresay that even the leaders of the Meiji period who hoped that the "wealth and power" of the "advanced Western nations" could be transplanted to our country would not have expected their ideals to be attained so quickly.

Behind the scenes, however, how many sacrifices did we really pay in order to attain this "miracle"? To what chaos was our spirit led by these drastic changes in our way of life, as forced upon us by necessity? How did the demands of this cruel age distort the living spirit that had to accommodate itself to them? Aren't these the most urgent questions posed to us by our country's "modernity"?

In our country, the word "modern" has until now generally been used with the same meaning as that of "Western." This ambiguous if widely accepted idea still firmly dominates our consciousness, primarily because it posits the following two facts as the basis of reality.

First, all the cultural phenomena considered "modern" in our country are Western imports; and second, we see only "modernity" when we look at the "West." Even if it goes without saying that modernity is a striking feature of contemporary European culture, this is only one aspect of culture, it is not everything. Just as Japan has a long history, so, too, are all the nations of Europe old. Socrates lived more or less in the same period as Confucius, and the history of European thought is as old as that of the Orient. This eternal tradition flows continuously in the blood of contemporary European culture, just as the influence of Confucianism does in ours. Whether Greece, Rome, or Christianity, all of the elements that helped form the West's distant past represent living ideas that shape the spirit of contemporary Europeans.

Now why in our country is this simple fact generally so difficult for people to understand as common sense? Why has that shallow misconception that regards the "West" as synonymous with "modernity" lingered so strongly in people's hearts?

Even in the domain of culture, for example, why have we repeated our disgraceful behavior of pursuing Europe's supposed newness and failing to understand its age? Why have there appeared such major errors in perspective today within our commonly accepted view of Europe?

In order to investigate the reasons for this, we must look back upon the ways that we have incorporated so-called European civilization since the Meiji period.

Broadly speaking, there are two cases in which a national culture is subjected to the sudden inflow or influence of a foreign culture: (1) when the former is conquered by the latter and (2) when it conquers the latter. Unfortunately, the introduction of Western culture in our country since the Meiji period has taken place under conditions that more closely approximate the first of these two cases.

As I stated earlier, the introduction of Western civilization was a matter of life and death for our country in the initial stages of its opening. The very fact that this issue of adopting a foreign culture was presented to the people in such a dire manner bespeaks the depth of the crisis surrounding the survival of our country at the time. It was the threat of the "black ships" that directly hastened the opening of our country in the closing days of the Tokugawa government. In order to achieve survival as a state in the face of Western coercion, the most urgent task was to attain equal military and economic power.

The introduction of Western civilization during the Meiji period was entirely carried out in line with this basic necessity. The Western things that our people first studied were guns, steamships, trains, spinning and weaving machinery, the factories required to set these machines in motion, and banks and companies. It was as if the West at this time both threatened and dazzled our people through the scientific civilization put to use in the late nineteenth century. I would even say that the introduction of Western civilization then basically consisted of nothing more than importing machinery and acquiring the technology to operate it. By virtue of its superior utility, this new and apparently magical scientific technology served to hasten the revolution taking place in the people's way of life, whether they liked it or not. Lanterns were ousted by lamps, which were in turn exchanged for gaslights. For people at this time, Western civilization meant above all machines and a society that was suited to their use. It was precisely for this reason that intellectuals felt that the present state of affairs in our country was far behind that of the "advanced nations of the West." Even if such a view of the West was certainly appropriate to the pressing need to address our deficiencies regarding the survival of our country as a state, it was in itself superficial and one-sided.

Of course even at this time there was vigorous debate concerning the need to go beyond a mere "external" understanding of Western civilization so as to grasp its "spirit." However, this "spirit" of the West that attracted everyone's interest generally referred to nothing more than the "people's independent spirit," which was the cause of their "wealth and power," or to those concepts of political organization that were suitable for the development of modern industry.

In a sense, all of our people during the Meiji period (with the exception of a few pioneers) regarded Europe through a kind of polarizing prism consisting of "the West qua scientific civilization and material culture." This prism was brought about by "state necessity." Thus despite—or rather precisely because of—its one-sidedness, such a view of the West, with its powerful basis in reality, naturally became the womb from which emerged immensely influential social tendencies. The unquestionable superiority of the West's so-called material civilization naturally created a sense of credulity toward the West in every other cultural field. The fervency of this credulity existed in proportion to the shallowness of people's understanding of the West. When seen merely as a sign of the times, the so-called civilization and enlightenment tendencies that appeared here are now already a past event. Nevertheless, isn't it the case that such deeply rooted tendencies as planted in the spirit of our people are still perceptible all around us even today?

Earlier I wrote that the introduction of Western culture was for our country early in its opening during the Meiji period a question of life and death, and that this question was imposed upon us by the superior utility of Western scientific civilization at the time. Ultimately, however, these two things are the same. For if a certain national culture were not overwhelmingly superior to others with respect to its utility, then its importation would not be necessary for the survival of these latter.

Even in this sense, it was quite natural that the importation of Western culture during the Meiji period would focus on scientific civilization as shaped for practical use. However, in considering such phenomena as the opening of domestic railways, the creation of steamship service, electric wires traversing the countryside, the development of lamps from gaslights to electric lighting, and the introduction of horsecars followed by the running of streetcars, are we to simply believe, as did people then, that these are signs of "civilization"? Even if such things represented a change in our everyday lives, are we to see them in terms of human life's "progress"? More concretely, are we to think that by importing these practical goods we have incorporated science from Europe?

As goes without saying, science represents one function of the human spirit, for it is a way to know nature through the intellect. Thus, science is fundamentally the result of rigorous intellectual training, one based on long tradition. Like art, science is essentially a gratuitous activity of the human spirit. From the perspective of science itself, its application to real life is always the result, regardless of how surprising this may be, rather than the goal. This gratuitousness is the essential life of science, as it is of art. Just as the utilitarian emphasis in art easily leads to decadence, so too in a sense is the social valuing of science strictly for its usefulness an unfortunate situation for true scientists. In this regard, it is certainly no coincidence that such geniuses as Leonardo and Goethe have disappeared in post-nineteenth-century Europe, where the utilization of science has increased with astonishing force.

Needless to say, then, it is clear how European "science," which was imported together with the coercive pressure of practical goods, was incorporated in our country. I would even go so far as to say that it was no longer science but merely a pile of ready-made scientific knowledge. In terms of the need to use such practical goods, what was imposed upon our ancestors was the acquisition of ready-made knowledge and technology, which generally stand as the opposite of the work of true scientists. Many of our ancestors were not even given the time to truly digest this acquired knowledge so as to establish their own ideas. The nature of machines is to induce constant improvement and invention, and countless of them were brought to our country from their native Europe in the form of bewildering new knowledge. At least in terms of ideas, our country then was in a way incessantly conquered by the West's "new knowledge." Rather than poorly think about things oneself, a shortcut to advancement consisted in borrowing the West's "progressive" knowledge. The overwhelming majority of so-called scholars were mere wholesalers who imported new Western knowledge in quick and ready-made fashion.

In terms of the introduction of machine civilization, these methods of course represented the most painless but fruitful shortcut. Such an introduction of "science" formed a central point in the importation of European culture at this time, however, as a result of which the kind of hurried and easy spiritual habits that were thus formed spread deeply if unconsciously throughout other cultural spheres and came to dominate them as an irresistible trend of the times. What we can see here, I believe, is both the essence of the age of civilization and enlightenment in the sense I described earlier and, in another sense, the greatest harm inflicted upon our people's spirit by the importation of Western culture.

If we are too rash in cramming ready-made knowledge into our heads, then we will lose that much ability to think about things ourselves. In every country and in every age, countless examples can be found of erudite scholars who turn out to be nothing more than poor thinkers.

However, isn't the greatest sacrifice imposed upon our country for introducing Western culture the fact that this kind of spiritual deformity produced a general taint on the era?

When Western knowledge acted as the driving force for all drastic reform in the domains of politics and economics, it was natural that the "West" would preside over other cultural spheres with a certain symbolic superiority. Even in the domains of philosophy and literature, the "new knowledge" of the West was regarded as an indispensable condition for those living in the "new era."

As the West itself represented for our country at this time an immense new discovery, there was no reason whatsoever for an unhealthy situation to arise in our pursuit of the nourishment provided by its new knowledge. Yet the problem here lay in the quality of this imported knowledge. If I were to use an extreme example in order to simplify matters, didn't we incorporate Western literature and thought as if these were steamships or telegraphs, in the fashion of ready-made goods that were new to us alone? In the field of literature, isn't it the case that only a few authors at the time truly studied the lives of Western writers despite the strong influence of their works? And in the field of thought, isn't it true that the new ideas incorporated from the West by scholars were nothing more than knowledge of the theories and systems of Western philosophers? Just as those writers who skillfully imitated the gist of foreign works were seen as champions of new literature, so too did clever interpreters of Western philosophy pass as philosophers and thinkers. Just as in the domain of literature foreign works were read as immediately useful models, in the domain of thought, too, knowledge about ideas functioned as their substitute.

Of course I am not saying that all the work of writers and thinkers during the Meiji period was wasted on foolish things. All of the best writers and thinkers opposed these outrageous tendencies. But such foolish things certainly existed as a trend of the times. Regardless of whether people scorned this trend or made use of it, no one could avoid being more or less swept up by the force of this period.

As literature can never be produced no matter how much knowledge one accumulates about it, likewise even the broadest and deepest knowledge about thought is insufficient for the creation of thinkers. The possession of knowledge about ideas is not the same as understanding them, that is, truly grasping their vital meaning. It can be said, moreover, that we first make ideas our own only when we confirm their meaning through our actual lives.

If this represents the true form of ideas in their influence on man, then it should be clear just how shallow was the West's influence on our country's literature and thought from the Meiji period.

That is to say, thanks to the then dominant tendency to fear the West rather than the tendency to worship it, foreign literature and thought were, even in their crudest forms, overcirculated and overvalued, because of which they weren't given the chance to take root in our country's soil. Certain ideas were imported, enjoyed a brief popularity, and were then forgotten without any time to assimilate them, whereupon they were then replaced by other ideas that were again imported as "new knowledge." These latter ideas were likewise only welcomed during the time they remained novel as knowledge, after which they were soon forgotten, just like the previous ideas.

As a result, literature wandered about searching for new plots from abroad like the constant importing of new machines, while philosophy simply produced many "philosophers" who lacked any ideas of their own.

As Masamune Hakuchō wrote, "Since the Meiji period, Japan's distinctiveness lies in the fact that its people are quickly fascinated and restlessly stirred by new foreign objects."

The Meiji and Taishō periods in our country are generally described as a time of digesting Western civilization. When seen from the inside, however, wasn't this time actually one of spiritual indigestion given the importation of a bewildering Western culture that was suddenly imposed upon us? In his *Sore kara* [*And Then*], Sōseki assumes the voice of Daisuke to compare Japan at this time to "a frog competing against a cow": "Hey, its stomach is about to burst!"

Since space is running out and I should hurry to my conclusion, I should say that I do not regard the things I have discussed thus far simply as the social conditions of the past. The Meiji and Taishō periods are the eras in which we were born and raised. As with all cultural legacies, we are not entitled to a limited inheritance consisting of only those culturally advantageous aspects of previous ages.

In recent years, voices calling for the people's cultural self-awakening have increased together with the rise in our country's strength. Given how deeply rooted are our spiritual deformities as unconsciously formed through the long oppression by foreign culture, however, isn't it the case that these can in no way be cured through mere changes in journalistic trends? On the contrary, by thinking only of "restlessly" adapting oneself to the superficial trends of the times, isn't it the case that the owners of this spirit that has lost the habit of thinking for itself will even gradually see their numbers increase? Many such spiritual cripples can be found even among those who advocate reviving the classics or who speak of history and tradition. In a way, these people peddle our country's classics in the same way that they once peddled the West. I, for one, cannot believe that the serious project of a people's cultural self-awakening can be achieved through such facile spiritual work. The Meiji policy of civilization and enlightenment, which was in every respect the womb of our present-day society, has in its reverse side perhaps now come to take its revenge against us.

If this is the sad reality of that "modernity" in which we are actually living, then a sound first step toward overcoming modernity consists in clearly recognizing such spiritual crisis as an internal enemy to be fought.

If the fact that we have fallen into such confusion through the West's particular influence is truly our own responsibility, then it is unlikely that our rejection of Western culture at this point will save us from the source of this illness.

Nevertheless, if the cultural confusion our country has endured since the Meiji period is based primarily on the imbalance of power that existed between the West and Japan as well as the resulting distortions and inadequacies in our understanding of the West, then isn't the best opportunity to truly understand the West precisely *now*, when we have admirably recovered from that imbalance and no longer feel such "restless" pressure?

We only fully escape our useless fascination and fear of people and things when we clearly discern their true form. This represents both the logic of individual maturation and the real course of maturation for a country's culture.

A Note on "Overcoming Modernity"

SUZUKI SHIGETAKA

WHILE URGENT SOLUTIONS to the world's problems are now being sought in both East Asia and Europe, these problems have already gone beyond the stage of scholarly debate and entered that of policy management. At this stage, a defective tendency can easily arise in which all roundabout theories with no direct relevance to vital countermeasures are either ignored or shunned under the name of abstractions. Above all, the most superficial popular views of such theoretical thinking offer coldhearted criticisms of this latter, as if it were bereft of any practical fervor. This is the environment from which spring all poor policies and circular arguments. Despite the fact that our present situation necessarily calls for urgent countermeasures, we must nevertheless prepare ourselves for the realization that the ultimate solution to these problems cannot be reached by piling up such measures. As goes without saying, herein lies the reason the demand for guidance at the level of ideas exists on the reverse side of the demand for concreteness in the formulation of countermeasures.

There are today a great many "principles," however, whose excessive numbers might be seen as deriving from the narrowness of thought. Even if it is implicitly if only vaguely understood that there exists a kind of commonality between the so-called principles of regulation, organization, culture, national defense, and so forth, there are no attempts to establish any logical consistency between them. Or perhaps it is simply claimed that one of these principles is dominant, such that it comes to replace all of the others. In effect, all of these principles remain fixed, stipulated, and regional; they are unable to become ultimate principles that touch upon the ground of such stipulation itself. Just as, for example, the idea of the Co-Prosperity Sphere cannot yet become a truly ultimate idea when it is not supported by reflection and insight into the entire world order, so too do all solutions to the world's problems require further steps if they do not pursue thinking at an ultimate level.

Although the world is currently in the process of unprecedented change, this view that the "solutions" to its problems require further steps might actually be true, and it seems that people have become aware of such. That is to say, the measures being taken today are yet nothing more than shortsighted solutions, as intellectuals now realize that the truly ultimate problems are to be found at a deeper level. Even though the current situation is of such urgency as to preclude any fundamental tracing back of the world's problems beyond shortsighted solutions, it is nevertheless crucial for us to always seek out and recognize the site of fundamental problems. When we broadly consider the fate of the world as a whole apart from the question of actual interests, we realize that its problems are of such gravity as to go well beyond the fortunes of a few specific nations. If we fail to understand how fundamental the consequences of the current changes will be, moreover, we will neither be ready to pay their price nor know how to position ourselves for what is to be our own new era.

The notion of overcoming modernity consists of problems found at this level, which at the very least emerge in the quest for the ultimate. This involves, for example, the overcoming of democracy in politics, the overcoming of capitalism in the economy, and the overcoming of liberalism in thought. The notion of overcoming modernity is diverse in its most general aspects and extremely grave in its implications. At perhaps its deepest level, this notion gives expression to those problems faced by the world today: not only those of the internal structure of the state and the relations between states but also issues relating to the basis of worldviews and the nature of civilization.

However, here we should note that the notion of overcoming modernity has today been put forward mainly by Europeans, whose notion of modernity refers of course to *European* modernity, with its strong implications of a European and twentieth-century manner of thinking and feeling. It is not the case that this term "modernity" can be applied to Japan and East Asia with the same meaning. For example, today's problems can be seen in the fact that a place like China has not yet fully solved the question of how to achieve modernity. Even in the case of Japan, the point is that the meaning of overcoming modernity here differs from that of Europe. Nevertheless, this issue of overcoming modernity must in one sense be seen as related to us, since European civilization has today already become deeply internalized within our country and is no longer merely an alien civilization but actually now a part of us. In other words, the modernity that is to be overcome exists not only in Europe but indeed within us as well. Above all, to the extent that the European civilization that has been incorporated within our country is one of capitalism, individualism, and liberalism, that it is in other words part of a nineteenth-century civilization that has now reached what Europeans regard as a stage of decline in need of reexamination and liquidation, then this problem necessarily demands the keenest reflection on our part. In Japan today, such a European civilization has provoked a Japanese-style intellectual crisis in which a confrontation is called for between such oppositions as foreign civilization and national civilization, Western spirit and Japanese spirit, and imported civilization and native civilization. On the other hand, since Japan has already become one of the great modern powers, the fact that a simple rejection of Europe's foreign civilization is unable to resolve this question of overcoming modernity merely serves to deepen these contradictions. This state of affairs suggests nothing more than how deeply the issue of overcoming modernity is situated within our country as well.

In Japan, moreover, the situation has become even more complicated since this issue of overcoming modernity overlaps with the more specific issue of overcoming Europe's world domination. Also, in Europe itself the notion of overcoming modernity is not necessarily univocal; reflections on the meaning of the modernity to be overcome are not necessarily uniform. To put this more directly, there is some question here as to whether modernity refers only to the nineteenth century or, more broadly, to the whole modern era since the Renaissance. For such men as Hans Freyer, Dürckheim, and other German thinkers, it seems that modernity is conceived primarily in the former fashion, while for Berdyayev and Dawson the errors of modernity are found by tracing back its roots to the Renaissance. Consequently, there are calls for a second coming of the Renaissance as well as demands for overcoming it. If the nineteenth century represents the necessary result of the development of the spirit of modernity since the Renaissance, then this latter view of tracing modernity back to the Renaissance must of course also be recognized as well grounded.

Based on the preceding reflections, I would like to raise the question of overcoming modernity in terms of the following points:

1. We must clarify this question of "overcoming modernity" based on its original—that is, European—meaning.
2. We must position this question in terms of its Japanese angle and clarify its meaning as a specifically Japanese issue.
3. We must examine whether the modernity that is to be overcome refers to the nineteenth century or to the Renaissance. While this question is of course included within the first point, a historical approach to this matter carries its own special meaning.
4. The overcoming of the Renaissance naturally touches upon the basic problems of *l'humanité* as well as upon the question of religion. It must also be related to the future of Christianity.
5. The questions of machine civilization and humanity are related to the question of science. That is to say, we must investigate the role of science and its limits in resolving the crisis of civilization.

6. In terms of historiography, we must examine the overcoming of the "idea of progress," which is the issue most profoundly related to this discipline. We must also explore the fundamental problem of overcoming historicism, which is particular to historiography. The overcoming of historicism, in other words, represents the overcoming of modernity in historiography.

Concluding Remarks to "Overcoming Modernity"

KAWAKAMI TETSUTARŌ

FROM ITS INITIAL conception, the symposium has taken approximately one year to be realized. Kamei Katsuichirō eagerly proposed a meeting of this type at the beginning of this year [1942], and, with the participation of Kobayashi Hideo and myself, plans were drawn up. These plans were finally put into practice in May, when we selected participants and sent out invitations. Everyone accepted (only Yasuda Yojūrō was unable to participate due to a sudden inconvenience at the time of the symposium). We then immediately requested copies of the papers, printed them out, and had them distributed to the participants to look over. The symposium took place over a course of eight hours in the intense heat of July 23–24. A stenographic record of the proceedings was then distributed to all the participants and substantially revised, and this together with the papers was published in the September and October issues of the journal *Bungakkai* [*Literary World*]. The present volume is based on these issues, although several participants added material and made changes to their papers when asked to make further revisions.

I do not yet know whether the symposium was a success. It is an undisguised fact, however, that it was organized at a time of intellectual trembling during the first year of the war. We intellectuals were certainly at a loss then, for our Japanese blood that had previously been the true driving force behind our intellectual activity was now in conflict with our Europeanized intellects, with which it had been so awkwardly systematized. This resulted in the strange sense of chaos and rupture that dominated the symposium. Informed persons will recognize that this is a faithful recording of that desperate fighting, which indeed continues today. The war's final outcome will be known only after we have cleared away the dust of the battlefield.

Symposia of a similar format were held about ten years ago at the League of Nations by the Committee for Intellectual Cooperation, with several chaired by Paul Valéry. There one could see the mobilization of intellectuals as a stopgap measure for preserving the Treaty of Versailles, whose contradictions had already begun to be exposed. Toward this end, it was skillfully contrived that the topic for discussion be "How Are Europeans Possible?" First-rate intellectuals thus exhausted their minds in trying to strip the body from the intellect. The attempt to ban political statements from the proceedings succeeded re-markably in the end in strengthening the political effects of their discourse as a whole. Although versed in intellectual etiquette, the participants' chorus sounded empty amid the emasculated if apparently rich and gorgeous harmony. Their forlorn hopes are revealed today by the real state of European politics.

In any event, the course of our symposium is quite different. Somewhat prior to the start of the Greater East Asia War, most people had begun chanting in unison slogans about Japan's new spiritual order. All intellectual efforts and capacities were suppressed behind this unison. The crisis was thus only superficially averted and everything tidied up under mere conceptual pretexts. The aim of our symposium was to break through such easy torpor. This was not done as defiance against "being unable to say what one wishes," which is merely sentimental self-confession. Rather, we wanted to discuss "how" we were present-day Japanese.

It had already been pointed out several years ago that our culture's various fields were isolated from one another, and I am sure that many readers of the present volume would concur with this. Disparities could be seen everywhere, in such aspects as terminology, intellectual methodology, and historical stages of work. We spoke to one another like comrades in neighboring cells who communicate by beating against a wall. We were so impatient in communicating all of our long-cherished convictions that we did not desist even in our useless conflicts. This was faithful to our original goal. It was with unspeakable joy, then, that the Overcoming Modernity symposium appeared like a beacon that faintly pierced these walls and shone into our eyes.

In this regard, the themes and methodologies of the symposium did not so much aim for truth in general but were rather mere mileposts for passing inquiry. Perhaps the symposium was inadequate in stopping only at the discovery or establishing of such mileposts, with nothing left to teach us about any subsequent course of action or form of conduct. Actually, there have been several participants who have impatiently expressed such dissatisfaction. Yet this represents another project. For the present, let us be satisfied with this foundation. It is wholly owing to the blessing of the Japanese nation, moreover, that such a group of unknown men could come together and undertake this project.

Roundtable Discussion

Day One

KAWAKAMI: Let me thank you all very much for coming such a long way in this heat to meet here today. As the organizer of this event, I am extremely pleased that so many first-rate people have agreed to express how their thoughts have been troubled by certain urgent issues that are shared by all of us.

However, it seems that the theme I proposed for this conference was not an altogether sensible one. The phrase "overcoming modernity" is actually a kind of sign or mark, one that I thought might appeal to the feelings all of us share. This was my original aim in proposing this theme. But having now read through more than half of your essays, I'm afraid that such a careless proposal may have actually made matters more complicated. I would thus like to restate my feelings.

If I may be allowed to say so, all of us here haven't lived through this current era—which stretches from, say, the Meiji period onward—in entirely the same way. In other words, each one of us has encountered the present from different angles. Nevertheless, our emotions have assumed something like a single pattern to them, particularly since December 8. This emotional pattern can in no way be expressed in words, that is to say, it is what I am here calling "overcoming modernity." Our *aims* for this conference, as it were, consist in departing from this pattern so as to inversely discover our individual traits and characteristics; to express various thoughts about our own qualities while listening to the remarks of others; and finally to convey to the outside world that present-day Japanese culture is operating smoothly upon one track. Having read through your essays, it seems that my very careless proposal for this conference has resulted in differences even about, for example, the single word "modernity." Such differences are to be expected, but the meaning of this term differs, for instance, among Mr. Nishitani, Mr. Yoshimitsu, and Mr. Tsumura. Nevertheless, a reading of these essays should yield an understanding of everyone's notion of modernity, so that I no longer need to first rigorously define this term. However, let me try by way of suggestion to synthesize the central themes of our roundtable discussion as these appear in your essays.

This roundtable discussion must progress, in other words, by first problematizing the notion of Western "modernity." This problem then comes to be linked to Japan, given its influence by that modernity. From there we will be led to Japan's original or proper form ("original" not necessarily in the sense of old), that is to say, the form of present-day Japan. These three steps, I believe, represent the major framework leading to "modernity." But this issue is even more complex, as many general abstract concepts emerge in this context. Dozens more such concepts can be considered here, such as science, humanity, and historical progress. These individual abstract concepts will also be examined in the course of our discussions on modernity. By way of proceeding to our first step in this framework, then, we should begin by problematizing the notion of Western "modernity." For the sake of convenience, this has been organized as follows:

The meaning of "modern" Western thought is discussed chiefly by Mr. Nishitani, while the meaning of "modern" Western science is taken up by both Mr. Kikuchi and Mr. Shimomura. "Modern" Western music is examined by Mr. Moroi, and finally the topic of "modern" Western literature is undertaken by such people from the literature camp as Mr. Kobayashi, Mr. Nakamura, Mr. Kamei, and myself.

We must also discuss the question of the Renaissance, given its status as the origin of Western "modernity." While it is certainly true that Western "modernity" derives from the Renaissance, I would like Mr. Nishitani and Mr. Suzuki to discuss how long this period continued. This is a strange way of putting it, but what I mean here is how far the Renaissance extended: until the end of the eighteenth or nineteenth century, or has it reached into the twentieth century? In addition, I'm sure that we will all have much to say about the meaning of the transition in the West from the eighteenth to nineteenth centuries.

Next we deal with the movement of Western "modernity" to Japan through the Meiji period forces of "civilization and enlightenment." Here Mr. Kamei's essay addresses mainly the question of the advantages and disadvantages of this movement for Japan. Somewhat relatedly, Mr. Tsumura's essay touches upon the question of Europe's present and future.

We will also examine such concrete issues as Europe-U.S. relations and the question of Japan's status therein. Here as well, I'm sure that many similar problems will be raised.

We thus arrive at the question of Japanese culture as it has been influenced by Western "modernity." This gives rise to three issues.

The first concerns the meaning of the "present" in the Japanese classics, in regard to which Mr. Miyoshi raises some very important questions in his memorandum.

The next issue involves the proposition that present-day Japanese history is world history and, as such, should be greeted by us with a particular sense of hope and idealism. This question must also be conceived on the basis of thought in its most practical sense. I'm sure that this understanding of contemporary Japanese history as world history is of concern for all of us.

Third, there is the question of how present-day Japanese people have become possible. Mr. Hayashi Fusao deals with this issue in an extremely specific and yet straightforward manner. Such treatment is not necessarily the only way to approach this question, which indeed can be said to guide our entire roundtable discussion.

In the wake of this issue regarding the possibility of present-day Japanese people, the concrete problem that immediately comes to mind concerns the intellectual confusion that has reigned in Japan during the Taishō and Shōwa periods. This is an extremely concrete problem, one that is of particular gravity and interest. It is taken up in Mr. Kamei's essay, and I would very much like Mr. Kobayashi Hideo to discuss it as well.

In the foregoing, I have referred to several points from everyone's arguments. While I really didn't wish to do this, I thought that for the sake of convenience it would be better than exchanging greetings in order to get the conference going. Of course my outline can in no way be relied upon and was intended solely for your reference. Let us now proceed to more substantial discussion.

THE MODERN MEANING OF THE RENAISSANCE

KAWAKAMI: If we begin our discussion by analyzing nineteenth-century Europe, then the question that first comes to mind concerns the fact that we have all been educated on the basis of European civilization. Mr. Suzuki, how do you conceive of the Renaissance? While I really don't know anything about this period, I do have the vague sense that Renaissance tendencies reached their peak in the eighteenth century, whereas the nineteenth century revealed the aberrations of "modernity" in the negative sense.

SUZUKI: I'm not quite sure where to begin. Generally the Renaissance is seen as the beginning of "modernity," but what exactly does this mean? Recently the notion has become widespread that European modernity is false or mistaken. If we were to identify the starting point of this false modernity, virtually everyone would point to the French Revolution. Assuming that "modernity" can be genealogically traced back to this point, this would involve democracy in the political realm, liberalism in the realm of ideas, and capitalism in the economic realm. All of these notions can be seen as products of the nineteenth century. However, there is one other point that is not restricted to the nineteenth century, and which is discussed by Mr. Nishitani in his essay: this is the largely correct idea that modernity is something that is essentially European. In this equivalence between modernity and Europe, the latter does not simply refer to itself but rather possesses a more global meaning. Such equivalence thus refers to Europe's world domination, whose overcoming is the reason the Greater East Asia War is currently being fought. This, too, can be understood as one way to overcome modernity.

While thus changing the outer forms of the world order has become an urgent question today, I believe that we must also consider changing what amounts to the spiritual or internal order. It seems to me that we can in no way touch upon the question of overcoming modernity in its deepest and most radical sense if we restrict ourselves to changing the external order alone. Rather, such thinking requires that we trace back more deeply beyond the determination of "modernity" in the common or narrow sense as the era following the French Revolution, and this can be done by investigating the spiritual origins of "modernity." In other words, while the nineteenth century that followed the French Revolution represents "modernity" in its most typical sense, this century was in effect a development of the "modernity" that preceded it and whose time had simply reached its end. Hence the question arises of more deeply tracing back modernity's spiritual origins. No doubt most people believe that such a tracing back leads to the question of the Renaissance and Reformation.

When historians examine the Renaissance in a more scholarly fashion, however, matters become considerably more difficult with the emergence of various scholarly issues. Particularly in Western academia, it seems that there has been quite a lot of debate about this period in the past dozen years. Even in regard to the question of the nature of the Renaissance, for example, there are those who see this era as the revival of antiquity, while others regard it as the discovery of man and nature or else as the discovery of the ego, and yet again still others who define it in terms of the transition from the God-centered ideology of the Middle Ages to humanism. Among historians, however, such conceptual determinations alone have become inadequate, thus giving way to a host of scholarly questions. Even in Japan, people such as Dr. Ōrui have written on this subject as well. Because these questions represent a very specialized form of scholarship, there is no need for laymen to get too caught up in them.

HAYASHI: How do you personally conceive of the Renaissance?

SUZUKI: In fact, I am not really a Renaissance specialist. I focus on the Middle Ages, and so my views might be somewhat biased in that regard. But it seems to me that most theories of the Renaissance either excessively modernize this period or else regard it in too oppositional a fashion vis-à-vis the Middle Ages. The Renaissance represents the negation of the Middle Ages and yet at the same time remains very much indebted to it. Clearly historians have tended to adjust this view and will continue to revise many traditional theories of this period.

KAWAKAMI: In other words, are you saying that the Renaissance represents the conclusion of the Middle Ages?

SUZUKI: I'm not sure I would use the word "conclusion," but in simple terms such usage should be fine. These days there has been a rather influential notion that "modernity" in the true sense of the word emerged only after the eighteenth century. In this way, the Renaissance would not yet be seen as truly modern, for up until the eighteenth century, many social and intellectual elements remained that were quite medieval in nature. In France, this period has been called *l'ancien régime*. On the other hand, however, the Middle Ages were not suddenly overthrown with the emergence of the Renaissance. Here it is quite striking that the Middle Ages underwent a gradual transformation from about the thirteenth century. There now seems to be a growing trend that locates the Renaissance at the middle stages of the long and gradual historical transition from the Middle Ages to modernity. Various notions can thus be found in the field of historical research, but there is no harm done in allowing laymen to hold on to their own ideas of the Renaissance, whether these be based on the discovery of man and nature, the revival of antiquity, self-consciousness, or the birth of humanism.

KAWAKAMI: Let me ask in passing on what theories or phenomena do you base your view on the completion of the Renaissance, that is, the transformation of the world in the eighteenth century.

SUZUKI: It matters little which aspect one addresses in approaching this problem, but perhaps the dimension of spiritual life is the most familiar. From this perspective, the eighteenth-century Enlightenment played an enormous role. While it is often said that the Renaissance was the era of man's liberation from religion, for example, the major historical issue after this time was nevertheless religious wars. After all is said and done, then, it was faith that shaped history. A truly secular history had not yet taken place. In this sense, post-Enlightenment thought and spirit have come to develop very differently from the thought and spirit of early modernity. From the perspective of social life as well, the Industrial Revolution had its beginnings in England around 1760. Together with this development there emerged a civil society—or capitalist society, in the narrow sense of the term—and this in turn brought about the liquidation of all the many feudalist remnants that yet remained within modernity. Prior to this time, modernity was still characterized by a social structure in which the modern and feudal were intertwined, with the vestiges of the latter still very much in abundance. The dissolution of these feudal elements by the French Revolution at the end of the eighteenth century was a major development. There is also one other factor about which I must ask Mr. Kikuchi and Mr. Shimomura: this concerns the presence of scholarship, and particularly its use of scientific methods, as a major feature of modern culture. While the signs of such modern scholarship can perhaps be found in the Renaissance, the obvious presence of an independent scholarly system with its own rules or principles is undeniably a post-eighteenth-century phenomenon. The methodological scholarship proper to modernity derived from this system. Such methods provided scholarship with its own autonomy, so that it could no longer be governed by any external authority. For me, this is one of the major features of modernity. In addition to this independence of scholarship in modernity, we also see that scholarship now governs civilization. That is to say, scholarship has gone beyond its status as truth and come to determine the nature of civilization and society, even creating such new modes as scientific civilization. This development strikes me as characteristic of modernity. The appearance of such phenomena can be understood in terms of the post-eighteenth-century world, which in this sense must be regarded as eminently modern.

Thus your remark about the eighteenth century as the height of the Renaissance is in a certain sense correct, Mr. Kawakami. For although the Renaissance more narrowly understood took place in Italy during the fifteenth and sixteenth centuries, modernity only truly emerged much later, in the eighteenth century.

YOSHIMITSU: I would like to explain my essay for this symposium in very simple terms. When given the topic of "overcoming modernity," I wrote mainly about my views on the entire span of European spiritual history, and it was on this basis that I defined "modernity." It seems to me that the ordinary or commonsensical notion of European spiritual history as divided between the Middle Ages and modernity is seriously mistaken. While I of course do not believe that Christianity represents the Western spirit, Hegel's "Christian Germanic world" is nevertheless one of this spirit's arenas, as it were. Postclassical European spiritual history has been determined as a unified entity, within which there exist such minor period divisions as the division between the Middle Ages and modernity. This European world continues to exist today. I believe that a certain point of view is being expressed when we try to arbitrarily characterize this one world through such terms as "modernity" or "the Middle Ages." For me, the spiritual historical question of "modernity" is rather a continuation—or perhaps a modification—of the spiritual historical question of the Middle Ages. As Mr. Nishitani discusses in his essay, a unity existed in the Middle Ages between religion, culture, and national ethics, whereas in modernity this unity disintegrated when these individual moments each came to seek their own autonomous principles. In other words, what in the Middle Ages existed publicly in a single, unified fashion was now destroyed with the emergence of modernity, or perhaps the universal logic that had earlier united these individual elements now disappeared. As such, despite the division between the Middle Ages and modernity in terms of unity and the loss of unity, the questions here are ultimately the same. I believe that today, when the problem of "conquering modernity" is often discussed, we have come to the question of how to newly revive this universal principle of unity. There have thus appeared claims to rebuild this spiritual order through discovering the unifying principles of religion, that is, by rediscovering God and establishing a cultural order from a spiritual standpoint (this involves such questions as the internal relations between this order and science, metaphysics, religion, general culture, and social ethics). In effect, the crux of the problem lies in how Europe can once again rise up now that it has faltered in its Christian faith. The so-called modern European culture with which we have come in contact is actually a culture that has lost sight of God. Hence, the question of how the European spirit can rediscover God has come to be intrinsically related to the question of how God can be rediscovered within Japan's own thought and culture given the influence over this latter by modern European culture. That is to say, these two aspects share something in common in terms of the category of religiosity.

I thus believe that the question of European modernity, as understood from both a historical and metaphysical standpoint, is at the same time the question of us present-day Japanese people. Such a spiritual historical standpoint must now be adopted even when praising or criticizing the Renaissance for its medieval or modern features. I find the Renaissance's promotion or perhaps creation of the cultural values of ancient humanity to be essentially indistinguishable from those things that developed out of the logos of the medieval cultural spirit. However, if one understands the Renaissance in terms of the "confusion of the orders" of culture and spirit, then I would locate the Renaissance man's original sin in the loss of that true, living religious spirituality characteristic of the medieval logos and its consciousness of humanity and values. I would also claim that this loss results in the Renaissance's inability to concretely revive classical humanity in its true sense. In the final analysis, ancient man in his concretely historical form is a religious man. He must not be understood in terms of the Renaissance reaction against religious man; rather, he is someone like Virgil, a creature of natural morality who requires salvation.

SUZUKI: We can by no means ignore the fact that the Renaissance was a classical revival. Historians have traditionally regarded the Middle Ages and antiquity as unrelated, given the major discontinuity between them. Until recently, the Renaissance was widely seen as a revival of antiquity, that is, that it was related to antiquity but unrelated to the Middle Ages. Such determinations of the Renaissance as the discovery of man or of nature cannot be conceived apart from this understanding of antiquity's revival. This is how the Renaissance has been perceived. While it is true that such a perception has come to be substantially revised, a classical revival nevertheless means a revival of classical antiquity. Furthermore, since classical antiquity was a pagan era and so more or less opposed to the Christian Middle Ages, it seems to me that antiquity represents one possible way of determining the Renaissance.

YOSHIMITSU: While the modern Renaissance has been called a revival of antiquity, this period ignored the profound state of ancient man's soul in his search for salvation. Such a revival was nothing more than nostalgia for what amounted to an idealized and abstract ancient culture. I also see in the spirit of the modern Renaissance both a substantial connection to and a spiritual estrangement from the religious man of Christianity. What is essentially lacking in the religious arts of the modern Renaissance is the religious soul. In this sense, I find the Renaissance to be of little importance.

SUZUKI: The Renaissance notion of antiquity was of course an idealized one.

NISHITANI: What has been referred to here as the medieval Renaissance and the modern Renaissance (in the original sense of this word) raises the question of their continuity. Forgive my layman's remark, but I wonder if Henry Thode, for example, believed that the seeds of the Renaissance could be found from the time of Saint Francis. Such artists as Cimabue and Giotto, for example, would thus be included in that period. Yet as you just remarked, Mr. Suzuki, the Renaissance is seen as fundamentally religious given that, from the perspective of its own internal spirit, it is bound up with the medieval church. In contrast to this, for example, there has appeared the attitude of l'art pour l'art, that is, the notion that art is made purely on the basis of its own autonomy as art. As one can see in scholarship and elsewhere, many fields have thus been secularized by becoming independent of religion. These fields have acquired their own autonomy. Such a development no doubt represents a fundamental change in spirit. Mr. Yoshimitsu stated that "modernity" is a variation of the Middle Ages. While I understand this point, it nevertheless seems to me that a very fundamental discontinuity or gap exists between the Middle Ages and modernity, and that this latter cannot truly be problematized without acknowledging as much. What are your thoughts on this?

YOSHIMITSU: When I used the word "continuity," I meant it in the sense of the metaphysical questions of spiritual history—that is, how has modernity resolved the questions of the Middle Ages, or again, despite the fact that modernity is seen as the overcoming or advance over the Middle Ages, wasn't it in fact the faltering of the Middle Ages that determined the fate of modernity? In other words, I understand the Middle Ages more comprehensively, such that the questions of modernity become part of the questions of that period. I regard the Middle Ages not simply in opposition to modernity but rather in terms of the eternal questions of humanity that live on even today.

NISHITANI: Of course these questions themselves can be described as identical. Hence the Middle Ages was fully unified based on the understanding of one's relation to God. In contrast, modernity is characterized by the fact that man has lost sight of God while at the same time fundamentally seeking Him, as you have just remarked. This is true enough, but isn't it the case that modern man has not sought God in the same manner as did men of the Middle Ages?

YOSHIMITSU: To put it plainly, then, modern man is not a simple unbeliever. Rather, he is a tragic figure who has lost his faith. He must thus rediscover God through his self-consciousness. Until he does so, he will remain a tragic figure whose essence lies in his irredeemable anxiety. Although the Renaissance man abstracted and idealized ancient man in terms of his own liberation or salvation, I rather find hope in grasping the latter more concretely through more serious reflection on the aspect of human existence. As the logos of ancient culture, the Renaissance's cultural will and autonomous intellectual inquiries have been granted a new and healthy life in the new order of medieval spirituality, one that should continue and develop. However, all culture becomes a Tower of Babel when the soul cannot be saved. We must criticize and overcome the modern Renaissance spirit in order to rebuild a healthy human culture. Natural man and religious man are existentially one. It is my belief that a return to nature and to human nature must necessarily also be a return to God.

SUZUKI: Ultimately, I believe that the Renaissance is most fundamentally characterized by man's self-renewal. This desire for self-renewal emerged from within medieval spiritual life, and in this respect the origins of the Renaissance lay in the Middle Ages rather than antiquity. While the Renaissance is thus related to the Middle Ages, it nevertheless revolted against this latter by discovering a new type of man in antiquity.

Therefore, while the Renaissance fundamentally emerged from the Middle Ages, it did so with the intent to revolt against that period. Therein lies a fundamental problem, I believe. That is to say, despite the fact that modernity takes the Middle Ages as its objective point of departure, modern man nevertheless subjectively believes that this departure took place by his negation or rejection of that period—and that this rejection was correct. Here we see the contradiction of modernity. Now then, must we not overcome this contradiction? As, for example, John Macmurray has argued, there is something wrong about modern man's spirit of rejecting the Middle Ages, and so we must look back to that period. It seems to me that this represents one way of overcoming modernity.

MODERNITY IN SCIENCE

KAWAKAMI: My layman's common sense tells me that science underwent great changes after the Renaissance. Mr. Shimomura, can you offer any explanations about science as it relates to the discussion thus far?

SHIMOMURA: For me, it seems dishonest to view modernity all too simply as the "unfortunate era." To be sure, the formation of modern science represents the most striking development of the post-Renaissance, or *kinsei*, period, and it bore a decisive influence on that culture. However, the notion that science unilaterally influenced such fields as religion, ethics, and politics presupposes that by this time it was already fully formed and existing independently, and this is quite strange. Such an understanding views modern science as the origin of modernity, but even science is something synchronic that exists in coordination with other things. In relation to the question of the Renaissance, there is no doubt an aspect of modern science that represents a revival or continuity with the Greek spirit of antiquity, but this alone cannot fully account for the nature of modern science. Fundamental differences can be found within science: in ancient times geometry was regarded as the model of science, whereas in the post-Renaissance period, science was represented by mathematical physics. Such essential distinctions clearly exist within science, regardless of whether these be seen as differences in the nature of science or in epistemic concepts. Here the origin of the nature of modern science comes into question. Yet this origin is not unique to science, for science is a product of the same ground as all other modern phenomena. The Middle Ages were unlike either antiquity or modernity in having no scientific contributions of their own. In other words, the seeds of modern science can be seen from about the thirteenth century, during the transition from antiquity to modernity. When one looks at the circumstances surrounding the concretization of modern science in the Renaissance period, an opposition appears between the astrological theories of Pietro Pomponazzi and the magic-based theories of Marsilio Ficino. Astrology was based on the notion that the world was ruled by a fateful necessity, in which the position of the stars was related to man's destiny. In contrast, the will to establish the individuality of man's soul and the freedom of his spirit manifested itself in the desire to overturn this notion of fateful necessity through "magic." There can be found at the root of this spirit of magic something like the "will to power," which I suspect leads to the methodology of modern science, that is, the experimental method. Since magic aims at producing things that do not otherwise exist naturally, it is connected to the spirit of the experimental method. For the notion of experimentation means that one does not simply observe nature purely objectively, or as it exists as such; rather, one tries to create something that does not exist naturally through intervention. Experimentation involves looking at nature in terms of its potential rather than its existence. The fundamental spirit of the experimental method can be found in the attempt to externalize that which is internal to nature. In this sense, the experimental method is interconnected with the spirit of magic. Modern scientific methods came to be established when this experimental spirit united with the astrological notion of necessary causality, that is, natural necessity. These methods were consciously formed in the era of Descartes and Galileo. The epistemological character of modern science consists in extracting the potential from things rather than in intuiting their essence or eidos, as in antiquity. Here science does not regard things statically but rather dynamically or kinetically—it tortures nature, so to speak, so as to make it answer its questions. In this sense, the epistemological character of modern science is technological and formative, as it were; it does not lie in purely objective observation or in the intuition of the essence of things themselves. Descartes also stresses the technological character of knowledge in his *Discourse on Method*. I believe that this character of modern science is shared by all modern thought. We see this perfectly in the philosophy of idealism, which possesses the general characteristics of modern thought. Idealism can be described as the attitude whereby the immediacy of being is recognized only as something mediated by the subject. This spirit of idealism informs such modern philosophies as so-called empiricism and positivism, as well as the spirit of the Reformation. According to Luther, all things—even, for example, natural reason—lack value in and of themselves, for they can be made meaningful only on the basis of faith. Basing oneself on experience and faith represents the spirit of idealism, which aims at subjective mediation. In this way, modern science can be described as unique in relation to antiquity but not particularly uncommon in relation to other modern phenomena, for it is grounded upon the same modern spirit.

SUZUKI: I just recalled something related to your remarks. You have just explained that modern science has a very different origin from, say, the Renaissance in its status as a classical revival. That is to say, modern science derives from something entirely new and is thus not a revival of something that existed long ago. That is quite fascinating. Mr. Nishitani clearly makes the same point in his essay, which I read with a great deal of interest. I agree with Ernst Troeltsch in his listing of the four "traditions" that formed present-day

Europe. The first of these is classical Greece, the second is Christianity, and the third is the German spirit. Assuming that these three factors are correct, the fourth tradition cited by Troeltsch is the scientific spirit, which is viewed as fundamental in the formation of modernity. Troeltsch believes that this fourth element is of a different type than the other three, that is to say, the source from which science derives is utterly unique. It seems that there is an aspect of science that derives from something that never before existed in history, and it is this source that has endowed modernity with its unprecedented and unique coloration. For me, this is partly why the question of overcoming modernity necessarily entails somehow resolving the problem of science. It is often said that the overcoming of modernity is the overcoming of the Renaissance, and this is certainly true. However, the question of overcoming modernity also involves the question of science, and this makes things much more difficult and complicated. Mr. Shimomura, I would like to ask what you mean by saying that the experimental spirit that determines science derives from magic. Given that the average person regards science and magic as irreconcilable opposites, I would be grateful for some elaboration on this point.

SHIMOMURA: While it seems paradoxical to claim that modern science derives from the spirit of magic, I believe that the notion of "reason" presupposed by the experimental method of modern science is fundamentally different from ancient reason—that is, logos-based reason—which expresses itself through language and debate. I prefer to distinguish the fundamental nature of positive proof in modern scholarship from the argumentative proofs of ancient scholarship.

SUZUKI: In any event, the scientific spirit is utterly impersonal or transpersonal—I believe that Mr. Nishitani refers to it as the "spirit of indifference"—and this seems quite unlike the project of discovering man found in Renaissance humanism. It is science along with the machine civilization that derives from it that is seen as provoking a crisis in humanism. I think that it would be very significant if the origins of science were found to exist outside of the Renaissance.

SHIMOMURA: It seems that one must view science as unique only when one regards it from the perspective of its results. However, the motivation and spirit behind the formation of modern science share the same ground as the Renaissance's notion of human consciousness, as, for example, its utterly person-based will as found in the belief in the freedom and independence of man's soul. Hence the question arises of the source of science's impersonal nature. It seems to me that there must have been a change or transition here, much like the shift from Luther to Calvinism in the Protestant spirit.

KOBAYASHI: Regarding the common nature shared by modern experimental science and primitive magic, isn't it the case that magic was always based on its actual usefulness and ends and means within primitive life? On the other hand, isn't it the case that the major difference between ancient science and modern science lies in the fact that the former was part of natural philosophy?

NISHITANI: In fact, these points have long been debated in the field of religious studies. For example, James George Frazer states that magic represents the science of primitive man, as you have just remarked. For Frazer, man turned to religion when he sensed that magic was wrong, and then again to science (in the original sense of this term) when he felt that the religious standpoint alone was wrong. Magic, religion, and science all came into being when man, living in the natural world, sought to secure his own survival. Whereas magic and science are informed by the same attitude, however, this is regarded as the opposite of the religious attitude. In other words, magicians shape the hidden forces of nature with their various magic rituals and incantations—as, for example, making rain fall. As Mr. Shimomura said, there is the sense here that nature is coerced by human forces. In this regard, magic and science share something in common. In religion, man mourns his own powerlessness and grounds himself upon the absolute, whose authority he submits to and embraces. This attitude is seen as fundamentally different from the attitude of coercion, and yet the notion of magic has in certain respects come to be revised. Recently, there have been many objections to the excessively intellectual understanding of magic as the science of primitive man. Magic is now no longer seen simply as an attempt to shape or know nature but rather as part of man's life—for example, his social life—as well as something that was originally part and parcel of the religious attitude. Nevertheless, there seems to be no harm in recognizing the presence of scientific elements within magic.

SHIMOMURA: Sociologists agree that primitive man did not simply deal with everything on the basis of magic, that he rather clearly distinguished between magic and ordinary experience. I am not claiming, then, that the relation between modern science and magic lies merely in the fact that science also contains a simple, primitive stage. (This should be obvious.) I mentioned the connection with the spirit of magic because I was thinking about the sources of modern science's methods and nature, which consist in experimental formation and positive proof, for example, rather than in the intuition of eidos or argumentative proofs.

YOSHIMITSU: In regard to this issue of science and magic, it seems that you, Mr. Shimomura, understand magic-cum-modern science as purely technological in nature. However, I wonder if this point doesn't bear some scrutiny.

SHIMOMURA: It is meaningless to speak of technology except in its modern character.

YOSHIMITSU: Do you mean that it aims for the practical domination of nature?

SHIMOMURA: Not only that, for there is no such thing as technology that is not practical. Although the phrase "domination of nature" is also ambiguous, I would have to say that modern scientific knowledge results in the formation of machinery. Modern machinery does not simply involve bodily extension or supplementation, nor the application or use of natural power, as in pre-modern machinery. It is not a mere imitation or analogy of nature but rather the reorganization, reconstitution, and remaking of nature. That is what is meant by machinery in the modern sense. Modern scientific knowledge lies in knowing how to form such machinery, just as modern technology is technology that is mediated by this modern scientific knowledge.

YOSHIMITSU: I would like to ask you about the possible connection between science and the Greek spirit. Even in Descartes' case, the spirit of scientific inquiry meant in part the technological domination of nature. When Descartes speaks of the "search for truth" in his *Discourse on Method*, for example, it seems that he is referring to science's logos-based nature as well as to its technological nature. I believe that there is in this logos-based nature of science something that is bound up with the Greek search for logos. From this perspective, the scientific spirit in no way begins with modernity but rather goes back all the way to the philosophical spirit of the Greeks. The Greek spirit of metaphysics and philosophy still lives on in the scientific spirit of the search for truth in modern philosophy, albeit in a different and distorted form. The Greek search for logos that appears in modern science emerges during the Middle Ages in the intellectual investigations of theology, but there it takes the form not of a false science but rather of a logos-based, metaphysical search for spirit. In this sense, I am able to conceive how the modern spirit of scientific inquiry is connected to the intellectual investigations of metaphysics.

SHIMOMURA: Of course I also recognize the ancient moments or elements to be found within modern science. However, the question here is not whether such moments exist but rather whether they are dominant for modernity. Although the ancient logos of course exists within modern philosophy and science, the question is its dominance. In other words, modern philosophy and science could not have been formed on the basis of logos in its original sense.

YOSHIMITSU: In terms of this discussion of "conquering modernity," I believe that the relation between physical truth and metaphysical truth comes into question. What is required today is for us to newly establish natural philosophy and a "theory of scientific knowledge," but this point must be further explained.

SHIMOMURA: I think that physics and metaphysics must for the time being be kept clearly divided and independent of each other, for this is tantamount to the need to keep science and metaphysics pure or purified of each other. The relations between them must first presuppose such division. This point is important in the context of the question of overcoming modernity.

KOBAYASHI: I wonder if there is anyone who has more adroitly described modern science than with the words "torturing nature so that it reveals its secrets."

THE LINK BETWEEN SCIENCE AND GOD

YOSHIMITSU: I would like to ask Mr. Kikuchi his opinion on the following. Until the end of the nineteenth century, it was believed that the standpoints of scientists and those who thought about religious truth or human spirituality were mutually contradictory. Hasn't this belief long dominated the popular view of science? From your own perspective as a scientist, could you please discuss how this belief is currently regarded? I think that this matter will also bring us to the question of overcoming modernity.

KIKUCHI: I also feel that science must be overcome, but I am not confident to speak about how this overcoming should be accomplished. It seems that perhaps the only way to accomplish this task is through an appeal to the notion of nothingness, as described by Mr. Nishitani.

YOSHIMITSU: One should also note that today's top scientists have considerably changed their views on religion and science as compared to scientists of the past. This can be seen, for example, in Max Planck's relatively recent work "Religion and Natural Science."

HAYASHI: I believe that scientists should become servants of the gods.

KAWAKAMI: There are three craftsmen present here: the poet Mr. Miyoshi, the musician Mr. Moroi, and the physicist Mr. Kikuchi. All craftsmen are servants of the gods.

YOSHIMITSU: I would like to touch upon something that actually relates to Mr. Nishitani's essay. Given your belief that the scientific standpoint is *not* related to the question of God's existence, it would appear logical for you to understand religious truth on the basis of the standpoint of absolute nothingness, which links together the question of science with that of religion. In Europe, however, science has been a source of distress for the realm of ideas, as such tenets of religious truth as God and man's soul have been seriously pursued as real truth. This tragedy cannot be saved by the logic of nothingness. But if scientific knowledge can be systematized along the lines of an "order of truth," in which science becomes part of the search for truth as it relates to nature, then I believe that such a chaotic situation might be saved. Then we have the problem of physics and metaphysics, to which I referred earlier. For me, the notion that science is unrelated to the thought of God's existence must be conquered directly rather than from the standpoint of the logic of nothingness. It is this direct method that represents the standpoint of philosophy.

NISHITANI: I don't really think that science and the question of God's existence are ultimately contradictory. To speak frankly of my own feelings, there does appear to be some inconsistency between the notion of God as commonly understood in Christianity—of course I am referring here only to this common understanding—and science. (I don't actually know much about science, and so it is difficult for me to speak about it.) Even with regard to the notion that God created the world, for example, isn't it the case that the scientific viewpoint has thus far existed through its exclusion of that notion? The same can be said of history. The notion that history is ruled by divine providence has thus far been rejected by modernity, but isn't it the case that we must recognize a certain progress in this modern historical viewpoint? It seems, then, that the question here is how to search for God and the religious standpoint and so on after having endorsed our present historical consciousness. Even in the West, isn't it the case that mysticism—that of Meister Eckehart, for example—developed out of its struggles in dealing with this same kind of problem? (This is my own personal view.) In my essay I discussed the Buddhist notion of "nothingness," which can also be seen as an expression of Buddha-nature. This notion can be understood as the manifestation or revelation of God and may be described from man's perspective as the negation of each and every "I." In the history of Christianity, isn't it the mystics who have most thoroughly explored this problem of God and science? It thus seems to me that the element of mysticism within Christianity is extremely important.

YOSHIMITSU: Depending upon what mysticism means, either pantheism or a theistic and supernatural experience of grace, the question of God's existence will be linked to the theological roots of mysticism.

NISHITANI: You just mentioned pantheism, but that is fundamentally different from true mysticism. In pantheism, there is no soul or subjective standpoint—that is to say, it is not the standpoint of existence. On the other hand, theism could be supported by the standpoint of nothingness, but here the meaning of God's being becomes an issue. Putting aside the question of theism as experience, the common understanding of theism as idealized within theology is quite problematic. In other words, these views conflict with both the scientific view of nature and man's historical consciousness.

YOSHIMITSU: I cannot agree with the various writings of the Kyoto professors about conquering the system of theism, given their view that scientific knowledge is unrelated to the notions of Christianity, God, and man. When the standpoint of nothingness leads to the standpoint of mysticism, as you have just claimed, then isn't it at this point that the standpoint of theism can be perfectly conceived as religious experience? In other words, isn't it the case that the truth of man's religious existence and his scientific or intellectual inquiries can be tied together in Christianity?

NISHITANI: In both Greece and the post-Renaissance period, philosophy can be said to have come into being out of the conflict between science and religion. Hence this question of science and religion is a fundamental one. This question has also been fundamental in Protestant Germany, whereas in France it has shifted between the two poles of Catholicism and atheism.

YOSHIMITSU: In order to solve this question, one must grasp the nature of the truth of reason. Furthermore, the truth of religion is not simply spiritual enlightenment but is rather approached through the standpoint of real "truth." Here I believe that people are making new efforts in this new project of intellectual truth.

NISHITANI: Well, it seems to me that mysticism is an extremely significant part of these efforts. Mysticism is primarily characterized by an absolute and transcendent God *and* a living union between God and oneself. Here, of course, one finds the negation of the "I."

YOSHIMITSU: But of course this question falls within the category of religiosity. I am completely convinced of this, but the problem today lies in the continuation between religion and scientific intelligence.

KIKUCHI: With what did you say that science must be logically connected?

NISHITANI: The issue here is whether religion and science must be directly linked together. Yet science has its own standpoint and . . .

YOSHIMITSU: But if one adopts Mr. Nishitani's standpoint in order to systematically explain that apparently contradictory standpoints are not contradictory, then one falls into the problem of idealist philosophy.

NISHITANI: When I spoke of the concept of "nothingness," this actually means something like "no-self." If, for example, we can interpret Shinran's call to surrender oneself to the Buddha as an example of such "no-self," then it seems to me that this no-self subjectivity also offers a way to resolve the question of religion and science. From this perspective, the question of how one should speak about issues of theism and theology also comes to be clarified in inverse fashion.

KIKUCHI: What does it mean to speak of God's existence? What is the meaning of "existence" here?

YOSHIMITSU: Just as you and I exist, God exists within our soul when we personally encounter Him. In other words, existence means spiritual and personal existence.

KIKUCHI: Isn't the issue then not one of God's existence but rather whether one believes in Him?

YOSHIMITSU: That is the providence of God.

HAYASHI: Western mythology involves battles between gods and men, whereas Japanese mythology centers on battles between the gods themselves.

Ever since Prometheus, man's weapon in his fight against the gods has been science.

OUR MODERNITY

KAWAKAMI: Allow me to interrupt for a moment. Despite the fact that our discussion of the West was progressing along well and some of you perhaps still have much to add, I would like now for reasons of time to change the topic more directly to modern Japan. Since it is too troublesome to rationally determine the meaning of modern Japan here, I would appreciate it if everyone could simply speak about modernity on the basis of your own personal feelings.

KAMEI: I have for some time now listened to the various interpretations of "modernity," which were all very instructive. Ultimately, my own sense of "modernity" lies in the very chaos I've experienced over these past dozen years. My education spanned the Taishō and Shōwa periods, during which time I came across various intellectual issues. In looking back now, I would say that, in a nutshell, the most basic shortcoming of modernity lies in its status as an era of faithlessness. I would describe this period in terms of man's misery in being exiled from the gods. Present-day Japanese, that is, those of us who have lived through the "civilization and enlightenment" program of the Meiji period to the Taishō and Shōwa periods, are people who have lost sight of the gods. In the field of literature, this phenomenon can be seen clearly since naturalism, but the same can be said of all other fields as well. Since the program of civilization and enlightenment, we have experienced such things as the spread of science and the influence of foreign thought, but out of all this misery and confusion the one faint hope that I glimpse can be expressed only through the phrase "gods and Buddha": this is the search for faith. Not the search for interpretations of faith, but for faith itself.

I wrote my essay for this symposium based on this idea. In other words, I listed several examples of the misery experienced by present-day Japanese people in our exile from the gods. Although I'm sure that other things could also be considered, my discussion focused on what I have perceived for some time now. That is, I made a diagnosis of how the poisons we received from the West have circulated within our body since the time of civilization and enlightenment.

Regardless of whether this diagnosis is correct or with what erudition and analysis we try to understand "modernity," it seems that there is something unhealthy in our minds to begin with. Since the China Incident, the classical texts have come to be widely read and one hears talk of a revival of the Japanese spirit, but will these things directly save us from modernity? I feel very uneasy and suspicious about such matters. When the question is raised about the possibility of overcoming modernity, people either hastily jump to conclusions or content themselves with detailed interpretations—although these same two attitudes can be seen now in regard to any question whatsoever. I am quite dissatisfied with this. Such things as faith, learning, and culture must not become standpoints of interpretation, nor must they even be used to save oneself. This represents my thinking on faith that I have arrived at during these past couple of years, and yet I do believe that it is important when speaking about faith to fight against the easy conviction that one has been saved. Through your discussions today, I have learned various things about Western modernity. The modernity that we have experienced since the Meiji period can surely be described as hell. Although many analyses and cures have been discussed, few people have earnestly tried to point out this virus. Everyone appears rather sanguine or carefree.

I wish to establish my faith not by speaking about it but by extracting the virus that all of us carry. While it is easy to think about one's own salvation idealistically, I see it as decisive training to spend one's whole life lodged within this worldly hell itself. It is on this basis that I would like to think about the question of overcoming modernity. I mentioned that present-day Japanese people have lost sight of the gods, but where are we to rediscover them? I write about this place in the essay I submitted for the symposium. What does it mean to speak about the existence of the gods? I would like to answer this question in words, but I suppose I have my entire life to prove the gods' existence—and that after my death, this question will be settled by future generations. In any case, providing that we have the strength to overcome modernity, my one desire is to have faith in the gods. The central issue for present-day thought is precisely the resurrection of the gods. It is my life's wish to someday state with conviction that the gods exist. My life's wish consists in saying the words, "The gods exist."

NAKAMURA: When a layman like myself thinks about "modernity," it seems that Western "modernity" has thus far appeared to the Japanese as something very grand. Ever since the Meiji period, Western "modernity" has appeared to us as unconditionally wonderful. However, it is we Japanese who grasp the real spiritual basis of that "modernity," that is, the substance of its spirit. If we did not truly grasp the inner workings of the modern spirit, then it seems to me there could be no overcoming of modernity at all. Roughly speaking, ever since the Renaissance, man's spirit has been thrown into some system or order of which he himself was ignorant: herein lies the specific character of "modernity." Although some of you have discussed various aspects of the discontinuity between the Middle Ages and the Renaissance, for example, the fact is that during the Middle Ages man's spirit was such that he believed in a solemn world order. Within this European world order, man lived in extremely good spiritual health. By the time of the Renaissance, however, the feudal and status systems that built medieval society had collapsed. The Europeans, who had previously regarded the world only in terms of Europe, then set out to discover the unknown worlds of America, Asia, and Africa and realized that they were going to have to live in relation with those places. On the other hand, these Europeans discovered that they must not believe in God unconditionally, as they had to confirm His existence for themselves. In the same way, they understood that they could not continue to rely upon their traditional concept of nature, for example, but rather had to actively experiment with nature themselves. Man's spirit was thus forced to live within this unknown order, and this brought about various kinds of confusion. It seems to me that herein lies the basis of the specific character of modernity. For example, such people as writers and artists basically think about the question of how to live within the chaos of this actual order. In modern society, even tradition exists less within this actual order than it does through the artist's resolve to defy that order. Doesn't the real form of modernity consist in a kind of spiritual state in which one is forced to always live among unknown things and search out the new? In this regard, can't it be said that modernity in its true sense has now begun to arrive in present-day Japan?

KAWAKAMI: Mr. Kikuchi, I would like you to say something.

KIKUCHI: About modernity?

KAWAKAMI: I read your book *Busshitsu no kōzō* [*The Structure of Matter*]. It was more interesting than any other commentary of this type, for you write about the joy of your research discoveries. Of course there are parts of the book that I will never understand, but the parts I did understand were quite fascinating. My impressions are doubtless the result of my own subjective reading, but I did feel that classical physics, although of course not absolutely wrong, was nevertheless something that became worn out through use. In contrast to this, on what basis did the quantum physics that you scientists practice today originate? Certainly this physics must have been based on advances in mathematical precision, but I sense that there was a kind of groping after the motives and methods of discovery. In other words, while you scientists clearly had to overcome traditional physics in order to practice a new form of physics, the difference between these two forms of physics seems to lie in the following: while Newton certainly saw the apple fall with his own naked eye, for example, you scientists don't grope for discoveries with your own flesh, that is to say, your new science is not based on an entire life of collaboration.

KIKUCHI: In my opinion, however, there can be no modernity or antiquity in science.

KAWAKAMI: When I listen to Mr. Moroi's theories of music, I feel that there is something very analogous to physics. There is something similar between the sensuousness of modern music and the logic that grounds the mathematical hypotheses of modern physics. By the nineteenth century, for example, classical physics had evolved and electrical science made great advances, and it was through electric power that you actually split the atom. This fact is quite symbolic, given that the atomic nucleus represents the foundation of classical physics. According to my argument, this fact appears as the overcoming of traditional science through the force of modernity itself. In this way, however, quantum physics has come to signify a new type of metaphysics.

KIKUCHI: Since scientific progress is of course historical, each period has its own issues. However, I don't believe that there is any direct relation between the question of science itself and its zeitgeist.

KOBAYASHI: This is perhaps a silly question—no, of course it's a silly question. Kepler, for instance, wrote in his diary that God disclosed the universe's secrets only to him. For me, this is an extremely beautiful and religious cosmic image. Are scientists still able to feel this way even now in the twentieth century, when physics has come to be so specialized? Don't scientists, or you yourself [Mr. Kikuchi], for example, have the sense that you are no match for the men of old?

KIKUCHI: Yes, I do.

KOBAYASHI (*laughing*): Then everything's fine!

KIKUCHI: But this brings us back to the question of the relation between religion or the world of value and the world of things.

KOBAYASHI: Kepler believed that these two worlds were in fact one.

KAWAKAMI: I wonder if this discrepancy isn't due to Mr. Kikuchi's lack of skill in providing a historical view for his own work. I somehow have the sense, Mr. Kikuchi, that your comments are different from your work.

MODERN JAPANESE MUSIC

KOBAYASHI: I would like to ask Mr. Moroi if modern music aspires to older music. Does modern music sense that it cannot equal the old?

MOROI: Do you mean consciously?

KOBAYASHI: Or even in your own consciousness.

MOROI: Having listened to the discussion now for some time, it seems to me that the concept of modern music is quite different from the way others here understand it. The modernity that I would speak of occupies a very narrow range and refers to more limited things. I do not know whether modern man thinks that he is any match for the classics, but I have long been convinced that we must extract ourselves from modernity. I don't even know whether I am any match for the classics, but I do at least think that modernity must be overcome.

KAWAKAMI: I have read your essay for this symposium, Mr. Moroi. To summa-rize, you list three schools after romanticism: impressionism, expressionism, and primitivism, and after these you cite neoclassicism. The three schools of impressionism, expressionism, and primitivism are exactly how we regard modernity, but don't you buy a little bit too much into neoclassicism as the way to overcome these?

MOROI: I don't think so. If in Europe today there are some attempts to over-come modernity, then this is the form they have taken. The problem is that these attempts persistently remain within the limits of Europe, and in this respect perhaps I have bought too much into them. Considered more deeply, modern Western music in the broad sense is ultimately a music of feeling or sensation. Thus, even harmonics and other theories are based on the prin-ciple of sensation, and their beauty is of a sensuous nature. If we are hence-forth to create music that is unprecedented and new, and that marks a great advance over Europe, then it must be essentially spiritual. This is what it means to fundamentally change the past ways of thinking about music. Since we are talking about music, of course, this new form must involve the sense of hearing. Yet this is only a means. What is important here is not how this music sounds but rather how it braces our spirit and appeals to our hearts.

TSUMURA: But such music can be found in the Western classical tradition.

MOROI: There are figures like Beethoven. Beethoven's personality was such that he wished for great sincerity and justice within humanity, and so he had to write music that was based on these things.

KAWAKAMI: I completely agree. Such spirituality that reflects man in his entirety never appeared after Beethoven.

MOROI: I would also like to add the following idea. There are no doubt various ways to think about the scope of modernity, but as a separate issue, I think we must recognize that modernity contains periods of both progress and decline, for in our discussions it seems that many believe that modernity has been entirely negative. We must after all learn from those periods of prog-ress. When one thinks about modernity in a broad sense, one must consider such progressive eras as a plus.

YOSHIMITSU: Even in present-day Europe, discussions of overcoming moder-nity from the standpoint of Catholic religiosity have emphasized the "pre-dominance of spirituality" for culture as a whole. In Jacques Maritain's metaphysical reflections on music and poetry, it is this "predominance of spirituality" that is stressed. In this respect, Maritain has given high marks to the spirit of music informed by Spanish mysticism, as attempted by such composers as Arthur Lourié. Along with the new appreciation of Gregorian music, this European tendency shares something in common with the ques-tion of overcoming modernity.

MOROI: At present, Europeans don't believe that they can grapple with the question of overcoming modernity, at least as far as music is concerned. Thus, I believe that the light is in the East. But I don't wish to speak about this matter lightly. I think that one should put all one's energy into one's work. As I wrote in my essay, certain nations have always occupied the center of music, thus making the whole world into a pyramid structure: music of the fifteenth and sixteenth centuries was centered in Italy, that of the seventeenth and eighteenth centuries was centered in Germany, and that of the late nineteenth and early twentieth centuries has been centered in France. In this sense, I believe that Japan's future is of great significance for music—and of course all of the other arts—from here on in.

NISHITANI: On what basis do you think that European music is unpromising?

MOROI: I cannot speak about this theoretically, but I just can't find anything promising in this music after Beethoven. If I were to predict the future of European music as based on its recent history, I feel that it will experience at least one period of decline.

KOBAYASHI: I completely agree.

MOROI: I have for quite some time now resigned myself to accepting reviews of my work as "Germanic music." But I don't think that I'll have this reputation for long.

KOBAYASHI: Where did you receive the hint to create more spiritual music rather than music with a different sound? Did this come from the tradition of Japanese music?

MOROI: No. I have been writing music for a long time now, but everything began from my conviction that music must be something that strikes our hearts. I had to study many different things in order to achieve this effect. It was for this purpose that all of us had to make a thorough study of European music. This involved not meekly studying the surface of this music but rather appreciating its essence.

KOBAYASHI: Do you dislike Japanese music?

MOROI: No, I don't.

KOBAYASHI: Do you find it quite poor?

MOROI: I would say rather that it lacks a sense of development.

KOBAYASHI: Have you not made any discoveries in looking back through the Japanese music tradition?

MOROI: I am doing that now. There have been times when I found traditional music to be very beautiful. I certainly do not reject such music in its entirety. It is just that I think negatively about the idea of incorporating it as part of our attempt to create music for the future. Some people receive hints from studying the *Man'yōshū* [*Collection of Ten Thousand Leaves*], while others receive hints from completely devoting themselves to modern music. All I am saying is that I have not received any hints from traditional Japanese music. In other words, the same problem would occur if one devoted oneself only to European music. I am therefore not saying that it is wrong to receive hints from the koto and samisen.

TSUMURA: It seems that you are talking about creating a new Oriental music by marrying it to Western music. The problem here is whether the structure of Western music actually goes well with Japanese music as a means to express part of the Japanese *Geist*. Don't you have any doubts about whether such music would work well as an expression of the Japanese spirit?

MOROI: It is not that I have no doubts about this, nor can I declare that this problem could be resolved within a few years. But I do think that the only way to create a new Oriental music is to actually attempt what I have just discussed.

TSUMURA: As for Japanese musical composition, I have no authority to say how awful it is. Based on recent works, however, I think that not only lyrics but also vocalization in Japan have been badly influenced by Western music.

MOROI: This means that there is no real Japan.

TSUMURA: One reason I have thought about this issue relates to the culture film *Yamato*, which you scored. When I listened to Okuda Ryōzō sing in this film, I felt that his style completely ruined the spirit of the music you were trying to express.

MOROI: Even when one writes a new score, the vocalist has to understand how to actually sing it.

TSUMURA: When I consider Japanese music today, I think that it shares a similar fate with Japanese film. That is to say, there have long been attempts or efforts to create contemporary music using pure Japanese instruments, but these have not been successful. I find the pure old music of Japan to be much grander and more beautiful than this strange school of New Japanese Music. Mr. Moroi, it seems that you are determined to express the Japanese spirit through such techniques of Western music as instrumentation and composition methods, and I think that this direction is ultimately a necessary one. For example, I have grave doubts about using Japanese instruments to create a symphony that could appeal to people today. Nevertheless, there are difficulties and contradictions involved in trying to use Western musical techniques to express the Japanese heart, as was mentioned earlier. In fact, these difficulties are very familiar to the top filmmakers in Japan. While Japanese film techniques were basically learned from American and Soviet films, most of what was expressed through these techniques has been fake, showing neither real Japanese customs nor the Japanese heart. There are now people working hard to devise Japanese-style film techniques to express the Japanese spirit, and we are seeing the chaos of this transitional period today. Yet even if we try to express the Japanese heart through film, we ultimately run into problems, since this mechanism of film originally came from abroad. It seems to me now that such difficulties will always appear whenever we try to make the Japanese heart flourish through the tools of Western musical instrumentation. Although it is comparatively easy to express the westernized aspects of present-day Japanese customs, we immediately confront these difficulties when making historical films. Perhaps the most direct sign of this can be seen when one actually uses Western musical techniques in scoring such historical films. If one thinks about it, it is rather strange to use Western music when making a movie about *Chūshingura* [*The Forty-seven Ronin*]. To speak more plainly, this problem can be understood by considering how it is virtually impossible to use the mechanism of film to express the essence of Noh theater and Japanese dance, for example, as well as such things as *sabi*, *yūgen*, and *iki*. I am interested in how future Japanese films will resolve this issue, and I myself would also like to reflect upon it.

NAKAMURA: Mr. Moroi, is Western music really suitable for the Japanese people?

MOROI: I would reply by saying that Western music in its current form is not suitable. But if one could create a completely new style of this music, then I think it would be suitable.

NAKAMURA: It seems to me that there is something very idealistic about how the Japanese people today appreciate Western music. Although Westerners fully enjoy music that you describe as new and sensuous, the Japanese lack any appreciation for it. In this sense, I feel somewhat that it is the emotion of Western music that is so unsuited to the Japanese.

MOROI: I think that the most basic element in European music is the feeling one experiences when singing. From the perspective of the audience, it is the enjoyment of this feeling that is fundamental. I believe that in Oriental art, the essence is narrative. Thus, I would like to write narrative music. Here it seems that the manner of reception does not consist in the audience's enjoying the song but rather in the narrative intentions of the writer permeating the audience.

KAWAKAMI: Your works are clearly narrative music. That is why you must work so hard, and yet your work is not easily understood.

NAKAMURA: Does such narrative music exist in Europe?

MOROI: Not in the sense to which I am referring.

HAYASHI: I was once at a provincial hot-spring resort listening to songs on the radio performed in the Western vocalization style. Everyone in the room listening to the radio was in their sixties and seventies—illustrious old men of various careers—which left me in my forties as the youngest person present. After about twenty minutes, I got up and exclaimed, "How disappointing!" The old men, all of whom were imperial university graduates, then interrupted their silence. "Do you young people also find this music disappointing? That is a great relief, since we actually all felt this way but decided to say nothing out of politeness." And with that they turned off the radio. I wonder if Western musicians will try to understand the misgivings of these Japanese people.

TSUMURA: Japanese vocalists sing in a disastrous manner. Someone like Okuda Ryōzō is typical in this regard, but Fujiwara Yoshie has the same vocalization style. Fujiwara sings Japanese folk songs with a strange Western-style vocalization, and it is ridiculous to see the ovation he receives from Japanese people. Even if one writes musical compositions that are filled with a new mood and spirit, the manner of singing remains rather comical and ill fitted to them. This might be due to the influence of the Ueno School of Music. This problem is also related to film scores, as such comic instances can often be seen in culture films. I have thought urgently about this problem, which is now imminent for Japan. Although the movie *Yamato* was quite boring, the Japanese people would in any case still understand the atmosphere of the battleship *Yamato*, on which the film was based. Nevertheless, the songs in the film actually made one want to burst out laughing, and they destroyed the work's atmosphere. I am very concerned about the urgent question of whether we should somehow correct this Western vocalization or realize that there is something about Western singing methods themselves that don't fit Japan. Now, however, it is high time to export to the south the music that expresses the Japanese spirit.

HAYASHI: As can be seen in both Japan and China, Oriental music involves a kind of straining of the voice through overtraining or overuse. Does this same thing happen in the West?

MOROI: No, it doesn't.

HAYASHI: Won't this be important in the future?

KAMEI: I wonder if the Buddha wasn't the first person to strain his voice in this manner. To depart slightly from this topic of music, the melodies of Noh chants contain a great many notes from Buddhist sutras. As goes without saying, these sutras are the voice of Buddha. In chanting these sutras, one attains religious ecstasy through the echo created by chanting Buddha's voice. However, since Buddha practiced religious austerities while experiencing all of the world's suffering, then I would imagine that his voice would naturally become strained. In other words, since Buddhist sutras consist of life's painful groans transformed by the Buddha into something like a song with stanzas, then it would be natural for the Noh chants, which incorporate notes from the sutras, to make one's voice strained and hoarse. While it is true that this kind of straining of the voice is part of artistic training, it would be more correct to say that it essentially occurs as a result of one's training as a human being. I believe that this represents a major feature of Oriental music. If one does not regard serving music as equivalent to serving the gods and Buddha, then one could never strain one's voice in this manner.

KOBAYASHI: When did people begin straining their voice in this way? Surely this did not happen long ago.

MIYOSHI: Noh chants became popular from the Ashikaga period, and they were performed in a strained, hoarse voice. The texts recited in these chants did not appear out of the blue but rather are said to be derived from the utterances of esoteric Buddhism, which thus makes them quite old. People probably began chanting in this manner from about the time of the *Man'yōshū*.

KAWAKAMI: We do not know who practiced this strained form of chanting, as there are of course no records. Yet even if such records existed, we would not know what musical meaning this practice conveyed to people at that time. This represents the unknowability of music history, which goes beyond literature and the arts.

MIYOSHI: Even now this strained form of chanting continues to be handed down in such places as Mount Kōya. It is said that chants from Tenjiku are handed down there in their original form.

KIKUCHI: Was that during the Ashikaga period?

MIYOSHI: It was probably much before that.

Roundtable Discussion

Day Two

KAWAKAMI: Yesterday we discussed Western modernity, broadly speaking, and so today I thought we would explore the question of Japanese modernity.

As such, our first topic of discussion concerns the situation since the Meiji period as represented by the phrase "civilization and enlightenment," that is, the process and forms through which Western civilization entered Japan and the subsequent state of Japanese civilization. Next, our second topic involves the question of how present-day Japanese people—or Japanese culture or perhaps Japanese intellectuals—are possible in the light of the circumstances we are facing today, as well as the question (but this ultimately comes down to the same thing) of the nature of future Japanese culture and Japanese people. I would like to proceed with our discussion by focusing primarily on these two issues from a variety of perspectives.

Mr. Miyoshi has suggested—and both Mr. Kamei and Mr. Hayashi agree—that the present-day meaning of the Japanese classics has become a matter of interest. I think that this topic can rightly be placed in the context of Japan's current problems, thus affording us an opportunity to discuss it.

First, however, in what ways has Western civilization entered Japan since the Meiji period? While I am sure that all of you have opinions on this matter from the perspective of your own specialized fields, I would for the moment like Mr. Kobayashi to provide us with a general discussion of this phenomenon as a whole.

HISTORY: THE MUTABLE AND THE IMMUTABLE

KOBAYASHI: I don't like general discussions, and so, as a reference point, I'm going to speak about my own personal experiences.

Although it is said that Western civilization has since the Meiji period been incorporated on the basis of the principle of civilization and enlightenment, this ideology was nevertheless not embraced by writers. Yet it is absolutely impossible to conceive of Japanese literature since the Meiji period apart from modern Western literature, for it is clear that the former developed through the extremely powerful influence of the latter. It is only recently, however, that we have come to reflect on the ways in which we received this influence, as we are doing here and now. It is only recently that there has appeared the spirit to discern the true aspect of modern Western thought and literature, as the history of Japanese literature since the Meiji period has been—to put it in the extreme—the history of misunderstanding modern Western literature, for everyone has been busy nourishing themselves on their own arbitrary misunderstandings. Now, when we have finally begun to see some sound and proper instances of reflection and research on modern Western literature, political crisis has broken out. We must somehow discover Japanese principles, and yet it is quite difficult to achieve this. If someone were to ask me whether it were not this very difficulty that was responsible for inaugurating our present type of roundtable discussion, then I would have no reply. Of all the great writers of modern Western literature, I have found Dostoyevsky to be the one with the richest questions. Feeling the need to examine these questions more thoroughly, I quickly discovered Dostoyevsky to be surrounded by layers upon layers of misunderstanding. Both Dostoyevsky and Tolstoy are lionized here, and so it is strange that the Japanese people have so arbitrarily misinterpreted their works. I never felt the slightest desire to embrace the Japanese view of Dostoyevsky, and I still don't even now. Indeed, I have only tried to correct this image of Dostoyevsky as it has been distorted in the style of modern Japanese writers. I have learned many things about Dostoyevsky in examining his path from social revolution to his discovery of the Russian people and Russian God, but for our present purposes I would like to speak about only one of these: this is that Dostoyevsky was *not* someone who expressed modern Russian society or nineteenth-century Russia—a point that Mr. Yoshimitsu has also written about. Rather, Dostoyevsky successfully fought against these things; his works stand as a record of triumph over them. When one realizes this fact, one begins to see with particular clarity the shortcomings of positivist and scientist forms of literary scholarship, which were quite fashionable when we began studying literature. I do not know about mediocre writers, but great writers are always those who have successfully fought against the conventional ideas of their own society and era. The shortcomings of those views in which literature is regarded as a mere expression of its society and era, then, can be found in their neglect of the victories of these great writers. People often criticize Western individualism and rationalism, but isn't it important to see that the great men of the West have successfully fought against these notions? One makes a great fuss over such things because one is fooled by the shallow historical view that states that individualist literature is created during periods of individualism. Western modernity is a tragedy, and thus the West has brilliant tragic actors. In its rush to imitate the West, Japanese modernity is a comedy, for brilliant comic actors appear only in plays. No matter how one examines the social or historical conditions that formed literature, these are merely the dregs or ruins left behind by great writers in their victory. It is impossible in this way to grasp these writers' spirit of triumph. Although we live in the modern age and speak of overcoming modernity, it is clear that the great men of all ages discovered their purpose in life in trying to overcome their own times. In focusing on this fact, of course, we realize the need to fundamentally change the view of history that has so powerfully influenced us. Generally speaking, the modern view of history is a theory of historical change, and yet it seems to me that a theory of the historically unchanging would also be possible. For example, if in the field of mechanics the theory of changes in force is called "dynamic," then a "static" theory about various forces in equilibrium should also be conceivable. I have come to suspect that the weakness of modern man lies in the fact that he has been carried away by the dynamic of historical forces, thus causing him to forget their static quality as well. Of course my thinking here derives in part from the familiarity I have always felt with literature and art, as these always appear in the form of harmony and order. Literature and art appear as an equilibrium rather than as a change of force. Is it impossible to conceive of an extremely propitious situation whereby such harmony and order are achieved by a leveling of forces in the confrontation between the writer and his era? This is what it means for an artist to triumph over his own time. Great men neither submit to their era nor stand apart from it; this relation is rather characterized by a static state of tension. In this way, I have discerned extremely profound analogies among classical texts as well as among great writers of both East and West, ancient and modern. From this standpoint, it seems to me to be an enormous mistake to view history always in terms of change or progress. Always there are the same things, and always people struggle against these things; those who attain this sameness are, in other words, eternal. It is from this standpoint that I have also thought about Japanese history and the classics.

KAWAKAMI: Your comments are extremely important, but I wonder if they must be understood as history.

KOBAYASHI: How should they be understood if not as history?

KAWAKAMI: Rather as something like anthropology in a more universal sense.

KOBAYASHI: Or perhaps as a certain kind of aesthetics.

NISHITANI: As represented in your remarks, the view that history contains both things that change and things that never change can also be seen in the way we think about history today. Yet the question is whether these two aspects of change and changelessness exist separately from each other or always cleave together. If the latter, then even what one calls the "eternal" in the literary world is always a product of history. For example, even great writers, in living through their era, both transcend history and exist utterly within it, and yet it is in this transcendence that they become all the more deeply embedded within history. In this regard, it seems to me that, despite Mr. Kawakami's objections, your remarks should be understood less as anthropology than as history in an even more fundamental sense. Even the notion of eternity cannot be conceived apart from history. It is because we live through the era that we so utterly inhabit that we can encounter the eternal. Eternity is something utterly historical.

KOBAYASHI: But isn't your view of history precisely that of modern dialectics? Modern dialectics belongs to what I call the theory of historical change.

NISHITANI: The notion of dialectics can be conceived in different ways. Even in Hegel, for example, it simply means a theory of change understood as process. But it can also be understood entirely differently.

HAYASHI: As I mentioned last night, I don't believe in the theory of evolution. We are all tired of such evolutionary principles. I was surprised to discover that there are many more things in the world that don't change rather than do. Bashō used the term *fueki ryūkō*—"permanence and change"—but in our education, with its emphasis on evolutionary theory, we were taught only about those things that evolve and change (that is, *ryūkō*) and were thus shielded from the existence of the permanent, or *fueki*. Evolutionary theory is really a modern superstition.

KAWAKAMI: Well, I don't think that Mr. Nishitani is claiming that history is evolutionary. But I would like to ask Mr. Kobayashi the following question. Why, for example, was Kusunoki Masashige born sometime in the second millennium whereas you were born now? How would you explain this phenomenon if not through history?

KOBAYASHI: That's right. Putting all theoretical talk aside, let me say that I have spent these past several years reading Japanese history and have become bored with all its historical interpretations and historical views. History contains something against which our interpretations and historical views are ineffective. Gradually I have come to understand that history remains unmoved by our modern interpretations. It is in this sense that I first recognized the beauty of history. No matter how much we interpret or criticize history in our modern fashion, we can never approach its beauty. The beauty of history lies in the fact that such dead men as Kusunoki Masashige existed in such a form as to surpass all our interpretations of him. To see this form is to understand history. For example, it is absolutely impossible to understand the Kamakura period by determining its nature, how it emerged as a result of the Heian period, and then how it influenced the next period. Regardless of how we explain the Kamakura period, either through such causal interpretations or dialectical interpretations, its form remains unmoved. I have come to understand the importance of sensing this form. No matter how one interprets Mount Fuji, it is necessary when sketching it that one's interpretation not change the mountain's form. It is an important secret that historical facts be seen in just this manner. Works of art from the Kamakura period exist right before our eyes, and their beauty is of an independence and self-sufficiency that surpass all our criticisms and interpretations thereof. I must perceive the customs, manners, and thought of the Kamakura period just as I do these artworks. Such a notion is not mere fancy, nor is it impossible. I believe that this view is quite different from contemporary historicism.

NISHITANI: Yes, it is different.

KOBAYASHI: Recently I feel that I have finally understood Plato's greatness. His theory of ideas is not mere fancy.

NISHITANI: Great writers, for example, are those who have successfully struggled against their own era. Eternal beauty derives mainly from this struggle. One can of course regard such eternity in terms of, say, beautiful form or aspect. As you remark, those who have truly come in touch with eternity from within history did so directly by surpassing in a single leap their own period and its various conditions, whatever these may be. However, these men encountered eternity not through such completed things as form and aspect in their eternal beauty, as you state, but rather by virtue of their own efforts or spirit, which created that form and aspect. Of course man's efforts or spirit appear within these latter, but form and aspect are already completed and belong to the past. Nevertheless, it is *we* who must possess the effort or spirit through which eternally beautiful form and aspect are created. We encounter this same spirit by being placed in our present age and having to live through it.

KOBAYASHI: What do you mean by the words "same spirit"?

NISHITANI: I mean the same spirit that lived in men from long ago. Spirit should be regarded not in terms of aspect or form but rather as something that belongs to us. As someone remarked long ago, "Do not seek the traces of the ancients; instead, seek what they themselves sought"—that is, one must treat the spirit of ancient people as one's own spirit. You just spoke of the utterly permanent, or *fueki*, but this is precisely what I mean by spirit. For example, it is impossible for us today to grasp Plato's thought system as such. Plato is considered a "godlike" philosopher, and we who study philosophy must understand the various concepts of his thought. However, what Plato regarded as the most important issue was philosophy itself in the sense of the

purity of the soul, that is, the very spirit that philosophizes. Without rigorously understanding this point, one fails to grasp the basis of Plato's thought.
It is from this basis that Plato's various concepts derive, and this basis doesn't
change even if today we do not accept some of his thoughts. In our present day many new questions have emerged, and these questions require new
solutions. However, the spirit that constitutes the basis of Platonic philosophy remains utterly unchanged. At the same time, if Plato were born today,
he would no doubt create from that same spirit a different philosophy than
that of the Plato of old. Hence, while it is extremely important to both regard
and revere the beauty of Platonic philosophy today, we must at the same time
occupy our own present position and, in a certain sense, seek what Plato
sought from within our struggle (as you have said) with the present day. Isn't
this latter task also necessary? It indeed appears strange to imitate such a
great man as Plato, but this is of course what we must do if we study philosophy. Accordingly, there exist within history such immutable or eternal things
as form and aspect while at the same time a permanent spirit is also at work
that expresses itself therein. Today we have inherited this spirit and must
make it our own. In this sense, history necessarily changes while remaining
permanence itself. From the historian's position, it is natural to place before
one and regard, as it were, both history in its constant change and those
immutable elements that exist within history. For writers, thinkers, and religious men, however, such an approach is inadequate. In their struggle to
find their own way to live, these people understand that the mutable always
emerges from out of the immutable.

KOBAYASHI: Yes, I understand your point.

NISHITANI: As such, history cannot be conceived apart from the fact that we
exist within it. If history is understood in this way, then wouldn't the mutable
and the immutable that I just mentioned always cleave together as one?

KOBAYASHI: I understand your point, but since our viewpoints are so different
from each other, this becomes a fruitless argument. Basically, the question
is whether one privileges the traces of the ancients or those places that they
sought after, but here the meaning of such terms as "traces" and "places" has
changed. However, I was merely speaking about my own personal experiences for your reference. The past is the past; if Plato were born today, he
would surely create a new philosophy. Since I live in the present, I also create
new things. But is it the case that, as based on the reasonable notion that I
will and indeed must create newer things than did the ancients, those things
will actually be created? Is it not the case that the creative standpoint actually
has no need of the new? The ancients achieved everything possible in the
classics. The fact that we people today exist in the present age and need different materials to create simply means that different things will be created.
I am thus humbled by the fact that we are absolutely incapable of achiev-

ing anything that surpasses the achievements of the ancients. I feel that this sense of humility is lacking among people today. We readily embrace our utterly meaningless sense of superiority in having been born in the present day. We flatter ourselves by thinking that, while the ancients were great, we people of the present still have other tasks before us and different paths to explore. Nevertheless, our self-flattery characteristically disappears when we actually look at the work of a great artist. For example, a *tanka* poet such as Masaoka Shiki, who deeply understood the *Man'yōshū*, wrote poetry based on his insight into the incomparable greatness of this collection. In other words, the position that Shiki established allowed him to firmly recognize the classics as classics.

NISHITANI: Speaking from my own experience, I can tell you that in philosophy as well, virtually everyone at the start immerses themselves in the classics. One gets a sense of the greatness of such philosophers as Plato and Kant, for example, and then studies them with the aim of coming in touch with their spirit. At the same time, however, one constantly looks back at and problematizes oneself while also reflecting on the period and society within which one exists. Although it may thus be said that one fails to truly grasp Plato or Kant, there are nevertheless certain things within one that cannot be satisfied by these philosophers. One feels the need to at some point stop following the traces of others, even those of Plato and Kant. While I am speaking here of my own experience, I do think that this is something that everyone who studies philosophy (with the exception of historians of philosophy) has experienced at one time or another. However, Plato and Kant were great philosophers who took things as far as they could go, as everyone who studies philosophy knows. In such cases, I believe that one begins to truly understand the greatness of these philosophers only by struggling to resolve the questions that have been given to one from the basis of one's own present standpoint. Plato's thought will shine quietly for all eternity. When one considers this fact, it is easy to feel that one's own efforts are meaningless. Yet isn't it the case that one first discovers Plato's footprints from within one's own struggle to deal with such questions in one's own fashion? Without this process one simply regards eternity as beautiful form, which makes me wonder if the beauty of Plato's thought is truly being grasped.

YOSHIMITSU: I am from the same field of philosophy, or perhaps theology, as Mr. Nishitani, and yet from this perspective I arrive at the same conclusions as those of Mr. Kobayashi. At its limit, Mr. Nishitani's position, like that of Mr. Kobayashi, contains a metaphysical element whereby only the meaning of the soul is understood—the soul directly attains the soul—and external historical conditions are seen as mere dregs. Mr. Kobayashi no doubt regards the soul from the perspective of art. I regard the soul from the perspective of faith or theology, which is to say on the basis of Kierkegaard's spiritual category of *die Gleichzeitigkeit*, or simultaneity, that is, spirit is understood through spirit. If one can directly come in touch with the greatness of the soul or the reality of spirit, then ultimately modern philology, scholarship based on historical records, and many other viewpoints of objective truth come to fall beneath one's feet, thereby allowing one single thing to appear. Both scholarly and spiritual experience teach that what modern forms of interpretation and understanding try to understand in terms of their own measure is utterly false. The soul defies all dogmatism and exceeds the limits of criticism and interpretation. It also represents the ultimate response to what Mr. Kawakami referred to as "anthropology." Last night we discussed the theory of evolution, but in fact the reason I reject this way of thinking—putting aside the question of evolution in a biological sense—is that it has become increasingly clear in the spiritual world that the notion of "evolution" is false. It seems that herein lies the question of the reality of the soul. Ultimately, to understand the soul is to engage in metaphysics. The spirit or soul is not something that can be proved to one by others. Rather, the spirit posits itself as reality, and it is from this perspective that it participates in history. What one calls "history," therefore, is not meaningless. History, in other words, is that which takes the soul as its subject, it is the place within which the soul is situated. It is in this place that we undergo the same struggles as the soul and are given the same tasks. The classics are the classics: to follow and yet struggle with them in our own fashion represents what Mr. Nishitani calls our struggle and our task. I believe that we must metaphysically undertake this task that is always humbly given to us rather than ask what the ancients failed to achieve.

NISHITANI: I am not speaking of any ambition to achieve something that the ancients did not. I personally would have no objections whatsoever to immersing myself in every line of Plato's texts. In all honesty, I would be content to walk the very same paths as the great men of old. However, it seems to me that the essence of philosophy is such that we cannot and must not do this. This question can be conceived differently in the case of artistic appreciation or religious faith, although I would have my doubts about this. In any case, I would also question whether the ways of ancient men can be truly grasped outside of the real life within which one is placed. I admit that one can derive satisfaction by becoming one with the ways of the ancients, and in this respect I have no intent of self-conceit. However, it seems to me that one only begins to truly come in touch with the footsteps of the ancients by walking one's own path oneself.

KOBAYASHI: I am not unfamiliar with the position of philosophers. Previously mention was made of a preference for the notion of aesthetics rather than that of historical philosophy. Although I have never really studied this subject, the aesthetics that has been most influential for me is that of Bergson, despite the fact that he didn't especially write on aesthetics. What attracts me to Bergson is his lack of ambiguity, as can be found in the aesthetics of other philosophers. Bergson writes extremely clearly, without any such ambiguous terms as, for example, "concrete universal." If man could eliminate all the inevitable obstacles within his social life and approach the true shape of real life, then he would grasp beauty. It is difficult work for human consciousness to truly come in touch with such existence. Were this work easy, then any-body could do it, anybody could become an artist, and artists would thus no longer be necessary: such is the insight of a simple and clear aesthetics. I am deeply attracted to Bergson's viewpoint, in which historical and social beings are seen as masked and metaphysics is created directly from analyses of pure perception. Bergson was once popular, but the time will surely come again when he is read seriously in our country. However, this could be a fleeting dream. We moderns have stuffed inside our heads vast historical charts and maps, but these things are like demons that must be destroyed and aban-doned in our efforts to attain a certain reality.

NISHITANI: In a basic sense, that is more or less what I have been saying. It seems that this is what people mean today when they speak of surmounting historicism.

SUZUKI: As someone who specializes in the field of history, I feel that I under-stand Mr. Kobayashi's historical view. History does not consist of that which passes away; rather, there is something that, while passing away, nevertheless does not pass away. Although we historians also believe that history con-sists in eternal stillness, we must of course conceive of it as change. In other words, even the immutable must necessarily be grasped in terms of change. Nevertheless, it is certainly true that the historical views of the past, in their superficiality, made too much of change. Hence, it is extremely meaningful in our present age to stress, even in our scholarship, the immutable in history. We historians have also considered this point. We do not conceive of change in terms of evolution or progress. We have expressed this notion of change through the term "development," but these days even this word has not been fully accepted. Rather, there has been a demand to somehow go beyond the notion of development. Or, indeed, it is perhaps the case that the overcom-ing of modernity in the field of historiography consists in overcoming this notion of development. But it seems to me that it is extremely difficult to overcome this notion in one's scholarship, and historians have struggled with the fact that it is not easy to eliminate this concept. Mr. Kobayashi, where do you see instances of such immutability within the mutable—or what we might call "eternal permanence"—in the context of history?

KOBAYASHI: There exists neither time nor development in our admiration and respect for things. History resembles the classics in the sense that the artist's creative position is such that he invariably experiences the traces of the ancients as a model or standard. Here both time and development disappear. This message is taught even in the layman's experience of appreciating the classics. Such is our everyday experience.

SUZUKI: Among historians, it was Ranke who said that no one could write better historical accounts than Thucydides, just as no one could write better tragedies than Sophocles. As Ranke famously said, however, all ages are linked to God, which is to say that every age is different and yet absolute, that is, they are all linked to eternity. It seems to me that Ranke meant here that each era possesses its own unique characteristics—something proper to it that is utterly different from other eras—while at the same time being linked to eternity. I am not claiming that such eternity is to be found by eliminating the particular features of each era. Rather, it seems to me that one must conceive of the historical elements proper to each period while at the same time grasping those eternal elements that exist therein. In other words, eternity exists within the mutable rather than in the immutable.

KOBAYASHI: I think that's right.

SUZUKI: I was interested in your remark that creation consists not in the birth of something new but rather in the nonnecessity of the new. When I heard this, I recalled Winckelmann's statement that "creation is imitation." Is the meaning of Winckelmann's remark the same as your own?

KOBAYASHI: Yes, I believe it is the same.

THE PROBLEM OF CIVILIZATION
AND SPECIALIZATION

KAWAKAMI: Well, I think that the present exchange among these four gentlemen can more or less be summarized by the position that "history is a succession of perfection," if you will forgive my infelicitous phrasing. In his initial remarks, Mr. Kobayashi stated that Japanese civilization of the Meiji period incorporated too much imperfect Western culture as its material. In one respect, then, Meiji civilization assumed an unwholesome form, and today this must be eliminated. That is to say, the time has now come for us to reflect on Western civilization, as the demands from our external political situation are at one with the intrinsic demand that the various items of civilization now available be arranged in one complete and living form. Now then, I would like at this time to make the conversation slightly more concrete, as based on examples and personal experiences, and hear from your various perspectives about the incorporation of Western culture in its imperfect forms within Meiji civilization. Perhaps Mr. Kamei, who has written so extensively on this subject, might be kind enough to start things off for us.

KAMEI: While I don't have any set views here, it is important to recall that the opening of the country in the Meiji period took place in the context of Europe's nineteenth century, that is, the era in which European culture came to a close. I am convinced that one of the features of post-Meiji civilization is, in a nutshell, the loss of man's human nature as a whole. Various kinds of work became extremely specialized at this time, with specialists appearing one after the other. By becoming expert in their own fields, these specialists lost sight of a certain universality that they were supposed to attain. Specialists became cripples. This situation in Europe rapidly made its way to Japan, leading to what I regard as a major consequence: Japan's loss of spiritual unity. Naturally, there were people who fought against this tendency. Let me cite one example here so as to illustrate my point: Uchimura Kanzō was a fisheries technician who studied the science of fisheries, and without any so-called specialization sought the universal—that is, God—that dwelled within his work. Broadly interpreting the notion of theology, Uchimura stated that such fields as political science, economics, philosophy, historiography, and the natural sciences were correct only as part of theology. Although Uchimura went to the United States and entered divinity school, he wanted to become a great amateur or layman rather than to specialize as a pastor. In whatever work he did, Uchimura wished to remain pure to God, who dwelled therein, and it was with this conviction that he returned to Japan. Uchimura represents one example of Japan's struggle with modern European civilization. Since the time of civilization and enlightenment, various kinds of technology and knowledge rapidly entered Japan, where they were soon mastered. However, the excessive focus on these objects of specialization brought about a state in which man's metaphysical needs, such as one's internal service to the gods and Buddha, came to be completely absent. This tendency seems to have grown steadily worse from the Meiji to Taishō periods. Although intellectual curiosity about the world increased all the more during this time, the kind of personality that could grasp this knowledge grew extremely deformed. In other words, it was as if man did not exist. Another factor leading to this situation was the persistent utilitarianism that haunted civilization and enlightenment, in which only useful things were employed for immediate effect. Utilitarianism gave rise to countless specialists as well as academic Scholastic philosophers, thus leading to the disappearance of human nature as a whole, which itself might be called the sage of real life. When all is said and done, it is significant that we have lost sight of the Most High, which spirit must embrace. As I said, the essay I presented earlier consists of my extraction of the signs of decay of civilization and enlightenment.

KAWAKAMI: I would like to know what Mr. Shimomura and Mr. Kikuchi think about this loss of human nature as a whole, as resulting from scientific specialization.

SHIMOMURA: It is obvious that everything in modernity becomes specialized or differentiated. Nevertheless, such differentiation or specialization is not directly equivalent to decadence.

KAMEI: Specialization is not directly equivalent to decadence, for something is doubtless served by specialization. Indeed, I wonder if decadence does not lie in overlooking this something. The reason I raised the example of Uchimura Kanzō is because Uchimura tried to recover his own human nature as a whole through his belief in God and by acting as God's servant while at the same time working as a fisheries technician. In other words, my point is that Uchimura represents a great struggle against civilization and enlightenment.

SHIMOMURA: Losing sight of the whole in the interest of specialization certainly represents one form of corruption. We must recognize, however, that specialization is necessary and that its nature is one of development. This is an important point, which relates especially to the nature of the modern spirit as well as various other modern issues.

MOROI: What this means, I believe, is that specialization concerns basic attitudes about our lives, as Mr. Kobayashi remarked. It is not a question of whether we need specialists or not.

KOBAYASHI: That's right.

MOROI: I don't recall what you said, but our interpretation of this specialization is a secondary matter compared to these attitudes, which in any case is the most basic thing in our lives. I fully understand the remarks made by Mr. Kobayashi and Mr. Kamei. When I went to study in Europe, I too very much felt that Europeans think about how different they are from others in order to express their selves. I found it intolerable that Europeans devoted all their efforts to this. Art certainly does not consist in distinguishing oneself from others by poking so finely at individual differences. First of all, it is crucial to understand that people are about 90 percent the same. I actually couldn't stand being in Europe. In a musical sense, Japan is very limited, and in many ways one is blessed to be in Germany. But I felt strongly about returning to Japan. Such things as attitude are the most basic issues of life, and they don't lead to the question of whether specialists are unnecessary.

SHIMOMURA: The specialization of modern culture is a serious problem and is directly related to both the loss of unity of the so-called modern worldview and the question of overcoming modernity, as raised in the essays of Mr. Nishitani and Mr. Yoshimitsu. For example, the post-Renaissance, or *kinsei*, period is generally described in terms of the separation between science and religion, such that these two are seen as oppositional or contradictory to one another. But one must consider the nature of this conflict or contradiction. Viewed today, such a conflict appears as nothing more than an opposition between a certain religious dogma and a certain scientific theory; it was in a sense a conflict between one philosophy and another, or one science and another. This wasn't necessarily a real conflict between religion and science. Any science that conflicts with religion is not actually science but rather metaphysics or philosophy, just as any religion that conflicts with science is not actually religion but a mere sciencelike religion, that is, not a pure religion.

This problem is eliminated in modernity. In other words, in modernity science became special science and thus lost its status as a naive metaphysics, while religion lost its status as a naive science. In this sense, the specialization of learning along with the independence of science from religion and metaphysics marked the purification of science. At the same time, religion also came to be purified as pure religion. In the Middle Ages, for example, theologians raised various theological objections against the notion that the earth was round or that it moved. Here the standpoint of theology was actually nothing more than naive science, for from a religious perspective, such matters regarding the earth would be of no concern. In other words, in modernity religion lost its status as a naive science while science lost its status as a naive metaphysics. In this way, science first became aware of its own standpoint and established itself as such. Although the Middle Ages also recognized a distinction between physics and metaphysics, this was nevertheless a difference in rank and thus allowed for continuity between these realms. It is in the severing of this continuity that we see the specifically modern character of modern science. This point is related to the claim that the post-Renaissance period experienced a loss of unity in its worldview, in contrast to the Middle Ages, when such a unity still existed. The so-called disunity of the post-Renaissance period is thus not simply negative, for we must recognize the positive significance of religion and science becoming purified of one another by science losing its status as a general metaphysics and religion losing its status as a special science. To speak of something negatively as lacking unity is to say positively that it has become purified. In this sense, we must acknowledge that so-called specialization represents the positive character of the modern spirit. This of course does not settle the issue, however, for it is undeniable that specialization as such possesses the negative feature of being the opposite of unification. Of course specialization is not the final state of things, as there must be unity. Thus arises the concrete problem of overcoming modernity. However, I believe that it is meaningless as well as impossible to seek that unity by returning to the past for the unity of the Middle Ages. Here we need a negatively mediating relation, as it were, that takes into account physics and metaphysics and science and theology (in the broad sense of the term) in their independence rather than positing these fields as immediately connected or continuous. In this regard, specialization too is of fundamental significance.

KAMEI: According to my own real-life experiences, I believe that someone who is considered an excellent physician on the strength of his diagnosis of a disease also makes an excellent life teacher. I am convinced that one can become an excellent physician only by being a good teacher of life. Medicine is called the healing art; it represents the path of the Mahayana bodhisattva. In other words, I regard the loss of this awareness as the mortal wound inflicted by civilization and enlightenment. Various opinions have been expressed from the perspective of cultural history about our path of recovery, but I would return to the question of our reconfirmation of the Most High, as discussed yesterday. We have indeed recently seen a striking tendency for specialists to acquire all sorts of knowledge in a variety of fields. For form's sake, let me state my disapproval of this. For example, the bravest and most accomplished soldier on the battlefield unwittingly says the most penetrating things about life. In other words, this soldier understands both this world and God by virtue of his specialization as well as by his own life and death. I wish that all specialists could possess such understanding rather than for the soldier to speak superficially about politics and literature. I do not approve of any so-called overcoming of specialization through the vague spread of knowledge. I mentioned earlier that civilization and enlightenment has produced a group of crippled specialists, but I should add here that it has also produced some pretentious cripples who are not specialists but who are garrulous about everything.

THE ESSENCE OF CIVILIZATION AND ENLIGHTENMENT IN THE MEIJI PERIOD

HAYASHI: I see civilization and enlightenment in terms of Japan's adoption of European culture and its consequent submission to Europe following the Meiji Restoration. From an international perspective, the Meiji Restoration was both the Orient's final resistance and a brilliant victory against the West. India was destroyed and China defeated, but Japan alone was able to stem the tide of the West. In order to survive in its resistance against Europe, however, Japan was forced to accept European culture in the sense of its practical views. Civilization and enlightenment is nothing more than a culture of practical objects; there is nothing culturally fundamental within it. As such, Japan's resistance against civilization and enlightenment already began from the second decade of the Meiji period, as manifested in the call to oppose its culture of utility and return to what is fundamental in culture. Such an attitude can be seen in such figures as Uchimura Kanzō, Okakura Tenshin, Saigō Takamori, and General Nogi. Yet all those who raised this cry were defeated by the times, as civilization and enlightenment continued to claim victory. It seems that the Greater East Asia War has managed to put an end to civilization and enlightenment, but there are still many in Japan who endorse this way of thinking.

NISHITANI: Perhaps you are correct, but the one problem here is that Japan, in order to survive, was forced to steadily incorporate a Western-style form of practical organization in such fields as science, technology, economics, and government. In truth, it was in this way that Japan was able to live on. At the same time, however, there was something about civilization and enlightenment that attracted people at this time, and no doubt Western culture was also considered prestigious. Putting aside the ideas of such figures as Itō Hirobumi, most people in Japan did not simply feel that they could abandon Western culture if it was not necessary; even when they went dancing, for example, I suspect that there was something about that culture that attracted them. This trend continues even today. It seems to me, then, that the issue also involves why Western culture has so fascinated and captivated many Japanese people and continues to do so today.

HAYASHI: Civilization and enlightenment can be seen in such forms of expediency as, for example, mobilizing writers to give lectures or allowing scientists to wear shorts.

SUZUKI: In this respect, it is true that civilization and enlightenment was especially necessary for Meiji-period Japan, that it had to transform Japan into a great modern power, and that, as Mr. Nishitani just remarked, a powerful tendency existed among the Japanese people at the time to regard Western culture as prestigious. In addition to these factors, however, most people around the world in the late nineteenth century believed that this type of civilization—which can be called "material civilization," or simply "civilization"—was just. Such a worldview was then dominant. For example, the notion of utility was seen as extremely important. This worldview also dominated all of Europe at this time. Yet the reason that people in Japan today have come to criticize civilization and enlightenment goes beyond the desire to return to their Japanese roots; it is also related to the fact that civilization and enlightenment has come to be criticized in Europe, and that civilization has come to be seen as simultaneously an object of trust and criticism.

HAYASHI: Thinkers at the time of the Meiji Restoration were not so susceptible or loyal to Western thought as they are today.

SUZUKI: During the Meiji period, the Japanese understanding of Europe was extremely fragmentary and superficial and hardly penetrated to the root of things. This was a serious mistake. As a result, while it is perfectly fine to construct Japanese things, it seems to me that we must also gain a more thorough understanding of Europe so as to surmount civilization and enlightenment.

HAYASHI: That sounds excellent.

SUZUKI: Specializing in Western history has impressed upon me the need to gain a truly fundamental understanding of Europe.

HAYASHI: In addition to Europe, there is also the need for a greater understanding of China and India.

NISHITANI: Even in the case of thought, the ideas of, say, Spencer appear quite inferior when seen today. Particularly when set against ancient Japanese Buddhist thought, Spencer's ideas are incomparably superficial. Yet why were Buddhist and Confucian thought abandoned while such superficial ideas grew popular and were treasured; why did those ideas so captivate people at the time? Here lies the problem. In feudal times, distinctions in rank existed between the military, agricultural, industrial, and mercantile classes. The transition from this period, in which the lives of the common people were at the mercy of the samurai, to a period of general equality and freedom and popular rights was marked, in a negative sense, by individualism and liberalism. Without such an experience, however, it would have been impossible for Japan to achieve unity in the form of an emperor-based nation-state.

HAYASHI: All things considered, this transition was one of decadence.

NISHITANI: But isn't civilization and enlightenment bound up with freedom and popular rights?

HAYASHI: No, civilization and enlightenment was a bureaucratic policy—it was state policy, so to speak—whereas the Liberal Party movement was a form of resistance against this clan government principle.

NISHITANI: Yet weren't both civilization and enlightenment and freedom and popular rights bound up with the Enlightenment thought of the eighteenth-century West, which subsequently entered Japan?

HAYASHI: No. Only disastrous conclusions can come about when scientists subjectively make unreasonable connections.

NISHITANI: My point is that, while individualism has today become extremely negative, it nevertheless greatly contributed as an idea to the abolition of the frozen class distinctions of the feudal period.

HAYASHI: When Shimazaki Tōson went to France, what most surprised him was that the class system was still quite harsh. What surprised me when I went to Beijing was also the harsh remnants of the class system. This system no longer remains in Japan, however. Its abolition can certainly not be attributed to the freedom and popular rights movement but rather to the Meiji Restoration. The Meiji Restoration was a revival of the old. For the royalists at this time, the model for abolishing the class system was certainly not France or the United States. Rather, the prototype they had in mind was ancient Japan, a classless period in which the people directly served the emperor. Did such Western-style awareness of the individual once exist in Japanese history? Furthermore, I believe that we must reexamine whether the notion of the individual was in fact negated during the Edo period under Japan's feudal system.

THE WEST WITHIN US

KAWAKAMI: Mr. Suzuki, for example, stated that we must examine whether Western civilization has in and of itself reached an impasse. In any case, since we have studied certain types of Western literature and pursued the paths of Western writers, we have listened to these writers confess that Western literature has, from the nineteenth to twentieth centuries, reached an impasse and is now in the process of collapse. While listening to these confessions, however, we have also sensed our own unfamiliarity with Western literature. In any event, we must now distance ourselves from the Western literature that we had previously known so as to examine it more objectively. Here arises the question of self-expression in regard to how we should express this literature, for our expressions must at all costs still follow the language of our Western teachers of old. Although we can use such means of expression for the time being, there is now something unsatisfying about this, for we wish to use more of our own language. That is to say, we wish to—and believe we now can—express ourselves in a language based on our own immaculate tradition. It seems to me that this is more or less our present situation, but what do others think?

Mr. Miyoshi, you have for example recently written the very direct, unadorned, and forceful poem "News of Victory Arrives" [Shōhō itaru] while at the same time devoting yourself to translating Francis Jammes. Do you not feel any contradictions in these activities?

MIYOSHI: When I write, I generally feel the same way as when I speak to someone directly, and thus I don't feel any contradiction. When I read the newspaper, for example, I'm not particularly conscious that its language is Japanese. Likewise, I'm not at all conscious of where words come from when I write. I write in a very natural, everyday language, but when I read foreign works, as for example those of Jammes, I occasionally find passages that are unnatural and unclear, or are unpleasant. I like Jammes' writing, but there will always be such passages no matter how much one likes a poet. Although I like Jammes because such unpleasant passages are relatively rare, there are still lines that are incomprehensible to me. First of all, I do not understand the Catholic faith in God, and this is perhaps the most crucial part of Jammes. Thus, my mind works very differently when I write my own work as compared to when I read Jammes. No direct link exists for me between creation and reading, or between those things that I write and those I read. Although I myself cannot say how much I have been influenced by Jammes, it is probably very little. What is directly linked to my own writings are Japanese works, that is, works written in the Japanese language. In other words, because of the Japanese language itself, Jammes appeals to me only in his influence through translation, that is, through the Japanese national language into which his writings have been rendered. Yesterday Mr. Kawakami called me a craftsman, by which he meant that the making of a poem is exactly the same as a craftsman making something with his own hands. In my own case, any substantial influence and concern can only take place through the immediacy of the Japanese language.

NISHITANI: Speaking from my own experience, I tried to read the Japanese classics and literature of the past when I was in high school and college, but nothing really struck me. In terms of my own tastes, nothing appealed to me except Bashō and the *Man'yōshū*; my indifference extended even to such works as the *Kojiki*. In contrast, I read Western literature with the sense that it had been written especially for me. What do you gentlemen who are engaged with literature think about this situation?

KOBAYASHI: You raise an important question. Such experience is extremely common and no doubt shared by everyone our age. We all found Western works interesting, whereas even those works of Japanese literature influenced by modern Western literature were boring. It was the original that was interesting, whereas those Japanese works merely strove after them—and no one read the classics. To put it rather crudely, I have grown increasingly bored by thought the more mature I have become. In other words, what I previously found so interesting about Western works were the opinions, criticisms, interpretations, and analyses. It was from this interest that I learned as much as I could about these works. That is what I thought. In practice, I came to understand that theories can be applied to anything, and thus they came to bore me. Gradually I have come to feel such things as literature and thought bodily rather than intellectually. I have grown bored with the written content or events in literary works and now regard literature as an object of art, to be sensed by its form through sight and touch. Ultimately, the Japanese classics can be understood only in this way. There is but one absolute life, and the most important thing is to come in touch with this life. This must be done through the body, as absolute life cannot be understood intellectually. We must mature to this point in order to understand the Japanese classics. Young people are daydreamers and idealists and thus are naturally bored by the classics. The classics are written in such a way that one does not have to be clever in order to understand them. They contain nothing that could satisfy a young person's desire for knowledge and criticism. If we do not mature in such a way as to outgrow the novelty of such things as thought, ideas, theories, criticism, and interpretation, however, then the beauty of the classics will remain forever hidden. Regardless of how much one advertises the importance of the classics, it is impossible to directly introduce these works to today's youth. This is impossible no matter how much Japanese classical scholars keep up with the times and shout out the value of these works.

NISHITANI: Speaking from my own experience, I read Western novels with the sense that I was coming in touch with living people rather than understanding ideas or theories. This may well have been a mere youthful impression on my part, but that's what I felt. In contrast, such works as *Genji monogatari* [*The Tale of Genji*] lacked any characters in which we could see our own counterparts. Rather, it was foreign literature that provided us with the more vivid impressions. In engrossing myself in foreign novels, I did not think of their beauty or artistic merit but felt instead as if I were coming in touch with my own pent-up feelings. It seems to me that therein lay the charm of such works.

KOBAYASHI: As a youth one believes in ideas, which become very vivid in one's burning enthusiasm for them. I fully understand your point and agree with it. However, the striving of Japanese youths after Western literature was directed at modern Western poetry and fiction rather than at Greek tragedy. In effect, then, the surmounting of modernity is the surmounting of Western modernity. There is no problem in surmounting Japanese modernity. To slightly change the topic, both your essay and that of Mr. Yoshimitsu are extremely difficult. I would go so far as to say that these essays lack the sensuality of the Japanese people's language. We feel that philosophers are truly indifferent to our fate of writing in the national language. Since this language is the traditional language of Japan, no matter how sincerely or logically expressed, its flavor must appear in one's style as that which can be achieved only by Japanese people. This is what writers always aim for in their trade. It is linked to literary reality, and so either moves people or leaves them unmoved. Thought is contained within this literary reality. Philosophers are extremely nonchalant in this regard. If this attitude is not conquered, however, it strikes me that Japanese philosophy will never truly be reborn as Japanese philosophy. What are your thoughts on this?

NISHITANI: This is a real problem for us philosophers as well, and others constantly raise this same point. Certainly we don't find the present situation acceptable either. First of all, the language of philosophy is extremely difficult. I admit that at times specialists in philosophy will employ words that even other specialists cannot understand, and this is regrettable. However, generally all of us have studied Western philosophy, and the philosophy we practice now never previously existed in the Orient. Earlier I raised the question of Spencer's lionization. Because of the particularity of Western scholarship—that is, its particularity as learning in the broad sense here of science or *Wissenschaft*—such superficial ideas as those of Spencer have captivated people and replaced more profound philosophical principles, as for example those of Buddhism. In any event, we philosophers in Japan now find ourselves caught up in this situation as adopted or inherited from the West. In this context, it is extremely difficult for us to express our thought through only the Japanese words of the past. Even when we forcibly restrict ourselves to these words, it only results in greater misunderstanding. Hence, we have naturally come to express ourselves by creating new words in Japanese. The fact is that we lack the time to write in a language that would be easily understandable to most Japanese people. Frankly speaking, philosophers in Japan feel as if our interlocutors are Western thinkers, and we wish to advance beyond their insights. Our first thought is to break through the impasse that these thinkers have arrived at rather than to make ourselves understood by most Japanese people. For now, we can only press on in this manner. If in this process philosophy were truly to arrive in Japan, then it seems to me that a different form of practice would naturally emerge in time. Earlier you used the word "sensuous," Mr. Kobayashi, but even now there has appeared in the works of Japan's best philosophers a sensuality every bit the equal to that of foreign philosophers. It is simply that such sensuality manifests itself differently in the case of literature and philosophy. What I find so unfortunate in contemporary Japanese literature and philosophy is the absence of any major figure who occupies a middle space between philosophy and literature, such as Pascal or Nietzsche. It is the fault of both literature and philosophy that we have not prepared the ground for the emergence of such figures.

YOSHIMITSU: This might appear somewhat as self-justification on my part, but when I write I am intent only on the necessity and truth of thought. Writing for me is the same as the scientist's devotion to his work. However, it is due to the influence of German writings that we philosophers have come to write such prose. Although my own prose is not very standard, it seems to me that philosophical essays differ from art in their enthusiasm for a certain kind of intellectual abstraction. While philosophy does possess artistic qualities, it is nevertheless closer to the scientist's position in its logical pursuit of truth. I think we must continue to outgrow this logical pursuit of truth and go farther. However, I for one lack the time for this task. Something must be done in this regard, but my efforts are devoted elsewhere. Frankly speaking, although philosophical works exist that are written in an easily comprehensible manner, I find these a bit unpleasant because it seems as if one is teaching from a superior position. It is decadent to try to make oneself understood. Rather, when seriously undertaken, one's utmost efforts necessarily result in comprehensible Japanese. I apologize for my own trivial self-justification here, but of course something must be done about this problem.

KAWAKAMI: In the context of the literary world, I am a poor stylist. If one aims in one's writing for the "whole man," as Mr. Kamei remarked earlier, or for "spiritual improvement," as Mr. Kobayashi would say, then one's prose naturally becomes easily comprehensible. There is no particular need to aim for simplification or popularization. Thus, even Mr. Yoshimitsu's "earnest pursuit of the truth" naturally aims for a simple and fine style because of its seriousness and authenticity.

KOBAYASHI: I cannot agree that one should strive for simplicity in one's writing. For example, although Bergson's writing is simple, he does not strive to make it so. In other words, his style is not colloquial, and because of this it is clear but not necessarily easy to understand. However, Bergson interests me because he states things clearly while completely avoiding the traditional language of philosophers. He restricts technical terms to a very exact language, in which conceptual determinations are based on positive science. While understanding of the exact meaning of even one philosophical term requires a vast amount of preliminary knowledge about the history of philosophy, Bergson never uses such words. He writes in a clear literary style even in those cases where the inexpressible must finally be encountered (which is the fate of metaphysics).

NISHITANI: This perhaps has less to do with Bergson's style than with his thought itself, which is based on the notion of life. Really it is only Bergson who writes in such an easily comprehensible manner.

YOSHIMITSU: Actually, the French philosophical tradition is linked to the literary tradition of Latin humanism. In France, the history of philosophy exists within literary history. In a certain sense, German philosophy is an extension of Scholastic philosophy. Scholastic philosophy regards God's truth clearly, in the manner of scientists, and treats this truth objectively, in the manner of logicians and scientists. This is more or less Scholasticism. Yet this philosophy is faithful to ideas. If I may engage in a bit of self-justification, I regard my own devoted task as grasping God's existence. Even though my writing is complex, those things that I leave unsaid are quite clear. Yet insofar as this writing involves metaphysical thinking, it leads to a poetic vision. I am in any case engrossed in what might be called internal music.

SUZUKI: I would like to offer my impressions on this question of literature. Since I lack the understanding for such things as literature and art, my thoughts might be very different from those of the writers assembled here. But I have noticed as something related to my own field the recent appearance in the West of a kind of medievalism, which has appeared in a variety of domains. It seems that such medievalism can be seen even in literary and art movements. Yesterday we discussed the Renaissance, from which emerged the dominant course of modern art, as for example naturalism and realism. But recently there have appeared movements that aim at a kind of resistance against these, as can be seen for example in symbolism as well as in the reaction of surrealism against realism and expressionism against impressionism. Even in the domain of aesthetics, aesthetic movements have arisen that seek to discover a principle of beauty completely unlike that of the modern principle. Whereas the modern notion of beauty consists in fidelity to nature, medieval art stands on the principle of abstract beauty, as in Worringer's Gothic aesthetics. It seems to me that such medievalism signifies a kind of overcoming of modernity in the art movement.

These movements were for a time also influential in Japan. Particularly in painting, such schools as cubism, expressionism, and surrealism were once popular. We could not understand such works at all, as they did not strike or appeal to us. We believed that there was something false or inauthentic about such art. In Japan, especially, that art was introduced with the same meaning as the naturalism and realism of long ago. Its reception often took place as if merely translating it, without any understanding of what was fundamentally at stake. Nevertheless, I have grave doubts as to whether even in the West these movements have developed in any real way, for they may have just gone around in circles.

In any event, such movements advocating a kind of overcoming of modernity have already appeared in the past. In his comments yesterday, Mr. Moroi seemed to touch precisely upon, for example, the presence of certain real or eternal elements even within modern art. To conceive of a new art movement without understanding such elements clearly reveals some basic flaws. These movements surely could not produce any real overcoming of modernity.

In this respect, Mr. Kobayashi's earlier comments were highly suggestive. For example, he mentioned how Dostoyevsky is conceived in the context of modernity as struggling against or overcoming his own era. Regardless of whether these are historical views, it seems that an understanding of such conceptions offers us a hint about new directions for art. My own layman's impression is that more movements that strive to overcome modernity will continue to appear.

KOBAYASHI: In Romain Rolland's book on Millet, he recounts how Millet, destitute, hopeless, and ready to die, painted a picture of an artist committing suicide, whereupon he then decided not to commit suicide himself. This must be a true story since it was written by Rolland. Although this is an extreme example, it aptly reveals the nature of the artist's work. From our own standpoint of overcoming modernity, we must recognize that modernity is not something that can simply be replaced because of its faults. Modern man can triumph over modernity only through modernity. The materials that have been given to us lie before us today, and I believe that the key to victory must be sought within them.

AMERICANISM AND MODERNISM

KAWAKAMI: Cubism and expressionism are hysteric manifestations that naturally appeared as an extension of nineteenth-century European art. When these movements came to Japan, however, they were not considered to be hysteric at all. Japan introduced these movements in the same way it did realism, and it also outgrew them in the same way. Thus, although Japan fully incorporated nineteenth-century Western culture, it neither truly learned that culture nor followed its more productive or developmental aspects. Mr. Tsumura, you argue in your essay that Japanese culture here reveals its most hasty and inverted aspects, but don't you have something in mind here? In other words, take for example American culture. I can't recall your interpretation, but I see this culture as a certain development of European culture. You write that one of the oddest aspects of Japanese culture lies in the fact that American culture was introduced by Japan's "modern boys" and "modern girls," who led strange, rootless lives. But shouldn't you point out that such oddness is not attributable to this frivolous race of "modern boys" and "modern girls" and that, in any event, many other such instances can be found within what is considered to be Japan's first-rate culture?

NISHITANI: I read your essay with interest, Mr. Tsumura, but I wondered why Americanism has spread throughout not only Japan but even Europe as well. What characteristics of Americanism . . . ?

TSUMURA: There are many reasons for the spread of Americanism in Europe. First of all, the daily impoverishment and moral confusion in post–World War I Europe generally laid the ground for its reception of American cinema with all its optimism, speed, and eroticism. It was this war that provided the decisive opportunity for American film to make inroads into Europe. Second, there was the high productivity of the American film industry, which meant that films received an enormous amount of capital. Yet this was not simply a question of mass production; from the perspective of quality as well, the industry was able to invest up to one to two million dollars per film. Such figures were impossible in Europe, and so Europeans were naturally captivated by these films. Third, there was the important factor that the United States lacked its own traditional culture. That is to say, in order for American film to candidly reflect this fact, it had to create a global universality that was easy to appreciate. Since American manners, customs, and morality were not as complex as those of Europe, the cinema had to create these in a way that would be easily understood by all peoples. For example, although American film has long been extremely influential in East Asia, its westerns and comedies would be easily understood when shown to, say, the natives of Dutch India and Malaya. Basically, the spirit of American cinema consists in the privileging of speed and movement and doesn't really depend upon dialogue. Even in the case of talkies, these films ultimately try not to stray from movement. In this sense, they remain easy to understand, but also the use of English as a weapon puts it at an advantage over other languages. Yet the American cinema's lack of any sense of traditional culture has created, on the one hand, the appeal of universality and, on the other, a different appeal, that is, the novelty of the social customs of this "new world" so bereft of traditional culture. American society is constituted of such elements as radical democracy, machine civilization, its own particular sexual morality, and jazz (this lattermost has been especially powerful in making inroads into Europe). There is also the novelty of the American-type social structure, in which people of various races live together. As a result of this multiracial exhibition, the United States has also become the world's criminal society, in which crime continues to increase. It is, moreover, natural that such thrilling new customs as high crime have incited the curiosity of present-day Europeans, who enjoy excitement. In other words, Europeans are probably amazed at the emergence of such utterly new social customs in the United States. Fourth, there is the power of cinema in the form of the talkie machines. The era of the talkies is one in which the United States has wielded great power over European cinema through its patents for RCA and Western talkie playback machines. Extremely favorable conditions have thus enabled American film to conquer the European market.

SUZUKI: From a historical standpoint, it is quite interesting that the United States has actually gained influence over Europe and come more or less to dominate it through its unseen force. In Japan nowadays, it seems extremely common to think about the colored and white races in terms of a simple opposition between two worlds. However, one could describe the United States as less an extension of Europe than a nation currently in the process of forming its own independent world, which means that the white race has now come to occupy two worlds. From the perspective of world history, moreover, this creation of two worlds for white people is extremely important. In the traditionally Eurocentric context of Western history, the United States existed only in the periphery as a colony. From the standpoint of world history, however, this nation has come to have a new significance.

The Americanism as grasped through the medium of film in Mr. Tsumura's essay heavily influenced Japan in the past and is one of the things we must overcome. Despite our contempt for this Americanism and its influence in Japan through the figures of the "modern boy" and "modern girl," we cannot really make light of it. Indeed, Europeans traditionally regarded the United States as an inferior colonial culture. We Japanese intellectuals have likewise held Americanism in low regard and take this as a point of pride. In truth, however, the United States poses a problem insofar as it cannot be so easily dismissed. It is now unfortunately a fact that civilizations of quantity have come to carry a certain weight over civilizations of quality. While it is important to conquer this situation, my reading has taught me that there are actually two kinds of Americanism: the first is that described by Mr. Tsumura, which has influenced Japan through such things as film, capital, and mass production; and the second, which might be called the Puritan spirit, can be seen now, for example, in the American rejection of evolutionary theory and the controversy around the Prohibition law.

HAYASHI: American cinema has captured the hearts of people all around the world through democracy. The nature of American democracy consists in capturing the hearts of people in those countries that are more or less misgoverned.

KAWAKAMI: Even in Japan, American cinema has captured the earnest fantasies of people from certain classes. For example, there is the fantasy of someone with a monthly salary of thirty yen marrying overnight into a family of great wealth.

HAYASHI: Even in Japan, the popularity of lowbrow films reveals that cinema is the global pastime of the ignorant. American democracy has the ability to capture the hearts of the ignorant.

TSUMURA: In terms of the capacity of cinema, there exist films superior to those found today. If one conceives of film only on the basis of vulgar Japanese works or the rubbish produced in the capitalist framework of American cinema, then it may be described as a medium of the ignorant. But film culture is both broader and superior to that and should in no way be seen as such a medium. What you are referring to are the low-class fans addicted to cinema. Newsreels and documentaries, for example, are very instructive for the Japanese people, and consider how influential these have been. Even the Greater East Asia War cannot be fully understood through newspaper accounts. Yet we can compensate for this by viewing newsreels and documentaries, which stimulate the poetic imagination. Film can, of course, help us perceive Japan's fate. It is this ability that now constitutes the cinema's great strength in leading the people. This is true in the case of Japan, but even more so in Germany, where film has been used very effectively. Prior to the last war, film was used in Germany as diplomatic policy, and in both Germany and the Soviet Union it was used as part of the people's movement. In the future, countless films will even have to be used for educational purposes. Film is actually being used now in the field of medicine, but in the future it will be used in many other aspects of science education. In Japan, film was finally incorporated as teaching material in the national elementary schools in 1941, but the film education of other countries is still much more advanced.

SUZUKI: In relation to the notion of overcoming modernity, do you see Americanism as the representative form of modernism, or does it differ from modernism? It seems that you are arguing for the overcoming of Americanism.

TSUMURA: Americanism must be overcome—although I am not sure that "overcoming" is the right word here—or rather struggled against because of the great force wielded by the United States as a material and machine civilization. From the perspective of our present-day lives, however, machine civilization and the advances of scientific technology are to some extent undeniable. These are the trends of our time and cannot simply be rejected because of their emergence in the United States. The same can be said of radio, the talkie, and various electrical appliances, as well as the communication, transportation, and production of machine civilization. Many of these things first appeared in the United States. This poses a dilemma, but it is precisely because of this fact that Japan must fully struggle against such power. The human spirit created machines, but it has now become consumed by them. We must thus bring machine civilization under control so as to prevent its consumption of human life. What we need are ideas for a higher culture.

SUZUKI: It is fundamentally the same spirit that can be seen here. Democracy, machine civilization, and capitalism all derive from the same root and possess a certain commonality.

TSUMURA: Democracy is a movement that brings things down to the average. Material and machine civilization allow us to produce our daily necessities and live our lives as cheaply and as easily as possible. In this way, they are also part of this averaging movement and so linked to democracy. Furthermore, machine civilization functions to speed up human life beyond measure, and this poses another danger.

SUZUKI: One of the features of the United States is its high standard or average. This is both its strength and weakness. . . .

TSUMURA: Thus, the American ideal is to raise the people's material standard of living.

SUZUKI: It is this high average that is the problem. Here lies the essence of the United States. Since machine civilization cannot at the present time be denied, the question is how to surmount it.

TSUMURA: Although machine civilization is absolutely unavoidable, we must use its own force against it so as to master it ourselves.

KAWAKAMI: But it seems to me that machine civilization cannot become the object of any overcoming. Spirit cannot take such civilization as its object to be overcome, for it disregards machines.

KOBAYASHI: I agree. The soul hates machines and so cannot battle against them.

KAWAKAMI: Machines lack what it takes to be a rival.

HAYASHI: Machines are servants and should not be seen as anything more.

SHIMOMURA: There is more at stake here, for machines are also made by spirit. We must problematize the spirit that makes machines.

KOBAYASHI: It is true that spirit makes machines, but still spirit is spirit.

SHIMOMURA: My point is that we must problematize this machine-making spirit.

KOBAYASHI: There is no such thing as mechanical spirit. Although spirit may make machines, the machine-making spirit is still spirit. This is the same spirit that makes art.

SHIMOMURA: What is at issue here is the nature of this machine-making spirit itself. This nature is a new one. Such spirit actually lives inside us moderns, and so any simple expression of hatred for it merely avoids the issue. It cannot be explained away by conceiving of it merely in terms of the soul or one's sense of resolution. The soul is in a sense the spirit of old. Although we of course need such spirit for our inner depths, its overcoming will be problematized in the context of overcoming modernity in the same way that we problematize the machine-making spirit. Previously I referred to the notion of "reason," but I spoke more about the modern nature of reason than reason in the sense of logos, which expresses itself through language. More generally, however, this issue relates to our present discussion in that both the "spirit" and "soul" have undergone a change in modernity. Previously the soul was seen in opposition to the body, but in modernity the nature of the body changed. That is to say, the modern body no longer signified the fleshly body but rather an organism whose organs were regarded as a kind of machine. The old notion of the soul was no longer able to control this new body, and thus it became necessary to form a new nature for the soul. The tragedy of modernity lies in the inability of the soul of old to keep up with the machine-body. Here the problem was whether we should retreat or advance, but of course we could not retreat. The machine-making spirit is in no way materialist. Rather, it represents the same idealism as the spirit of modern science, in the sense I stated previously. Is it not the case that modern moralists and religious people still adhere to what is in effect the old notion of the soul? Shouldn't this problem rather be resolved by changing this notion itself? A new metaphysics is required for the mind-body relation. This issue exists on a massive scale and cannot be dealt with, as in the past, on the basis of such individual or subjective methods as involve the soul's training or introspection. Rather, what is required are social or political methods as well as a new wisdom or perhaps theology. This is the problem that will confront future discussions of science, without consideration of which it is impossible to examine the practical problem of overcoming modernity.

YOSHIMITSU: In Bergson's discussion of the mechanical and mystical, he finds that even in machine civilization something acts as a substitute for the mystic. Even in the technological scientism of modernity, there exists something that strangely enough leads to an interest in magic. Mythology and the mechanic are linked together, and there is also a tendency here to substitute for the metaphysics of spirit. Man's demand for a kind of infinity can be found in his interest in speed and demand for the infinite of the materially unlimited. These are actually inverted demands for the mystic. Hence, the demand for the mystic exists at the limits of the mechanic. If we truly realized the emptiness of the soul to be found at the limits of machine civilization, then the mechanic might voluntarily yield its domain to the soul, thus rendering *it* rather than the soul empty. Here, as well, we must conceive of the true "logos-centered order of spirituality" as the true overcoming of modernity.

KAWAKAMI: All of Valéry's conclusions in his theory of civilization reveal that he is nothing but a mystic of machinery, and for this reason I find him ultimately trivial. For me, therefore, the "spirit of geometry" is a kind of "spirit." The spirit of geometry is in no way a rival of spirit, nor is it directly related to the accumulation of the machine civilization of modernity. Why, in effect, does spirit consider machines trivial? The answer is that the *etwas Neues*, or "something new," introduced by machines never goes beyond the question of quantity. It is quite enough that we already have Chaplin and Don Quixote to fight machines!

YOSHIMITSU: The soul must be introduced in order to conquer the mechanic. Isn't it the case that "overcoming modernity" begins only when we sense the emptiness of the soul? Here the soul is no longer ruled by civilization and the mechanic, for spirituality rules everything on the basis of the primary standpoint of life. For me, in other words, the "overcoming of modernity" involves the question of the "soul's repentance." God and the soul must be rediscovered throughout both East and West. Only in this way can we become joined to the profound religious tradition of our homeland.

POSSIBILITIES FOR PRESENT-DAY JAPANESE

HAYASHI: Japan is clearly a country that has long been massively influenced by foreign or world culture. This influence has been so substantial that one can even write a Japanese history or cultural history as based upon it. Yet I would like to marvel at the sight of a Japanese person who has not been so influenced. There are parts of Japan that have firmly rejected foreign influence, and I would like to marvel at these. I wonder if that is possible.

KAWAKAMI: I very much agree with Hayashi's point, which hopefully will be one of the conclusions of this roundtable discussion. This point is also related to the question of identifying the true nature of the Japanese people as such—that is, the full humanity of present and future Japanese—as well as the question of how to recover this nature.

HAYASHI: An extract from Mr. Miyoshi's brief account reads: "Today one of the most eagerly researched fields consists in the discovery—or rediscovery—of the Japanese spirit through the study, exegesis, and commentary on such ancient texts as the *Kojiki* [Records of Ancient Matters], *Nihon shoki* [Chronicles of Japan], and *Man'yōshū* [Collection of Ten Thousand Leaves]. However, some reflection may be needed as to whether this field is now approaching the discovery of something that is fully sufficient to embolden us for the future."

Such a trend clearly exists. As Education Ministry policy, this has . . .

MIYOSHI: That's right. What I am especially concerned about here is the Education Ministry's way of doing things. I am disturbed by such opportunism that is so lacking in true procedures, as described by Mr. Kobayashi.

HAYASHI: We have all had the embarrassing experience of enjoying French novels and American films. After some painful experiences, however, I have now, at age forty, grown to the point where I finally understand and enjoy the *Kojiki*, *Nihon shoki*, and *Man'yōshū*.

MIYOSHI: You are not alone in this, for conditions have finally reached this stage. Through various efforts, this historical trend can become an ample driving force for the future. On the other hand, the forced and opportunistic interpretations of classical texts have now rashly gotten ahead of themselves. First of all, these interpretations reveal ideas that are mixed or impure: while recommending the promotion of the present scientific spirit, the methods of interpretation remain extremely unscientific. This is a troubling contradiction.

HAYASHI: I would like to address those who believe that the Japanese people are formed through the Education Ministry's methods of interpreting such ancient texts as the *Kojiki*, *Nihon shoki*, and *Man'yōshū* and ask them if they have undergone hardships. I would like to ask them if they know anything other than these texts, and whether they have even seriously experienced modernity. The fact that many people first understand such texts only at the age of forty bodes extremely well for the future.

MIYOSHI: That is my wish as well. It is annoying that the publications put out by government authorities, who are in such an important position of leadership, are merely forced interpretations bereft of originality. I would like to discuss this point. These books appear to provide quite scientifically detailed discussions, but in truth they are not scientific at all. The notions of grandeur and majesty that appear like pet phrases in them would, in a different context, strike us as beautiful and subtle. Yet as readers, we find their facile interpretations unconvincing.

HAYASHI: The classics don't need to be immediately understood by students. A national character in which one begins to understand the classics only at age forty is a sign of a true state. Japan is endowed with such a national character.

MIYOSHI: I am perfectly happy with this national character. The problem is that people today believe that they must seek out the Japanese spirit in the classics and apply it to our current situation. This shortsighted intention can be seen through very easily. As a result, the reading or interpretation of the classics has become extremely rash, inadequate, and at times irrational. I think that we must point out this fact.

MOROI: I completely agree.

KAWAKAMI: I am actually optimistic about this. Mr. Kobayashi remarked earlier that, while we all read such Western writers as Dostoyevsky in our youth, we now understand the interest of the classics. Our experience is similar, but it is in effect only because of our readings of Dostoyevsky and Baudelaire that our interest in the classics arose. I certainly don't regard that reading as a past sin. It was Western literature that provoked our interest in people, whom we have gradually come to understand over time, at least to this extent. In this way, we finally came to be struck by the finely wrought descriptions of people that appear in the classics.

MIYOSHI: That's true. The classics have come down to us as fragments, for not one of these texts is perfectly preserved. In terms of supplementing this absence, it is utterly impossible to arouse any real interest in these works if one has not undergone various kinds of training as a human being.

KIKUCHI: Since, as you have all remarked, we can embark upon our path to the classics only in our forties, what path should young people be following today?

KAWAKAMI: By way of responding to your question, I hope I am not being presumptuous by saying that we critics always check whether contemporary works are able to approach the classics or the highest levels of literature. Shouldn't we point out this essential path to young people?

KOBAYASHI: For me, the road to the classics was opened up by traveling all the way to what one believes to be the shores of modernity.

KIKUCHI: Is that what you encourage for young people today?

KOBAYASHI: I'm not sure. I don't have time for such encouragement.

NISHITANI: As an issue for the Japanese people as a whole, any true understanding of the spirit of the Japanese classics must absolutely involve the question of education. What do you think would be the best way to guide people to this path?

KOBAYASHI: It is not in my nature to guide people.

HAYASHI: Education must be such that, at the junior high school level, we first cultivate in these youths sufficient ability to read the Japanese classics. We ourselves were not so educated.

KIKUCHI: Wouldn't it be better to teach them a bit more, even if they could only sense the presence of higher knowledge?

HAYASHI: Of course it would. My point is that even such traditional forms of education as those based on the Nine Chinese Classics would suffice, as these texts are first merely read and recited, since understanding of their content comes about naturally only with age. It would be unfortunate if we did not have these youths study the national classics.

KOBAYASHI: Truth can be found even in such irrational methods as drumming into students material that they don't understand.

KIKUCHI: This might sound like flattery, but there would be great pedagogic value for someone like you (Mr. Kobayashi) to research the classics, as the students all know you. Simply your research of the classics alone would be of pedagogic value.

KOBAYASHI (*embarrassed*): Well, it's a bit difficult for me since my desire to finally explore the classics has coincided with my sense of the futility and deceit inherent in all explanation and persuasion.

NISHITANI: As you remarked earlier, Mr. Kobayashi, the path to the classics reveals itself only after we have abandoned various things. Yet isn't the question here how these things can be abandoned? The difficulty is that one cannot abandon everything. It is not that one does not wish to abandon these things, but rather that one cannot given the difficulty of doing so. Even if scientists were told to abandon their scientific materialism, they would be unable to do so. Likewise, even if philosophers wished to abandon rationality, they could not do so very easily.

HAYASHI: I marvel at Japan's military flight education, in which—to repeat this phrase, such as it is—a unity has been achieved between machine and spirit. This kind of education has truly opened my eyes.

NISHITANI: I agree. However, that education is possible only because it provides an isolated lifestyle in which one pure teaching is drummed in. Such an education would be quite difficult for the average student, who does not live isolated from society.

HAYASHI: Yet there are many people in Japan who possess that kind of spirit even in their forties and fifties. You and I received a modern education and so have lost such resolve, but that is basically the path we must take. This resolve can be found not only among the young airmen but also among most true patriots and soldiers. It is unfortunate that we did not receive such an education.

NISHITANI: Take, for example, a physicist like Mr. Kikuchi, who, on the one hand, conducts physics research as his profession while, on the other, must maintain a sense of resolve. However, these two things generally cannot be immediately unified. Compared to the resolve of soldiers, this situation is considerably more complex.

HAYASHI: My point is that all people—and not just children—can, with age, come to acquire such resolve. For me, this path represents the goal of life.

MIYOSHI: The spiritual strength of military education in general, and not just that of young airmen, is such as to strongly emphasize the notions of friendship and comradeship. In our everyday lives, such awareness and feeling among fellow soldiers is inconceivable. I have some experience in this, having once attended military school. Also, soldiers become linked together as classmates or by serving as officers in the same unit or members of the same flight corps and develop, in these situations, extremely strong friendships. The depth or height or these feelings is unimaginable from the perspective of the outside world, where the bonding with others is more diluted. Such spiritual strength, which is inconceivable in our own, ordinary world, can be described as a kind of environmental element.

HAYASHI: There are two standpoints regarding the education of these young airmen: either one absolutely affirms this kind of education as something happy and pure or one views it as extraordinary spiritual beauty. In Japan today, these two standpoints fight with one another.

NISHITANI: I see this education as healthy spiritual beauty. Even so, in order for the people as a whole to become endowed with such spiritual beauty, they must first become immune to various poisons. That is the difficult part.

KAWAKAMI: Now then, we have touched upon the issues very generally, if rather quickly, and since time is at an end, we must now adjourn. Thank you all very much for giving so much of your time in such hot weather. Quite frankly, I worried too much in the beginning about whether we had enough to discuss over so many hours, and so I prepared too many topics. That was my fault. I now understand that just one of these topics would have been quite sufficient if discussed thoroughly.

In any event, this format of a "comprehensive conference" has produced ample results. Above all, the more implicit secondary results of so many of us meeting here for the first time are enormous. Any mistakes or dissatisfactions that you may have experienced are entirely the result of my own failings, for which I beg your forgiveness. I do hope that all of you are able to join us when we hold our next conference.

Symposium Participants

HAYASHI FUSAO (林房雄) (1903–1975). Novelist, critic, and member of the Japanese Romantic school. Born in Ōita, Ōita prefecture, under the name of Gotō Toshio. Dropped out of Tokyo Imperial University, where he studied law. Imprisoned for leftist activities both before and during the war and, upon release, committed *tenkō* (ideological conversion)—which he did not recant after the war. Works include *Youth* (1932–1934) and the twenty-two volume *Saigō Takamori* (1940–1970). Famous in the postwar era as a writer of "middlebrow" fiction and as the author of *In Affirmation of the Greater East Asia War* (1963–1965).

KAMEI KATSUICHIRŌ (亀井勝一郎) (1907–1966). Critic and member of the Japanese Romantic school. Born in Hakodate, Hokkaido. Dropped out of Tokyo Imperial University, where he studied literature. Committed *tenkō* in 1930 after being imprisoned for several years for involvement in Communism. Works include *Literature in a Period of Change* (1934), *The Education of Man* (1937), and *Studies in Japanese Intellectual History*, which won the Kikuchi Kan Prize in 1965.

KAWAKAMI TETSUTARŌ (河上徹太郎) (1902–1980). Literary and music critic. Born in Nagasaki and raised in Iwakuni, Yamaguchi prefecture. Graduated from the Economics Department of Tokyo Imperial University in 1926. Noted for his translations of Valéry and Gide as well as of Lev Shestov's influential *Philosophy of Tragedy*. Works include *Nature and Purity* (1932), *The Autumn of Thought* (1934), and *Japanese Outsiders* (1959).

KIKUCHI SEISHI (菊池正士) (1902–1974). Atomic physicist who served as the first director of the Tokyo University Institute for Nuclear Study. Born in Tokyo and graduated in 1926 from the Physics Department of Tokyo Imperial University, where he later received an advanced degree. Works include *Introduction to Nuclear Physics* (1935), *The Structure of Matter* (1941), and *The Nuclear World* (1957).

KOBAYASHI HIDEO (小林秀雄) (1902–1983). Critic. Born in the Kanda district of Tokyo and graduated in 1928 from the French Literature Department of Tokyo Imperial University. Criticized universal ideas and systems of thought throughout his work, beginning in 1929 with the essay "Multiple Designs." Cofounded the journal *Bungakkai* in 1933 and became its editor in 1935. Works include *A Life of Dostoyevsky* (1939), *The Letters of Van Gogh* (1952), and *Motoori Norinaga* (1965–1977).

MIYOSHI TATSUJI (三好達治) (1900–1964). Poet and translator. Born in Osaka and graduated in 1928 from the French Literature Department of Tokyo Imperial University. Noted for his translations of Baudelaire, Francis Jammes, and Prosper Mérimée. Cofounded the Four Seasons poetry group in 1934. Works include *The Surveying Ship* (1930), *Sand Castle* (1946), and *After a Hundred Times* (1962).

MOROI SABURŌ (諸井三郎) (1903–1977). Composer and music theorist. Born in Tokyo and graduated in 1928 from the Literature Department of Tokyo Imperial University. Studied in Germany from 1932 until 1934 at the Berlin Musikhochschule, where he was influenced by Bruckner. Works include Violin Sonata, op. 11, Cello Concerto, op. 12, Flute Sonata, op. 15, and Piano Sonata no. 2, op. 20.

NAKAMURA MITSUO (中村光夫) (1911–1988). Critic, playwright, and novelist. Born in Tokyo under the name of Koba Ichirō. Studied French literature at Tokyo Imperial University, from which he graduated in 1935. Critical works include studies of such writers as Tanizaki Jun'ichirō (1952), Shiga Naoya (1954), and Satō Haruo (1962); novels include *Confessions of My Sexuality* (1963) and *False Idols* (1967).

NISHITANI KEIJI (西谷啓治) (1900–1990). Kyoto school religious philosopher. Born in the town of Noto in Ishikawa prefecture. Graduated in 1924 from Kyoto Imperial University, where he studied philosophy under Nishida Kitarō and Tanabe Hajime. Spent the years 1937–1939 in Germany studying under Heidegger at the University of Freiburg. Taught primarily at Kyoto University, where he received his doctorate in 1945. Works include *A Philosophy of Elemental Subjectivity* (1940), *Nihilism* (1949), and *What Is Religion* (1961).

SHIMOMURA TORATARŌ (下村寅太郎) (1902–1995). Philosopher of science. Born in Kyoto and graduated in 1926 with a degree in philosophy from Kyoto Imperial University, where he studied under Nishida Kitarō and Tanabe Hajime. Wrote widely on such topics as mathematics, natural science, and art. Works include *Leibniz* (1938), *Natural Philosophy* (1939), and *Renaissance Artists* (1969).

SUZUKI SHIGETAKA (鈴木成高) (1907–1988). Kyoto school historian. Born in Kōchi, Kōchi prefecture. Studied in the Literature Department of Kyoto Imperial University, from which he graduated in 1929 before receiving his advanced degree there in Western history. Taught at Kyoto University and Waseda University. Works include *The Formation of Europe* (1947) and *Studies in Feudal Society* (1948).

TSUMURA HIDEO (津村秀夫) (1907–1985). Film critic. Born in Kobe and educated at Tōhoku Imperial University, where he graduated from the German Department in 1931. Began his career as a journalist for the *Asahi News*, writing film articles under the pen name Q. Works include *Film and Criticism* (1939–1940), *A Man Called Mizoguchi Kenji* (1958), and *In Search of the Beauty of Film* (1966).

YOSHIMITSU YOSHIHIKO (吉満義彦) (1904–1945). Catholic theologian. Born in the town of Kametsu, Kagoshima prefecture. Graduated in 1928 from Tokyo Imperial

University, where he majored in ethics. Spent two years in France studying Scholastic philosophy under Jacques Maritain. Taught philosophy at Sophia University before becoming a lecturer at Tokyo University in 1935. Works include *Fundamental Problems of Cultural Ethics* (1936), *Literature and Ethics* (1937), and *Saint Augustine's Path of Conversion in His "Confessions"* (1945).

Glossary

Adam, Karl (1876–1966), German Catholic theologian whose best-known work is *The Spirit of Catholicism* (1924). Major authority on Saint Augustine.

Akireta bōizu (the Shocking Boys), extremely popular music and vaudeville trio formed in 1937.

Akutagawa Ryūnosuke (1892–1927), short-story writer and essayist known for his social criticism; author of *Kappa* (1927) and "In a Grove" (1922).

Alain (pseudonym for Émile Chartier [1868–1951]), French philosopher and essayist whose influential writings often sought to teach practical and moral lessons.

Arima Shinshichi (1825–1862), clansman of the Satsuma domain who advocated the ideology of *sonnō jōi* (revere the emperor and expel the barbarians).

Asano Akira (1901–1990), nationalist poet and critic who committed *tenkō* while imprisoned for his left-wing activities; leading member of the Japanese Romantic school.

Bakunin, Mikhail Aleksandrovich (1814–1876), Russian revolutionary and anarchist who was imprisoned for ten years and exiled to Siberia. Escaped and continued revolutionary activities in Europe.

Bankei (1622–1693), Zen Buddhist monk famous for his doctrine of the Unborn, which refers to the Buddha-nature inherent in all people.

Bashō (Matsuo Bashō [1644–1694]), foremost haiku poet whose travel accounts, especially *The Narrow Road to Oku* (1694), are widely known.

Berdyayev, Nikolay Aleksandrovich (1874–1948), Russian religious philosopher who often treated the question of man's freedom; author of *The Philosophy of Freedom* (1911) and *The Meaning of Creativity* (1916).

Bergson, Henri (1859–1941), French philosopher most noted for his theories of duration, memory, and vitalism. Awarded the Nobel Prize in Literature in 1927.

Chaplin, Charlie (1889–1977), Hollywood icon born in England most famous for his creation of the Tramp character. In *Modern Times* (1936), the Tramp fights against what is portrayed as the inhumanity of machinery.

Chikamatsu Shūkō (1876–1944), naturalist writer who incorporated autobiographical elements into his fiction; works often deal with protagonist's desire for prostitutes. Author of *Letter to My Former Wife* (1910).

China Incident (Shina jihen), euphemism widely used in Japan for the Sino-Japanese War of 1937–1945.

Chūshingura (also known under the title Genroku chūshingura [The Forty-seven Ronin]), 1941 film directed by Mizoguchi Kenji and commissioned by the Japanese Ministry of Information. A commercial failure.

Cimabue, Giovanni (ca. 1240–ca. 1302), Florentine artist considered the father of Italian painting; teacher of Giotto.

civilization and enlightenment (bunmei kaika), the Meiji-period policy of modernizing Japan through the widespread adoption and implementation of Western science, technology, and social programs.

Clair, René (1898–1981), highly influential French film director and writer whose works include Le million (1931) and Les grandes manoeuvres (1955).

Comte, Auguste (1798–1857), French philosopher considered the founder of positivism. Sought to bridge the gap between science and philosophy through the use of the former's experimental methods.

Cortés, Juan Donoso (1809–1853), Spanish author and diplomat whose political conservatism and anti-Enlightenment views are expressed in his Essay on Catholicism, Liberalism, and Order (1851).

Darlan, François (1881–1942), French naval officer and minister in the Vichy regime. Widely criticized for his collaboration with Nazi Germany.

Dawson, Christopher (1889–1970), prominent cultural historian who, following his conversion to Catholicism, wrote such works as The Age of Gods (1928). Attributed the rise of European civilization to the medieval Catholic Church.

Declaration of the Rights of Man (La Déclaration des droits de l'homme et du citoyen), document articulating the principles of the French Revolution; states that all men have certain universal rights.

Dempf, Alois (1891–1982), German Catholic philosopher and historian whose books include Mensch und Charakter (1931) and Staat und Geschichte (1932).

Dilthey, Wilhelm (1833–1911), German philosopher whose philosophy of life sought to understand man and the human sciences primarily on the basis of historical change.

Don Quixote, canonical work of fiction completed in 1615 by the Spanish novelist and dramatist Miguel de Cervantes. In one of the novel's more famous scenes, Quixote battles windmills, which he mistakes for giants.

Durbin, Deanna (b. 1921), Canadian-born Hollywood actress and singer who, from age fourteen to twenty-seven, dominated the box office. Hit films include Three Smart Girls (1936) and That Certain Age (1938).

Dürckheim, Karlfried Graf von (1896–1988), German diplomat, psychotherapist, and Zen Buddhist master. Lived in Japan for eight years; influential in disseminating Zen Buddhist ideas in Europe.

Essertier, Daniel (1888–1931), French thinker and sociologist whose works include Psychologie et sociologie (1927) and Formes inferieures de l'explication (1927).

Feuerbach, Ludwig Andreas (1804–1872), German philosopher who rejected distinction between man and God and sought to analyze religion strictly as an anthropological phenomenon.

Ficino, Marsilio (1433–1499), Florentine philosopher, philologist, translator, priest, and physician; sought to ground Christianity on Platonism.

Frazer, James George (1854–1941), Scottish scholar whose primary work is the enormously influential study of comparative mythology, *The Golden Bough* (1890–1915).

Freedom and Popular Rights Movement (Jiyū minken undō), Meiji-period political and social movement that took as its aims the establishment of civil rights and the formation of an elected legislature.

Freyer, Hans (1887–1969), German philosopher and sociologist whose conservative views found expression in his works *Der Staat* (1925) and *Machiavelli* (1938).

fueki ryūkō (permanence and change), principle of *haikai* composition set forth by the poet Matsuo Bashō arguing for the necessity of both change and permanence in this genre.

Fujiwara Yoshie (1898–1976), famous tenor, whose father was English; founded the Fujiwara Opera in 1934, which was Japan's first full-scale opera organization.

Fukuzawa Yukichi (1835–1901), social reformer, author, and educator, one of the leading advocates of Japan's "civilization and enlightenment" policy. Founded Keiō University in 1868.

Futabatei Shimei (1864–1909), novelist and translator of Russian literature, best known for writing one of Japan's first modern novels, *Drifting Clouds* (1887–1889).

gagaku, imperial court music introduced to Japan from China and Korea during the sixth and seventh centuries.

Genealogy of a Woman (Onna keizu), 1942 black-and-white film directed by Makino Masahiro and based on a story by Izumi Kyōka.

Genji monogatari (The Tale of Genji), Heian-period fictional text authored by Murasaki Shikibu chronicling court life as it revolves around Prince Genji; widely considered the greatest work of Japanese fiction.

George, Stefan Anton (1868–1933), German poet and translator influenced by French symbolism; works include *The Star of the Covenant* (1914) and *The New Kingdom* (1928).

Gesshō (1813–1858), Buddhist priest who supported the emperor in his opposition to the Tokugawa shogunate; died in his suicide pact with Saigō Takamori.

gidayūbushi, samisen music used primarily in Bunraku (Japanese puppet theater).

Giotto (1266?–1337), Florentine artist who studied under Cimabue and became the greatest pre-Renaissance painter in Italy. His frescoes are credited with revolutionizing painting in both style and content.

Gotoba (1180–1239), cloistered, or "retired," emperor who sought to wrest back imperial power from the Kamakura shogunate; ordered the compilation of the great poetry anthology the *Shinkokinshū*.

Haecker, Theodor (1879–1945), German writer, translator, and cultural critic. Converted to Catholicism and known today partly for his opposition to the Nazi regime.

Heike monogatari (The Tale of the Heike), epic narrative about the rise and fall of the Taira (Heike) clan from the early twelfth to early thirteenth centuries. Originally recited by *biwa hōshi,* blind monks who accompanied their narrative with lute playing.

Hirano Kuniomi (1828–1864), clansman of the Fukuoka domain in the latter stages of the Tokugawa regime noted for his adherence to the ideology of *sonnō jōi* (revere the emperor and expel the barbarians).

Hirata Atsutane (1776–1843), Shinto revivalist thinker who advocated the restoration of imperial rule; disciple of Motoori Norinaga.

honnête homme (gentleman), represented the ideal of proper society in seventeenth-century France. The gentleman discusses any topic but does so without bringing undue attention to himself; seen as a model of social intercourse.

iki, aesthetic ideal in Japan believed to have originated in the Edo period that connotes simplicity and straightforwardness.

imayō, imperial court music popular in the late Heian period involving shortened Buddhist chants sung in Japanese.

"imperial organ" theory (*tennō kikan setsu*), argument put forth by the legal scholar Minobe Tatsukichi that the emperor was merely an organ of the state rather than an absolute entity. In 1935, this theory was attacked by the ultranationalists and Minobe was forced to resign his teaching post.

Ise monogatari (*The Tales of Ise*), Heian-period fictional text combining narrative and poetry in the form of short episodes about romantic love at court; the protagonist has traditionally been identified with the courtier-poet Ariwara no Narihira.

itchūbushi, style of music that developed in the late seventeenth century featuring chanting accompanied by the samisen.

Itō Hirobumi (1841–1909), first prime minister of Japan, who ultimately served four terms in office; considered the major architect of Meiji Japan.

Izumi Kyōka (1873–1939), novelist and short-story writer whose tales often concern the supernatural; works include *The Saint of Mount Kōya* (1900) and "A Song Under Lanterns" (1910).

Jammes, Francis (1868–1938), French poet and novelist whose early works are pastoral in nature while his later works, written after his conversion to Catholicism, tend to be more religious.

Japanese Romantic school (Nihon roman-ha), group of nationalist writers and critics affiliated with the journal *Japanese Romantic School* (1935–1938), whose leading members included Yasuda Yojūrō and Kamei Katsuichirō.

Japanism (Nihonshugi), the nationalist belief that the Japanese traditional spirit must serve as the foundation for all aspects of Japanese society; generally traced back to 1888 with the founding of the journal *The Japanese.*

Jinnō shōtōki (*Chronicle of Gods and Sovereigns*), ideologically based historical text written by Kitabatake Chikafusa in 1339 to legitimize the power of the Southern Court.

jōruri, narrative music generally found in Japanese puppet theater that is sung with samisen accompaniment.

kagura, literally "music of the gods," this style is composed of Shinto music and dance and generally performed at shrines.

katōbushi, musical style of the Japanese puppet theater consisting of singing with samisen accompaniment.

Kierkegaard, Søren Aabye (1813–1855), Danish philosopher and theologian whose themes included man's free will and relation to God, as expressed in such works as *Fear and Trembling* and *Either/Or* (both published in 1843).

Kikuchi Kan (1888–1948), writer, editor of the literary journal *Bungei shunjū*, and one of the central figures of the Japanese cultural world. Collaborated with wartime authorities.

Kikuchi Takemitsu (1319–1373), pro-imperial general who unsuccessfully defended the Southern Court against the Ashikaga shogunate during the Nanbokuchō period.

kiyomoto, type of narrative music accompanied by the samisen that developed in the early nineteenth century.

Koizumi Yakumo (Lafcadio Hearn [1850–1904]), writer and teacher whose works introduced Japanese culture abroad. Preceded Natsume Sōseki as professor of English at Tokyo University at the turn of the twentieth century. start here

Kojiki (*Records of Ancient Matters*), oldest Japanese historical text; chronicling the country's divine creation, it was compiled in the eighth century by imperial order.

Kojiki den (*Commentary on the "Kojiki"*), Motoori Norinaga's nativist exposition of the *Kojiki* text written in 1798 and published posthumously by his students in 1822.

Kropotkin, Pyotr Alekseyevich (1842–1921), Russian prince and social philosopher most famous for his development of anarchist theories.

Kusunoki Masashige (1294–1336), general who fought on the side of Emperor Go-Daigo against the Kamakura shogunate; eventually forced to commit suicide in battle. During World War II, his image was appropriated for use by the military authorities.

Kyoto school (Kyōto gakuha), the group of philosophers and other intellectuals centered around Nishida Kitarō and Tanabe Hajime at Kyoto University. Members included Nishitani Keiji, Kōsaka Masaaki, Suzuki Shigetaka, and Kōyama Iwao.

"Lakeside Lodgings" (*Kohan no yado*), hit song of 1940 by Takamine Mieko. Officially banned at first because its sentimental tone was seen as discordant with the wartime atmosphere, it nevertheless later became popular with Japanese soldiers.

Literary World (*Bungakkai*), influential journal of literature and culture founded in 1933 by Kobayashi Hideo, Hayashi Fusao, and Takeda Rintarō; hosted the Overcoming Modernity symposium in 1942.

Lourié, Arthur (1892–1966), Russian avant-garde composer whose early works show the influence of late romanticism but who also wrote neoclassical and atonal music.

Macmurray, John (1891–1976), Christian moral philosopher born in Scotland. Most famous works are *Interpreting the Universe* (1933) and *Religion, Art, and Science* (1961).

Maistre, Joseph de (1753–1821), conservative philosopher, diplomat, and writer of French background born in Savoy. Passionate critic of the French Revolution for its overturning of established authority.

Manchurian Incident (Manshū jihen), plot organized by two Kwantung Army officers in 1931 to initiate fighting between the Japanese forces and the Chinese Nationalist government army so as to legitimate Japan's acquisition of Manchuria.

Man'yōshū (*Collection of Ten Thousand Leaves*), first poetry anthology in Japan, written primarily during the Nara and early Heian periods. Most of the nearly 4,500 poems included in the volume are *tanka*.

Maritain, Jacques (1882–1973), French theologian, philosopher, and writer who converted to Catholicism. Student of Bergson, whom he later attacked in favor of Aquinas's reconciliation of faith and reason. Major influence on Yoshimitsu Yoshihiko.

Masamune Hakuchō (1879–1962), naturalist fiction writer, playwright, and critic whose works include "Where To?" (1908) and "Glimmer of Light" (1910).

Masaoka Shiki (1867–1902), famed haiku poet who called for the modernization of traditional Japanese poetic forms; in his critical work, he sought to revive interest in the *Man'yōshū*.

Millet, Jean-François (1814–1875), French painter and one of the founders of the Barbizon school; known for his paintings of rural life and peasants. Subject of Romain Rolland's biography *François-Millet* (1902).

Mitsukuni (Tokugawa Mitsukuni [1628–1701]), powerful daimyo of the early Edo period who compiled the historical collection *Dai Nihon shi*.

mobo, moga (modern boy, modern girl), youths of the Taishō and early Shōwa periods who, upon the emergence of mass culture in Japan, sought to imitate Western fashions and customs.

Mori Ōgai (1862–1922), physician, translator, and pioneer of modern Japanese literature; author of "The Dancing Girl" (1890) and *The Wild Geese* (1911–1913).

Morita Sōhei (1881–1949), author of the novel *Baien* (1909); disciple and later biographer of Natsume Sōseki.

Mount Kōya, located in Wakayama prefecture, considered the center of Shingon Buddhism after the monk Kūkai established a religious community there in the early ninth century.

Nagata Mikihiko (1887–1964), popular writer whose works include *The Earth Shakes* (1923) and *Night Talks in Gion* (1925).

naniwabushi, type of sung narrative accompanied by the samisen that was popular in the Edo period.

Nariaki (Tokugawa Nariaki [1800–1860]), daimyo from the Mito domain who supported the imperial restoration and argued for fighting against the West in its attempt to open the country.

National Learning (Kokugaku), intellectual movement that, from the late seventeenth century to the end of the Tokugawa period, promoted study of the Japanese classics and sought to exclude all foreign (Chinese, Korean) influence.

Natsume Sōseki (1867–1916), one of the founders of modern Japanese literature in his capacities as novelist, scholar, and critic; author of such works as *The Young Master* (1906), *And Then* (1909), and *Kokoro* (1914).

New Village (Atarashiki mura), utopian Japanese village community founded by the writer Mushanokōji Saneatsu in 1918.

Nihon shoki (*Chronicles of Japan*), after the *Kojiki*, the second oldest Japanese historical text; completed in the eighth century, it weaves mythological elements in with the historical.

Nine Chinese Classics (Shisho gokyō), canonical texts of Chinese Confucianism consisting of the Four Books and Five Classics.

Nogi Maresuke (1849–1912), army general famous for capturing Port Arthur during the Russo-Japanese War (1904–1905). Committed suicide with his wife following the death of the emperor Meiji.

Okakura Tenshin (1862–1913), disciple of Ernest Fenollosa who advocated a return to traditional Japanese art. His pan-Asianist views are expressed in his English-language books *Ideals of the East* (1903) and *The Awakening of Japan* (1904).

Okuda Ryōzō (1903–1993), tenor known for his high vocal range and prolific output, which included love songs, German *lieder*, and film scores.

Ōrui Noburu (1884–1975), historian and noted authority on Japanese castles and fortresses.

Ōtomo Sōrin (1530–1587), powerful daimyo whose control gradually extended over seven provinces, such as Chikuzen and Chikugo.

Ozaki Kōyō (1869–1903), pioneer writer of modern Japanese literature whose novels include *Passions and Griefs* (1896) and *Demon Gold* (1897–1903); cofounder of the Society of Friends of the Inkstone.

Peace Preservation Law (Chian iji hō), law enacted in 1925 to halt the propagation of any thought considered dangerous to the political and social order, such as anarchism or Communism.

Péguy, Charles (1873–1914), French poet and writer known for his strong defense of Catholicism, socialism, and nationalism. Works include *The Mystery of the Charity of Joan of Arc* (1909). Major influence on Yoshimitsu Yoshihiko.

Planck, Max (1858–1947), German physicist regarded as the founder of quantum theory. Awarded the Nobel Prize in Physics in 1919.

Pomponazzi, Pietro (1462–1525), Italian philosopher whose ideas are considered anticipatory of the Renaissance; best-known work is *On the Immortality of the Soul* (1516).

Power, Tyrone (1914–1958), Hollywood leading actor who starred in romantic swash-buckling films, such as *The Mark of Zorro* (1940).

Ranke, Leopold von (1795–1886), German historian whose meticulous research and analyses can be seen in his *History of the Popes* (1834–1839); set forth notion of "moral energy" later incorporated by the Kyoto school.

Rolland, Romain (1866–1944), French novelist, dramatist, essayist, and music scholar whose best-known work is *Jean Christophe* (1904–1912). Awarded Nobel Prize in Literature in 1915.

sabi, traditional Japanese aesthetic ideal connoting transience and impermanence; often used in the context of such arts as flower arrangement and poetry.

saibara, accompanied vocal music that developed in the Heian imperial court based on ancient Japanese folk songs.

Saigō Takamori (1827–1877), one of the leaders of the Meiji Restoration whose unsuccessful rebellion against the central government in 1877, known as the Seinan War, forced him to commit suicide.

Satō Haruo (1892–1964), poet and fiction writer strongly influenced by Oscar Wilde, best known today for his novel *Rural Melancholy* (1919).

Scheler, Max (1874–1928), German philosopher famous for his phenomenological research. Later works reveal an interest in political developments, as, for example, his denunciations of Marxism, capitalism, and the early Nazi movement.

Shimazaki Tōson (1872–1943), poet and naturalist writer whose works chronicle the tensions of modernization in society; author of *The Broken Commandment* (1906) and *Before the Dawn* (1935).

Shimazu Nariakira (1809–1858), daimyo of the Satsuma domain whose extensive use of Western military technology made the domain one of the most powerful during the latter stages of the Tokugawa regime.

shinnai, ornate singing style performed with samisen accompaniment that became popular in the late eighteenth century.

Shinran (1173–1263), founder of Shin Buddhism who taught that enlightenment can be achieved through faith and the practice of reciting the name of Amida Buddha.

Shōtoku, Prince (574–622), ancient ruler who propagated Buddhism by building temples and sending envoys to China.

Society of Friends of the Inkstone (Ken'yūsha), influential literary group organized in 1885 by such young writers as Ozaki Kōyō and Yamada Bimyō; published first literary journal in Japan, entitled *Garakuta bunko*.

Spencer, Herbert (1820–1903), English thinker who sought to apply the scientific notion of evolution to the realm of philosophy and ethics. Author of *Principles of Psychology* (1855).

Tanizaki Jun'ichirō (1886–1965), novelist whose psychologically probing works deal with love and sexuality. Author of *The Makioka Sisters* (1943–1948) and *In Praise of Shadows* (1933), a defense of traditional Japanese aesthetics.

Tayama Katai (1872–1930), naturalist writer most remembered today for his story *The Futon* (1907), which created a sensation at the time for its pseudo-autobiographical depiction of the author's relations with a young woman.

Thode, Henry (1857–1920), German scholar of the Italian Renaissance who wrote extensively on Michelangelo. Opposed the dominant view of the Renaissance as a liberation from the Middle Ages by stressing the role of Christianity.

tokiwazu,, type of narrative music used in Kabuki theater that first became popular in the mid-eighteenth century.

Troeltsch, Ernst (1865–1923), German theologian and philosopher of religion. In his *The Social Teaching of the Christian Churches* (1912), he argued that Western culture was in a state of spiritual crisis.

Tsubouchi Shōyō (1859–1935), one of the chief architects of modern Japanese literature whose critical work *The Essence of the Novel* calls for a more artistic and less didactic approach to fiction.

Tsurezuregusa (*Essays in Idleness*), collection of essays on random subjects composed by the monk Yoshida Kenkō in the early fourteenth century.

Uchimura Kanzō (1861–1930), leading Christian thinker and activist educated in the United States who criticized Western missionaries for their colonialist attitudes.

Ueno School of Music, Japan's most prestigious music school, founded in 1887, now known as the Tokyo National University of Fine Arts and Music.

Umeda Unbin (1815–1859), Confucian scholar of the latter stages of the Tokugawa regime. Spiritual leader of those forces that worshipped the emperor and sought to expel the Western "barbarians."

Valéry, Paul (1871–1945), French poet and essayist influenced by the symbolists whose writings often deal with the opposition between reason and passion.

Virgil (70–19 B.C.), Roman poet whose first work, *The Bucolics*, composed of ten pastoral poems, established his reputation. The *Georgics* and the unfinished *Aeneid* earned him lasting fame.

Wang Yangming school, highly influential school of neo-Confucianism that privileged intuitive over rational knowledge; critical of Zhu Xi philosophy.

Winckelmann, Johann Joachim (1717–1768), German art historian and archaeologist whose great appreciation for Greek art contributed to the rise of neoclassicism in the late eighteenth century.

Worringer, Wilhelm (1881–1965), German art historian noted for his high evaluation of abstract art; most influential work is *Abstraction and Empathy* (1907).

Yasuda Yojūrō (1910–1981), nationalist leader of the Japanese Romantic school who wrote on German aesthetics and traditional Japanese culture; editor of the journals *Cogito* (1933–1944) and *Japanese Romantic School* (1935–1938).

Yoshida Shōin (1830–1859), scholar and teacher famed for his erudition whose students included Itō Hirobumi; executed by the Tokugawa shogunate for insurrection.

yūgen, traditional aesthetic concept signifying a faint and elusive type of beauty that cannot be grasped directly.

Index of Names